TIMES
THEY ARE 'A
CHANGING

MATTHEW 24 & THE END TIMES

RAYMOND GRANT

Published by Ad Fontes Press, Portland, Oregon 97205
www.adfontespress.com/times-changing/

Scripture taken from the NEW KING JAMES VERSION®. Copyright © 1982 by Thomas Nelson. Used by permission. All rights reserved.

THE HOLY BIBLE, NEW INTERNATIONAL VERSION®, NIV® Copyright © 1973, 1978, 1984, 2011 by Biblica, Inc.® Used by permission. All rights reserved worldwide.

All other Scripture is quoted from the KING JAMES VERSION or adapted by the author.

Printed in the United States of America

On the Cover: *The Siege and Destruction of Jerusalem by the Romans Under the Command of Titus, 70 A.D.,* Oil on canvas by David Roberts, c. 1850.

On the Title Page: *Der Engel zeigt Joannes Jerusalem* [The Angel Shows John Jerusalem], Woodcut by Gustave Doré, 1866.

Cover design, book layout and typeset by Matthew Barron.

ISBN 13: 978-1-946138-00-2 (softcover)
ISBN 10: 1-946138-00-2 (softcover)

Publisher's Cataloging-in-Publication Data

NAMES: Grant, Raymond W.
TITLE: Times—They Are 'A Changing / by Raymond Grant.
DESCRIPTION: 1st edition | Portland, OR : Ad Fontes Press, 2017 | Summary: Commentary on the biblical book of Matthew, the 24th chapter, concerning the historic fulfillment of the end-time prophesy by Jesus Christ.
IDENTIFIERS: LCCN 2017931249 (print) | ISBN 9781946138002 (softcover)
SUBJECTS: LCSH: Bible. Matthew XXIV—Criticism, interpretation, etc. | Jesus Christ—Prophecies. | Bible—Prophecies—End of the world. | Second Advent.
CLASSIFICATION: LCC BS2575.52 .G73 2017 (print) | DDC 226.207

LC record available at https://lccn.loc.gov/2017931249

TABLE OF CONTENTS

GOD HAS MADE US COMPETENT AS MINISTERS OF A *NEW Covenant*, not of the Letter (Law), but of the Spirit; for the Letter (Law) kills, but the Spirit gives life.

Now, if the ministry that brought death, which was engraved in letters on stone, came with glory so that Israelites could not look steadily on the face of Moses because of its glory, fading though it was, will not the ministry of the Spirit be even more glorious?

If the ministry that condemns men is glorious, how much more glorious is the ministry that brings righteousness. For what was glorious has no glory now in comparison with the surpassing glory. And if what was fading away came with glory how much greater is the glory of that which lasts!

— 2 Corinthians 3:6–11

PREFACE

EVERY ONCE IN A WHILE THERE IS A BROADWAY THEATRICAL PRODUCTION THAT'S so amazing that it's most appropriate for it to "hit the road." After a successful run on New York's Broadway venue . . . and after rave reviews by the press have piqued the interest of the *hoi polloi* nationwide . . . a hundred sweaty stage hands will pack up the many costumes . . . the backdrop scenery. . . the sound equipment . . . and all the props . . . and load them into a dozen semi-trucks and drive down the already over-crowded turnpikes to the next city on the docket.

A few troupe tramps, who can't get enough of the sensational performances and/or are star stuck, bedazzled by the voice or vision of the lead actor, will even join the Diesel caravan across the country from city to city. They will be joined by the insatiable, story-starved press corps who drool over any crumb of gossip that falls their way, or any bone of contention that is thrown to them by an under-paid, disgruntled/jealous member of the cast.

More often than not, it is not the expertise of the star actors . . . actresses . . . understudies . . . that moves the audiences to tears or rapturous joy, but the skill-fully written script and the memorable dialogue masterfully directed by the behind-the-scene theatrical genius. People walk away reciting the lines . . . repeating the soul-piercing theme . . . rejoicing in the moral.

MASTER PIECE

Such is the jaw-dropping, soul-searching, mind-boggling type of response that results from an interaction with the words of Matthew 23–26. This part of Holy Writ contains a most intriguing *prophecy* filled with all the pathos and ethos of a thousand Greek dramas. It reaches way down into the bowels of a man and grasps even the most private emotions, and pulls them up into broad daylight for full exposure. Awe, terror, contemplation, hope, despair, amazement, reflection, disgust, and disquieting . . . they're all brought to the fore.

In this case, it is not only the content of the script(ure), but the One who is carrying along the dialogue, that makes this section of the Bible come alive. The back-drop is eye-catching . . . the 36-acre religious campus with a 15-story Temple emblazoned with gold and polished bronze; the music is rhythmically hypnotic . . . festive Passover hymns with Levitical choirs in the background; the mood is overshadowed by a full moon in springtime. But the One who is speaking this prophecy is the main reason why anyone and everyone sits up and takes notice! The *Prophet* matters most.

The Prophet is none other than Jesus, called the Christ . . . the Teacher from Nazareth . . . the miracle worker . . . the self-acclaimed Savior, on the one hand, and yet the one attested to by John, Moses, and the *Father*, on the other hand! We are about to study, not the words of an ancient holy man nor the ranting of a mortal social activist, but the inspired words from the mouth of Him who inhabits eternity . . . *and* who walks the stage of Mt. Olivet.

It is therefore, incumbent that we pay close attention to what He said . . . rightly interpreting each phrase . . . understanding each verse . . . and applying each admonition spoken from His heart.

SHOWTIME

What would it be like if you were given expensive tickets to a play's exclusive showing, but you were told the wrong time and given the wrong date? Bummer, eh? It would be quite a disappointment . . . an appointment missed by a false informer. It would be so disheartening.

And so it is with Jesus's prophecy we are about to interact with. We expect to be given its meaning correctly . . . its interpretation accurately . . . its application precisely. It would also be disheartening if we missed out on knowing the correct timing and dating of its predictions. It would be quite frustrating if we were given the wrong applications concerning its foretelling of strategic events in the history of mankind.

We want to experience the *real* drama. We don't want to miss the punch lines . . . the nuances of dialogue . . . the final outcome or climax with all its sense of awe and wonder . . . nor the denouement which explains the resident mysteries we were unable to unfold, though try we may.

Unfortunately, the prophecy Jesus gave on Mount Olivet just before the acting out of His Passion has many detractors and misinterpreters. Some biblical teachers have a commendable zeal, but not according to knowledge (Romans 10:2). Others simply "rush in where angels fear to tread," and come on up with calculations and date-setting, and scenarios quite foreign to the script(ure). Most commentators ignore the setting in which Jesus spoke this awesome, spine-tingling prognostication. They delve into the juicy steak parts of the prophecy (Matthew 24) without even setting the table properly (reading Matthew 23), or cleaning up afterwards (examining Matthew 25–6). Their books are merely a regurgitation of preconceived notions.

REVIEWERS AND CRITICS

To be more precise and informative, when we begin studying Matthew twenty-four, we discover that some who review it tend to place most of the events described by Jesus, way off into the nebulous future . . . that is future from the stand-point of the first century when Jesus prophesied. Their interpretation is "futuristic."

They teach that it's the end-of-the world when most of the prophecy is to be fulfilled. This group of men are called *Futurists, Judaizers,* or *Dispensationalists.* The Dispensationalists are known for pulling out of this Olivet Prophecy such events as:

A Secret Rapture of the Church	Rebuilt Jewish Temple
The Great Tribulation	Restoration of animal sacrifice
The "parenthesis" of the Church Era	Antichrist covenant
Two or three Second Comings of Christ	Signs of the Times

They tend to place an emphasis on the alleged "favored-nation status" of Israel in the planned history of mankind; and consider the Church to be an after-thought in the mind of God, who wants to get it out of the way so He can continue exalting the Jewish people.

This type of interpreting, not only this prophecy, but the entire New Testament scriptures, was systematized around 1830 by the Darbyites and the Plymouth Brethren. They had been influenced by the clandestine trickery of Jesuit Catholic priests, Ribera and, later, Lacunza. Ribera wrote commentaries emphasizing a futuristic viewpoint, and Lacunza put emphasis on Jewish promises of a naturalistic sort. The Catholics dressed as Protestant ministers and infiltrated Great Britain with these strange doctrines, leading congregations like the Plymouth Brethren away from orthodox beliefs.

Before 1830 the overwhelming majority of biblical scholars had taught that the Kingdom of God (with local churches as its embassies) was *the* fulfillment and long-awaited-for anticipation of Old Testament prophecies. Jesus was its Messiah (incarnated, crucified, and coronated) which the ancient men of God longed to see. (1 Peter 1:10–12). Anything contrary to this belief would have been considered "a different Gospel" and something to be avoided.

The second group of prophetic critics see a *mixture* of end-of-the-world scenarios *with* specific prophecies about the impending Destruction of the Jewish Temple in the first century (70 A.D.). They recognize the cultural and chronological context of Jesus's prophecy, but are ill at ease in applying all of it to the Destruction of Jerusalem because of the grandiose verbiage Jesus used in conveying what He meant.

Many of the scholars in this group are known as *Historical Premillennialists.* However, several denominations of Christianity who would not consider themselves as "millennialists" would fit into this category of interpreters. And essentially, they all do not subscribe to the many unorthodox doctrines promoted by the modern Dispensationalists. The Church is their main focus.

Historic Premillennialists give weight to the traumatic episode that was about to befall the Land of Judea when the Romans invaded, but they look forward through the corridors of time and anticipate *two Comings* of Christ: one before an alleged Millennium (1,000-year era), and another coming at the end of the Millennium, which would occur at the end of the world.

The third major aggregation of this prophecy's interpreters agree with the previous group in that the major topic of Jesus is the corruption of Judea and its impending doom: a coming of Christ in judgment whereby the land would be ravaged and the majestic and sacred Temple would be desolated . . . destroyed into oblivion . . . not one stone left upon another!

The difference with the previous group, however, is that they emphasize the need to recognize the chronological *bookends* which Jesus gave at the beginning and at the end of His discourse, which limit the events described to the first century (to 70 A.D.). *Verily, verily, I say unto you, all this will come upon this generation (23:36, 24:34).* And the grand astronomical verbiage which Jesus employed with "overtime" emphasis, they contend, can easily be understood as a way of describing that Judgment by recalling the figures of speech common in Jewish scriptures and apocalyptic literature published at that time.

When Jesus eventually does discuss the end of the world in contrast to His coming in judgment upon the Temple, He specifically only mentions *one* climactic Coming, not two or three . . . just one Second Coming . . . one THE END!

1. THE BASIS OF THE MODERNIST PROPHECY "SIGNS OF THE TIMES" INTERPRETATION (DISPENSATIONALISM)

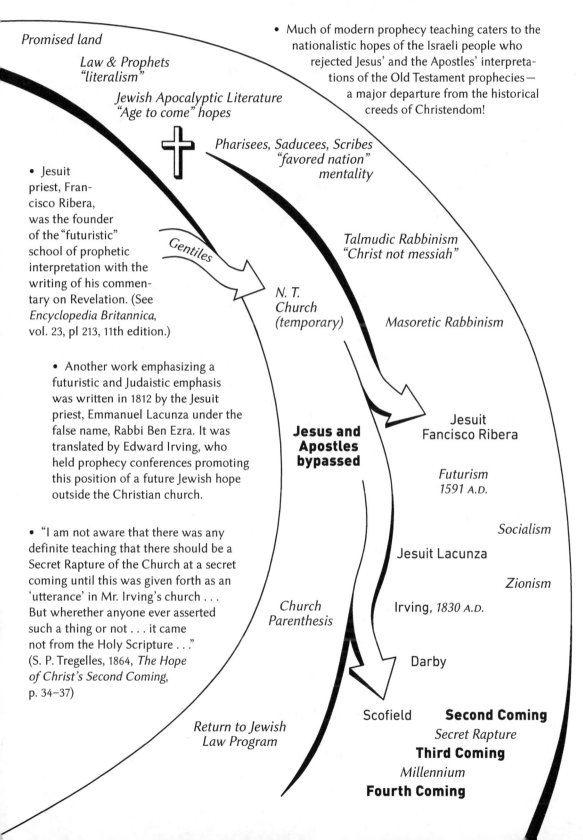

Promised land

Law & Prophets "literalism"

Jewish Apocalyptic Literature "Age to come" hopes

- Much of modern prophecy teaching caters to the nationalistic hopes of the Israeli people who rejected Jesus' and the Apostles' interpretations of the Old Testament prophecies — a major departure from the historical creeds of Christendom!

Pharisees, Saducees, Scribes "favored nation" mentality

- Jesuit priest, Francisco Ribera, was the founder of the "futuristic" school of prophetic interpretation with the writing of his commentary on Revelation. (See *Encyclopedia Britannica*, vol. 23, pl 213, 11th edition.)

Gentiles

Talmudic Rabbinism "Christ not messiah"

N. T. Church (temporary)

Masoretic Rabbinism

- Another work emphasizing a futuristic and Judaistic emphasis was written in 1812 by the Jesuit priest, Emmanuel Lacunza under the false name, Rabbi Ben Ezra. It was translated by Edward Irving, who held prophecy conferences promoting this position of a future Jewish hope outside the Christian church.

Jesus and Apostles bypassed

Jesuit Francisco Ribera

Futurism 1591 A.D.

- "I am not aware that there was any definite teaching that there should be a Secret Rapture of the Church at a secret coming until this was given forth as an 'utterance' in Mr. Irving's church . . . But wherether anyone ever asserted such a thing or not . . . it came not from the Holy Scripture . . ." (S. P. Tregelles, 1864, *The Hope of Christ's Second Coming*, p. 34–37)

Socialism

Jesuit Lacunza

Zionism

Church Parenthesis

Irving, *1830 A.D.*

Darby

Return to Jewish Law Program

Scofield

Second Coming

Secret Rapture

Third Coming

Millennium

Fourth Coming

2. THE BASIS OF THE HISTORIC PREMILLENNIALISM INTERPRETATION

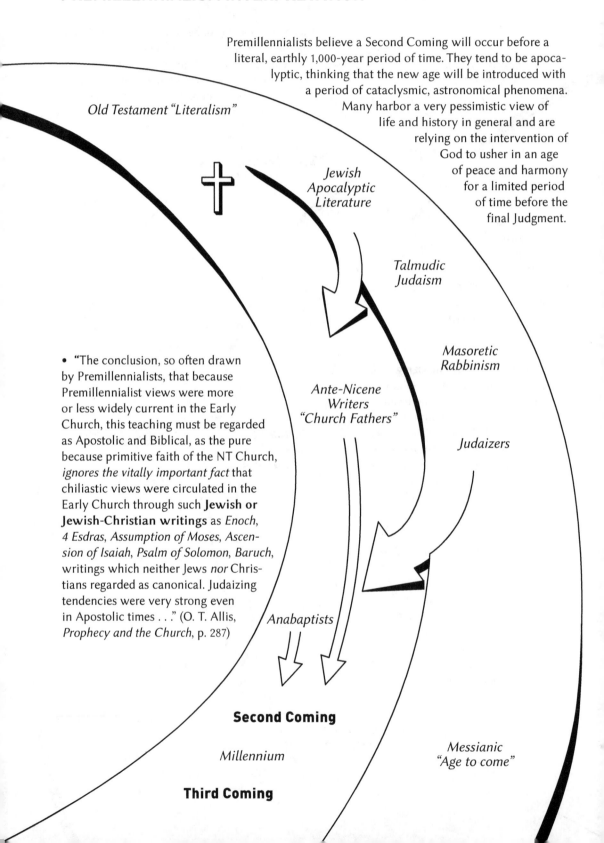

Premillennialists believe a Second Coming will occur before a literal, earthly 1,000-year period of time. They tend to be apocalyptic, thinking that the new age will be introduced with a period of cataclysmic, astronomical phenomena. Many harbor a very pessimistic view of life and history in general and are relying on the intervention of God to usher in an age of peace and harmony for a limited period of time before the final Judgment.

Old Testament "Literalism"

Jewish Apocalyptic Literature

Talmudic Judaism

Masoretic Rabbinism

Ante-Nicene Writers "Church Fathers"

Judaizers

• "The conclusion, so often drawn by Premillennialists, that because Premillennialist views were more or less widely current in the Early Church, this teaching must be regarded as Apostolic and Biblical, as the pure because primitive faith of the NT Church, *ignores the vitally important fact* that chiliastic views were circulated in the Early Church through such **Jewish or Jewish-Christian writings** as *Enoch, 4 Esdras, Assumption of Moses, Ascension of Isaiah, Psalm of Solomon, Baruch,* writings which neither Jews *nor* Christians regarded as canonical. Judaizing tendencies were very strong even in Apostolic times . . ." (O. T. Allis, *Prophecy and the Church*, p. 287)

Anabaptists

Second Coming

Millennium

Messianic "Age to come"

Third Coming

3. THE BASIS OF TRUE INTERPRETATION OF PROPHECY!

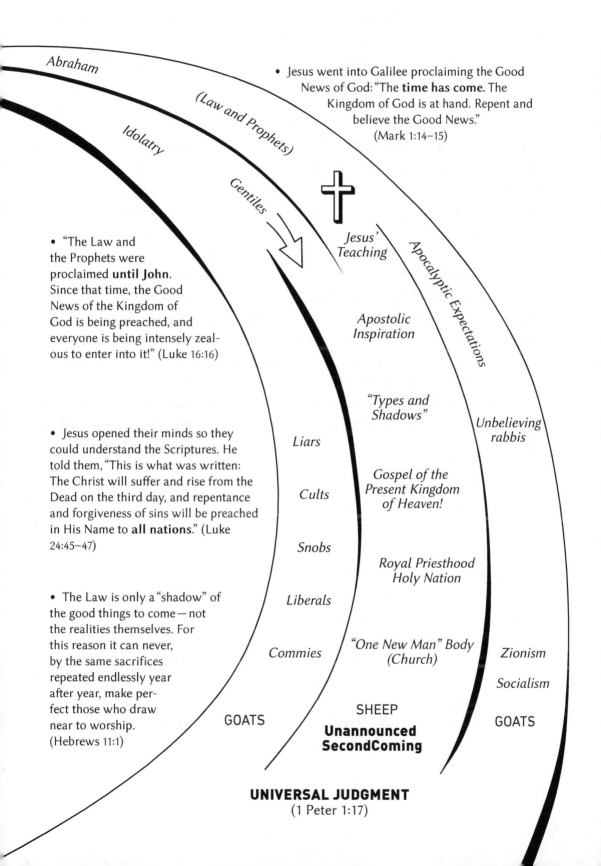

Abraham

(Law and Prophets)

Idolatry

Gentiles

Jesus' Teaching

Apocalyptic Expectations

• Jesus went into Galilee proclaiming the Good News of God: "The **time has come**. The Kingdom of God is at hand. Repent and believe the Good News." (Mark 1:14–15)

• "The Law and the Prophets were proclaimed **until John**. Since that time, the Good News of the Kingdom of God is being preached, and everyone is being intensely zealous to enter into it!" (Luke 16:16)

Apostolic Inspiration

"Types and Shadows"

Unbelieving rabbis

Liars

• Jesus opened their minds so they could understand the Scriptures. He told them, "This is what was written: The Christ will suffer and rise from the Dead on the third day, and repentance and forgiveness of sins will be preached in His Name to **all nations**." (Luke 24:45–47)

Gospel of the Present Kingdom of Heaven!

Cults

Snobs

Royal Priesthood Holy Nation

• The Law is only a "shadow" of the good things to come—not the realities themselves. For this reason it can never, by the same sacrifices repeated endlessly year after year, make perfect those who draw near to worship. (Hebrews 11:1)

Liberals

Commies

"One New Man" Body (Church)

Zionism

Socialism

GOATS

SHEEP
Unannounced SecondComing

GOATS

UNIVERSAL JUDGMENT
(1 Peter 1:17)

CHOICES

So . . . so then . . . so then which of these three approaches to Jesus's grand prophecy ought one to take? It's like trying to decide where one ought to sit in the theater to get the best view, feel the most emotions, and enjoy the play. Which side? . . . How high? . . . How distant? And how soft the seating?

We will examine *Rules of Interpretation (the study of hermeneutics)* later, but for now, we let common sense rule our decision: (a) We ought to let Jesus speak for Himself as much as possible without distractions from modern customs,. cults, or creeds; (b) We should see, and rely upon, time restrictions that are mentioned plainly; (c) and it would be prudent to also "walk a mile or two" in the sandals of Jesus . . . get His perspective on life (Jewish life in the first century) . . . slip into His mind for a minute . . . and then come to a conclusion as to what He is really trying to accomplish by giving this prophecy to His disciples.

Having considered all these, and further, realizing the "greater responsibility" that a teacher/minister has with Judgment Day in view, it is with humility and trepidation that the third perspective has been chosen for this book. More reasons will become evident as each verse is analyzed forthwith.

It is hoped that the greatest glory for Christ (for Christ and His Church) will be achieved in the direction this study takes. Perhaps the reader will gain a better perspective of the theme of the whole Bible (God's revelation to man), with the manifest continuity between the Old and New Testaments seen more clearly. And then, perhaps, we all can find our place in God's plan . . . our destiny in God's design . . . our peace in God's presence.

In God's presence, because this Prophet Jesus still walks the corridors of time, and skips through the halls of history, knocking on the doors of our hearts along the way.

By way of anticipation, it begs to be pointed out that Jesus did not leave His disciples in the throes of despair with the announcement of the desolation of the sacred Temple. But by further teaching and *by exemplary and astounding conduct*, Jesus introduced the grand theme of the beginning of a new Era: the confirming of the New Covenant era foretold by the Old Testament prophets!

The disciples were to experience a transition period that would be quite tumultuous, but also see with their own eyes how the new majestic Kingdom of God would affect the history of all nations . . . for good . . . for ever. *The Times, they were 'a Changing!*

PROPHETIC PROLOGUE

GOD HAS MADE US COMPETENT AS MINIS-
ters of a New Covenant, not of the
Letter but of the Spirit; for the Letter kills,
but the Spirit gives life.

— 2 Corinthians 3:6

AND IT CAME TO PASS, when He was come nigh to Bethphage and Bethany, at the mount called *the mount of* Olives, He sent two of His disciples, ³⁰ saying,

"Go ye into the village over against *you;* in the which at your entering ye shall find a colt tied, whereon yet never man sat: loose him, and bring *him hither.* ³¹ And if any man ask you, Why do ye loose *him?* thus shall ye say unto him, Because the Lord hath need of him."

³² And they that were sent went their way, and found even as He had said unto them. ³³ And as they were loosing the colt, the owners thereof said unto them, "Why loose ye the colt?" ³⁴ And they said, "The Lord hath need of him."

³⁵ And they brought him to Jesus: and they cast their garments upon the colt, and they set Jesus thereon. ³⁶ And as He went, they spread their clothes in the way. ³⁷ And when He was come nigh, even now at the descent of the mount of Olives, the whole multitude of the disciples began to rejoice and praise God with a loud voice for all the mighty works that they had seen; ³⁸ saying,

"Blessed be the King that cometh in the name of the Lord: peace in heaven, and glory in the highest."

³⁹ And some of the Pharisees from among the multitude said unto him, "Master, rebuke thy disciples." ⁴⁰ And He answered and said unto them,

"I tell you that, if these should hold their peace, the stones would immediately cry out."

⁴¹ ¶ And when He was come near, He beheld the city, and wept over it, ⁴² saying,

"If thou hadst known, even thou, at least in this thy day, the things *which belong* unto thy peace! but now they are hid from thine eyes. ⁴³ For the days shall come upon thee, that thine enemies shall cast a trench about thee, and compass thee round, and keep thee in on every side, ⁴⁴ And shall lay thee even with the ground, and thy children within thee; and they shall not leave in thee one stone upon another; because thou knewest not the time of thy visitation." ◄ **KJV**

Prophetic Prologue
LUKE 19:29–44

THERE IS NO MELODRAMA SO EXCITING AS THE ACTING OUT OR FORETELLING OF THE *End-times*, and nothing as spell-binding as the narrating of the *Signs of the Times* scenario which allegedly depict the end of the world as we know it. The human mind is easily enthralled by renditions of the Apocalypse and raging battles surrounding the idea of an *Armageddon:* the climax of the contest between good and evil.

These topics are a kaleidoscope of anxiety, curiosity, fear, and anticipation that change with the turn of the page in a Last Days book, or the movement of a prophet's hand behind a lectern. The casual student can experience a whole gamut of emotions as his eyes move from charts to paragraphs to artist's drawings of the spectacular End of all that is.

THE TRUTH, JUST THE TRUTH

Truth is such an elusive thing, especially during a political year. And there is so much pharmaceutical and nutritional carnival-hawking in advertising, one just doesn't know what to think! What's really real?

It is legitimate to ask, also, is there any truth to all this hype about the End of the World? Are the prophecy-teachers giving it to us straight, or are our emotions being manipulated? Are our concerns about the future being exploited by book-selling charlatans, and movie directors who are pulling our strings like we're marionettes? Puppets for their profit?

Let's assume that there is really an End to this world someday; still, is it going to happen the way that we are being told? Are there really signs when it is going to happen? And the big question: What good are premonitions if everything is going to end up, well, ended? Over with? Terminal? What could we ever do about it if we all are just going to be lint swept up and put into the dust bin of the universe, that itself might disappear into nothingness?

Are the Last Days novels a good source for information to answer our deep-seated questions? Are any of the *Left Behind* fear-flicks of use to inform us of what really is going to happen? Or, what of the workshops and lectures at all those prophecy conferences; could they quench our insatiable curiosity like even a drop of water on a rich man's tongue who is tortured in purgatory? Do these lecturers correctly present the truth about "the signs of the end" in a way we can trust to be true?

BIBLICAL TOPIC

There is one thing we can be sure of: the Bible does speak about the End of eras, End of ages, End of the world. It does present a finality about the plans and purposes of Almighty God, and of human history . . . whatever form they may take . . . however they may transpire . . . whenever they will occur.

And it is certain that *signs* of all sorts are mentioned in the scriptures: prophetic signs, messianic signs, miraculous signs, end-time signs.

It is as apparent as the Sahara sun on a cloudless day that the God of the Bible never wanted Him or His ways to be without signs that would confirm the truths relevant to people in His creation. He seems to have wanted faith in His principles and statutes to be founded upon credible evidence . . . especially faith in the teachings of His Son, Jesus. (Mark 16:20; John 2:11, 23; Acts 14:3; 15:12; Luke 2:12; Matthew 16:3; Luke 21:25) The Christian faith was to be founded upon facts . . . confirmed . . . verified . . . demonstrated. "Signs" were some of those facts.

The *signs* that have been given about past events are easy to understand today. The miraculous signs (healings, exorcisms, resurrections) were empirical evidences that were verified by family members, doctors (knowledgeable priests), and even admitted by hostile antagonists. The signs swirling around in the wind on Christmas night with heavenly back-up angelic choirs were confirmed by "going and seeing." The "sign of Jonah" which referred to the three days and nights of Jesus being in the grave, has been fulfilled. (Matthew 12:38–40) "The signs of the times" which referred to the decadent Jewish culture of the first century are confirmed by historians.

But the *end-time signs* are those that we have trouble distinguishing and determining. To which "end time" do they refer . . . the end of a nation. . . . the end of an era . . . the end of the world? And we ask, "Which phrases or statements are really 'signs . . . instead of literary metaphors or similes?"

The object of our study, Matthew 23–26, is quite often used as a petri dish that spawns a whole listing of end-time signs. "When will these things happen?" was the question posed by the disciples. Will the tragic event(s) be soon or later? Are the signs referring to something about to happen, or to some event years down the dusty road of history? Is this really all about a Second Coming that was spoken about, or just some desolation in the long tumultuous history of Judaism? Most of these questions have answers that relegate the signs of Matthew 24 to the great climax of the world at the Second Coming with all its concomitant events . . . according to modern evangelical telepastors . . . according to book sellers . . . according to movie makers.

But are they all right? Accurate? Truthful? It is incumbent to ask such. After all, for hundreds of years, many have pointed to "signs of the times" in their days and claimed . . . as their generation that would experience the End. Each generation, after each generation, prophecy teachers have made the same claim . . . with the same results: everyone has been wrong! The **failure rate** of prognosticators and teachers of "signs" is 100%. None of past prophecy interpreters have gotten it right! Zero! Nada! Zilch! That is sufficient reason to give us pause.

INTERPRETING SKILLS

How can we know what a passage of scripture teaches? Especially the Matthew 23–26 section with all its prophetic implications. How can we actually come to truth and line up with what Jesus really wanted us and His disciples to know? With such a failure rate on the part of men who seemed to have good Christian character and pastoral reputation, how can we even be certain our own interpretation is correct?

The answer lies in a field of study called *exegesis* which is based upon rules of interpretation known as *hermeneutics*. Exegesis (expounding) flows from commonly accepted principles which insure that the thought we draw out of a text is the same one the author intended to communicate.

For example, one of the major principles of hermeneutics is the *Context Principle*. A passage is to be interpreted within the context of the whole book in which it is laid: the literary context. Also, the historical, cultural, and religious contexts must also be studied to come up with an accurate understanding of a text.

Therefore, to draw out truths from Matthew 24 (wherein a lot of end-time signs allegedly are listed) a good student must consider Matthew 23–26, as well. Phrases must not be ripped out of Matthew 24 with no consideration of what preceded, and what transpired, later in the book.

In like manner, misinterpretations can be avoided like the plague if sufficient research is made concerning the Roman Empire during which the events of Matthew took place. The Romans and their puppet kings played a tremendously large role on the New Testament stage. Their historians complement much of the scriptures with insights often overlooked by modern prophecy lecturers.

The Jewish context is also of great importance. The cultural customs add window-dressing to the temporal, everyday events that Jesus and His disciples interacted with. Some nuances in the stories would be missed without a thorough study of Judaic life. The community activists, the religious institutions, the political intrigue, the economic inequities, the judicial oppression . . . all appear like a pop-up book during the life of Jesus . . . and they must be researched along with the culture.

Since Jesus mentioned by name the prophet *Daniel*—and used his terminology throughout all His life—then every effort must be made to read and understand his prophecies in the Old Testament. (See Matthew 24:15) One cannot understand the tremendous unfolding of events Jesus was warning about without mastering the book of Daniel, which spoke of *the Son of Man, the Kingdom, the abomination of desolation, the destruction of the Temple, etc.* And along with Daniel, the Psalmist and Isaiah are mentioned by Jesus, so they ought to be referred to for background material in understanding Jesus's teaching. (Psalm 118:26, Isaiah 13:10; 34:4)

FURTHER AIDS

To help make scriptures clearer another principle of hermeneutics is often solicited: Let scripture interpret scripture. This means that another passage found in the rest of the Bible will often shed light upon the verse at hand. What a verse means in Matthew 24 can be determined by seeing how the imagery or literary phrases were used before in Judaic literature. This prevents modern readers from imposing a modern-day definition upon words of ancient times that may have had a different shade of meaning. English words cannot "trump" Hebrew and Greek vocabularies, because the Bible was originally written in Hebrew and Greek, not English. Modern literalism cannot replace ancient figurative meanings of biblical words.

The Apostles were eye-witnesses of the life and times of Jesus. They received His teaching "first hand" and then were filled with the Holy Spirit on the Day of Pentecost so they might fully understand its implications for every-day living. Therefore, we ought to pay attention as to how they interpreted the scriptures, especially the Old Testament writings.

How the New Testament disciples related to the long history of the Jewish nation, *and* how they saw the fulfillment of the ancient prophecies unfolding, should take precedent over the opinions of modern day lecturers. The scriptures of the Apostles (and Luke) are better at giving an understanding of the Taanach (O.T., Jewish prophets and Law) than any modern novel or movie about End-times ever could. It is important that we leave behind any preconceived traditions of men—or recently contrived cultic teachings—and run to the classroom of the first century and sit down at the feet of those eye-witnesses of the majesty of the glory of Christ. (2 Peter 1:16–21)

Keep in mind that much of what passes as teaching about the End Times in modern days was never taught before 1830! According to their own admission, the advocates of dispensationalism state that their interpretations of prophecy—and especially their doctrine that separates the Church from Israel in the plan of God— were *new and novel ideas* never before taught by the church theologians. To put any stock in them, then, would not be prudent . . . no matter how much they are propagated by television media or published literature . . . no matter how sensational their movies are.

Another great aid in interpreting the Bible is the use of Synoptic Gospels, that is, the placing of the four Gospels of the Evangelists "side by side" in a parallel fashion. This especially helpful in the study of Matthew 24 because one verse in a first Gospel may show us what the same verse in another Gospel meant because of a little different wording or insertion of an idea that helps explain a point. By this method, we "let scripture interpret scripture."

Another idea to keep in mind when trying to understand verses is the practice of letting historical / literal verses interpret the symbolic ones, and not the other way around. Some have advocated beginning with the book of Revelation in their study. However, a reading and understanding of "Matthew to Jude" first, before delving into harder, symbolic books is highly recommended. It is quite reasonable that the "easier" should interpret the "harder". In other words, interpretations of symbolic passages cannot contradict the plain, historical/literal verses that teach the Gospel of Christ. Any conclusions drawn must fall in step with the preaching of the Gospel of the Kingdom of God. (Galatians 1:6–9)

In other words, any interpretation of the mysterious symbols, or of the figurative language, must not contradict the *plain doctrines* of the Gospel of the Kingdom that are clearly taught in the New Testament. The doctrines of "salvation" are so important for all ethnic nationalities. For some new or novel interpretation of prophecy to mess with them has eternal consequences, jeopardizing the precious souls of men and women. This should never be.

In all matters, it must be foremost in our thinking that Jesus is our "Master-teacher." (Matthew 23:10) His place of authority must not be usurped by any man, no matter if he be up-standing in our denomination, or seemingly of noble character, or no matter how charismatic and eloquent he may be.

And His Word is alone, our source for "rule and conduct" . . . and understanding of the End-times. Not any author of novels . . . nor any director of cinematic presentations. Just the Word of God. Not the tradition of men, which often nullifies or reverses the teaching of Jesus.

Sola Scriptura was the battle-cry of the Reformation, at a time when Bible students realized that the Word of God was to be the *only* arbitrator for establishing doctrines of creed and conduct. What had been called, "the Writings of the Church Fathers", were not to be the "source" of determining what was orthodox and what was heresy. The theological opinions of men a hundred and more years after the time of the Apostles, they realized, were not a good foundation for systematizing theology. And we ought to realize this as well.

Along this same line of thought, it is worth our while to notice that the commentaries and footnotes found in Study Bibles and Reference Bibles are *not inspired* writings, and are not part of the Holy Bible. They are not infallible interpretations of the scriptures. We are not to place them on equal footing with the Word of God. Many naive and gullible souls who have read the *Scofield Study Bible* have fallen into this erroneous habit, and have been led astray by many of his outlandish opinions. (For example: The grand Sermon on the Mount and the Lord's Prayer are not for Christians, only Jews; there is a distinction between Jews and Gentiles in the Church Age; etc.)

Finally, it is incumbent that we rely upon the Holy Spirit to lead us into truth, and not the spirit of our contemporary age; that is, the spirit of fear, anxiety, revivalism, or curiosity. (John 14:26) Nor the charismatic spirit of some telepastor or prophecy conference speaker.

The same Holy Spirit who inspired the prophets of Old to write concerning "the sufferings of Christ and the glories that should follow" ought to be our Guide through the modern maze of prophetic rabbit-trails and detours that complicate our understanding of God's awesome prophetic Word. (1 Peter 1:10–12)

He knows the way.

CURTAIN
RAISER

WHEN JOHN THE BAPTIZER SAW MANY of the Pharisees and Sadducees coming to where he was baptizing, he said to them: "You brood of snakes, who has warned you to flee from the *coming wrath*? Produce fruit in keeping with repentance, and do not think you can say to yourselves, 'We have Abraham as our father.'

"I declare that out of these stones God can raise up sons for Abraham. The ax is already at the root of the trees, and every tree that does not produce good fruit will be cut down and thrown in to the fire!"

— *Matthew 3:7–10*

THEN SPAKE JESUS to the multitude, and to His disciples, ² saying,

"The scribes and the Pharisees sit in Moses' seat: ³ All therefore whatsoever they bid you observe, *that* observe and do; but do not ye after their works: for they say, and do not. ⁴ For they bind heavy burdens and grievous to be borne, and lay *them* on men's shoulders; but they *themselves* will not move them with one of their fingers. ⁵ But all their works they do for to be seen of men: they make broad their phylacteries, and enlarge the borders of their garments, ⁶ and love the uppermost rooms at feasts, and the chief seats in the synagogues, ⁷ and greetings in the markets, and to be called of men, 'Rabbi, Rabbi.' ⁸ But be not ye called Rabbi: for One is your Master, *even* Christ; and all ye are brethren. ⁹ And call no *man* your father upon the earth: for One is your Father, which is in heaven. ¹⁰ Neither be ye called masters: for One is your Master, *even* Christ. ¹¹ But he that is greatest among you shall be your servant. ¹² And whosoever shall exalt himself shall be abased; and he that shall humble himself shall be exalted.

¹³ ¶ But woe unto you, scribes and Pharisees, hypocrites! for ye shut up the kingdom of heaven against men: for ye neither go in *yourselves*, neither suffer ye them that are entering to go in.

¹⁴ Woe unto you, scribes and Pharisees, hypocrites! for ye devour widows' houses, and for a pretence make long prayer: therefore ye shall receive the greater damnation.

¹⁵ Woe unto you, scribes and Pharisees, hypocrites! for ye compass sea and land to make one proselyte, and when he is made, ye make him twofold more the child of hell than yourselves.

¹⁶ Woe unto you, *ye* blind guides, which say, Whosoever shall swear by the temple, it is nothing; but whosoever shall swear by the gold of the Temple, he is a debtor!

¹⁷ *Ye* fools and blind: for whether is greater, the gold, or the Temple that sanctifieth the gold? ¹⁸ And, Whosoever shall swear by the altar, it is nothing; but whosoever sweareth by the gift that is upon it, he is guilty.

¹⁹ *Ye* fools and blind: for whether is greater, the gift, or the altar that sanctifieth the gift? ²⁰ Whoso therefore shall swear by the altar, sweareth by it, and by all things thereon. ²¹ And whoso shall swear by the Temple, sweareth by it, and by Him that dwelleth therein. ²² And he that shall swear by heaven, sweareth by the throne of God, and by Him that sitteth thereon.

²³ Woe unto you, scribes and Pharisees, hypocrites! for ye pay tithe of mint and anise and cummin, and have omitted the weightier *matters* of the law, judgment, mercy, and faith: these ought ye to have done, and not to leave the other undone. ²⁴ *Ye* blind guides, which strain at a gnat, and swallow a camel.

²⁵ Woe unto you, scribes and Pharisees, hypocrites! for ye make clean the outside of the cup and of the platter, but within they are full of extortion and excess. ²⁶ *Thou* blind Pharisee, cleanse

first that *which is* within the cup and platter, that the outside of them may be clean also.

²⁷ Woe unto you, scribes and Pharisees, hypocrites! for ye are like unto whited sepulchres, which indeed appear beautiful outward, but are within full of dead *men's* bones, and of all uncleanness. ²⁸ Even so ye also outwardly appear righteous unto men, but within ye are full of hypocrisy and iniquity.

²⁹ Woe unto you, scribes and Pharisees, hypocrites! because ye build the tombs of the prophets, and garnish the sepulchres of the righteous, ³⁰ And say, If we had been in the days of our fathers, we would not have been partakers with them in the blood of the prophets. ³¹ Wherefore ye be witnesses unto yourselves, that ye are the children of them which killed the prophets. ³² Fill ye up then the measure of your fathers. ³³ *Ye* serpents, *ye* generation of vipers, how can ye escape the damnation of hell? ³⁴ Wherefore, behold, I send unto you prophets, and wise men, and scribes: and *some* of them ye shall kill and crucify; and *some* of them shall ye scourge in your synagogues, and persecute *them* from city to city: ³⁵ That upon you may come all the righteous blood shed upon the earth, from the blood of righteous Abel unto the blood of Zacharias son of Barachias, whom ye slew between the temple and the altar. ³⁶ Verily I say unto you, All these things shall come upon this generation.

³⁷ O Jerusalem, Jerusalem, *thou* that killest the prophets, and stonest them which are sent unto thee, how often would I have gathered thy children together, even as a hen gathereth her chickens under *her* wings, and ye would not! ³⁸ Behold, your house is left unto you desolate. ³⁹ For I say unto you, Ye shall not see Me henceforth, till ye shall say, Blessed *is* He that cometh in the name of the Lord."

◄ KJV

CURTAIN RAISER
MATTHEW 23:1–39

A MELODRAMA IS ABOUT TO BE ENACTED ON THE MOUNT OLIVET STAGE OF HIStory. The characters are gathering, as well as the dark shadows of suspense. Dialogue will be spoken that will resound throughout time . . . and Church history.

But first, an introduction, a *curtain raiser*, a speech that will (a) give the background, (b) introduce the actors, (c) set the mood, and (d) reveal the theme. It is spoken by the Main Character / Director / Playwright, and He masterfully builds the suspense. He piques the interest of the common folk, arouses the napping minds of His disciples, and provokes the consternation of the antagonists. This provocative speech is recorded in the twenty-third chapter of Matthew's Gospel.

MATTHEW 23

The first twelve verses are exhortations directed toward the crowds among whom are standing the Twelve. The rest of the speech is an invective lambasting the religious elders of Judaism (verses 13–39). With jugular veins bulging, brow furrowed, and fist pounding, Jesus came the closest He ever did to swearing! His expression of fury and foam would make a Shakespearean actor purple with envy.

But Jesus wasn't acting. His script was not written by another. He was not reading the lines of another playwright. He "was telling it like it was." He was speaking His mind from His heart of hearts. And He was doing it with accuracy and precision; His descriptions of the wicked, and denunciations of the corrupt, were spot on.

Everyone listening pretty much had to agree. Both the Judaean crowds and the Jewish theologians (rabbis) were aware of the nature of the culture around them. The society, the economy, the politics, the Temple worship . . . were all marked by a conspicuous corruption. All were tainted with greed like catsup on the aprons of a

Bar-B-Que picnic. All were poisoned by sipping from the hot soup of power-laced with self-interest. Taxation was out of control. Assassinations by the Sicarii, *at the behest of the priests*, were all too common. The rich were getting richer, and the poor poorer. The courts belonged to the highest bidder / briber. The widows, orphans, and innocent victims never had their "day in court." Who needed the oppression of a foreign occupier when you had enough tyranny that was home-grown?

TEACHERS

Teachers of the Law and the Pharisees sit in Moses's seat, began Jesus. He then recounted what the people already knew: they were inconsistent in their function as ministers of the Mosaic culture. They went beyond Moses at times, and added layers upon layers of rules and regulations so that at any one time, anybody would be guilty of something! But meanwhile, these men would write in "loopholes" for themselves. *They bundle up heavy loads and put them on men's shoulders, but they themselves are not willing to lift a finger to help out.* (vs. 4) Picture an overloaded donkey with a fat man walking along side, giving it orders . . . beating it unmercifully . . . prodding it at will, his will.

It was true, a society can maintain its felicity and domestic tranquility only by the institution of some laws. As pertains to Judea, Mosaic Laws. But these teachers went beyond their civic and civil duty, imposing meticulous observance of the minutiae of the Law, and enjoined new precepts which were not based upon any authority given by the Law.

Everything they do is to be seen by men. (vs. 5) Along with power comes pride. They are twin sister uglies. Influence over others sends the soul of man up the escalator to the mezzanine of professional recognition and the balcony of undo honor. Looking down on the *hoi polloi* becomes second nature, then, baser nature.

Arrogance manifests itself in different forms, like a zombie that morphs when it is seemingly eliminated by one attack: religious paraphernalia and trinkets with deep mystical powers . . . garments that glitter and robes of ermine fur bedecked with rhinestones, outlined with lace and tassels that tantalize the eye . . . requests for seating at tables reserved for those with status and station . . . sitting in throne-like chairs on the platform of synagogues, cathedrals, and tabernacles . . . greetings that recognize their exaltedness, and salutations that tickle the ear like a feather in the hands of a lover. (vss. 5–7)

"Rab + bi" in Hebrew, means "my great (one)", such as a Briton would address royalty as "my lord" or "my lady" some historians think this title was begun by the great Hillel (b. 112 B.C.). The religious rulers were not content to be called this just once; "Rabbi, Rabbi", twice for emphasis, was more appropriate! It has a nice ring to it . . . unless it falls upon the ear of God; then it's the sound of a thud on a lead gong.

Thus Jesus gave the prohibition, *You are not to be called Rabbi!* "You" is quite emphatic in the original Greek sentence. "I'm talking to you!" "Listen up; this is a no, no!" "They may consider themselves 'great ones' but in reality, **you** all are *brothers*." (Do a word study on the use of 'brothers' in the New Testament, and especially, in the Church, and it will surprise you as to how much this is emphasized.)

Instead of human titles of honor, Jesus reemphasized the fact that just as there is One Lord, One Way, One Salvation, One Hope, etc, there really is only One Leader (Master, NIV), One Father, One Guide (Teacher, NIV). And these are not human beings on earth, but heavenly and divine entities.

The words translated as "Master" and "Teacher" (NIV) are the same in the Greek, *kathēgētēs*, and really mean *leader, guide*. In modern Greek, it means *professor*, and can refer to an instructor occupying a high position in academia, such as a School Master, or a University Professor. This word had the similar meaning in Jesus's day.

What is obsolete and aging will soon disappear. Hebrews 8:13

Has the modern Church obeyed this prohibition laid out by Christ? Since "rabbi" means "teacher" (John 1:38), and the Latin term for "teacher" is *Doctor* (its equivalent), the answer would have to be 'no'. For example, when we look at the introduction to the *Spirit Filled Life Study Bible* (Nashville: Thomas Nelson, 1991), we see that practically all of the contributors have doctoral degrees listed after their names!

They exult in being called "doctor" or "teacher" (reverend professor), if not "church father." (Some have even gone back to wearing "tassled" garments! . . . have their own parking space . . . private lavatories . . . high-backed platform seats.

There are two words that stand in stark contrast — rather, in warm contrast — to the haughtiness of the holy men: *brothers* (vs. 8), and *servant* (vs. 11). Within the Kingdom of God, and in its local embassies (local churches) there is no hierarchy. Though some are more scholarly than others, believers are all "brothers" with only One superior Authority, *our Father which art in Heaven* (vs. 9, Matthew 6:9). Those gifted men who are more literate serve their brothers in that capacity, and do not use it as an opportunity to advance themselves, or to establish a collegiate cadre of professors (theologians) who exploit the congregations.

> *Both, the One who makes men holy, and those who are made holy are of the same family. So Jesus is not ashamed to call them brothers.*   (Hebrews 2:11, quoting Psalm 22:22 and Isaiah 8:18)

It is mandatory, then, that every gifted person treat his brother with respect and "brotherly love." (Romans 8:29, 15:14, 1 Corinthians 9:11–13, Galatians 5:13–14; 6:1) *Whoever humbles himself in this manner, will be exalted* in the eyes of God . . . where it really counts . . . where it really matters. Therein lies greatness . . . nobility . . . royalty . . . charity.

WOE TO YOU

If you can't trust a policeman, who can you trust? Who can you run to for help? If a child can not trust a parent, where can he turn? And if a congregant can't trust a pastor, how can he learn of salvation for his soul?

There is nothing more heart-breaking than the perversion of religion. There is nothing more deleterious than false doctrines taught by corrupt ministers. There is nothing more egregious than light becoming darkness. (Matthew 6:22–23) But, thanks be to a holy and just God, there is also nothing more disastrous than judgment on those who are guilty of such corruption!

Verses 13–39 are a graphic presentation of that reality. *Woe to you!* is repeated eight times with the certainty of a gavel's thud on a judge's desk. This phrase, or interjection (*ouai humin,* Gk.) is not merely an expression of grief: Alas! Rather it is a dogmatic assertion of judgment, a denunciation that is just the opposite of "blessing." It is a curse from the Christ! (Compare 11:20–21, Luke 6:20–26) This divine Brother has our back. If anyone messes with His kin, He responds with justified anger.

To underscore the pointed judicial-decision, the words "to you" are added. The long finger of justice is directed at the robed rascals with overt certainty. None can respond with, "Who me?" *Woe to you!* And you, and you, and you . . . Jesus addresses the many facets of the crystal palace of the Pharisees . . . just before He envisions its crackling and crumbling into a thousand pieces of broken glass.

Hypocrisy, like the turn of a kaleidoscope, takes many forms. Jesus saw them all: Exclusive bigotry, perverting the converting, hair-splitting dogmatism, "straining at a gnat", external ritual without internal ethics, whitewashing character flaws, seething hatred for all that is holy and all that might expose their corruption.

"Hypocrisy", the nasty word that echoed through the Temple hallways until it found freedom and darted across the courtyard to the priests' chambers, bouncing here on the hard cobblestones and there off the hard hearts of the Pharisees . . . accurately described the pretense of virtue that dominated the religious scene of Judea. Mentioned seven times by Jesus, there was no way the rabbis could be mistaken as to whom Jesus was pointing His finger. They were all culpable, feigning even the sanctity of Moses's Law. And if Moses was disqualified from entering the Promised Land because he did *not uphold God's holiness* and *broke faith* with God in the presence of the Israelites, certainly dire consequences were to be in store for these men. (Deuteronomy 32:48–52)

SUN GLASSES

Four times Jesus diagnosed the condition of the religious rulers: *blind guides* (twice), *blind men, blind Pharisees*. He was hitting hard at the proud reputation — self-designated reputation — of these clerics. The Apostle Paul recorded their boast:

> *Now you call yourself a Jew . . . if you are convinced that you are a guide for the blind, a light for those in darkness, an instructor of the foolish, a teacher of infants, because you (think you have) in the Law the embodiment of knowledge and truth . . .*
>
> *You who brag about the Law, do you dishonor God by breaking the Law? As it is written, "God's name is blasphemed among the Gentiles because of you."* (Romans 2:17–24, quoting Ezekiel 36:22–23)

"Guides for the blind (unlearned *hoi polloi)!*" Oh really? Jesus had previously confronted the rabbis about their ophthalmological sickness because they *nullified the Word of God for the sake of their traditions.*

> *The disciples came to Jesus and asked, "Do you know that the Pharisees were offended when they heard this?"* . . . .

> *He replied . . . "Leave them; they are blind guides of the blind. If a blind man leads a blind man, both will fall into a pit."* (Matthew 15:6–14; compare Luke 6:39, John 9:39–41)

They had turned a blind eye to the righteous teaching of Jesus who zeroed in on the heart issues of piety. The sun glasses they wore were so dark they could not see the "light of the glorious Gospel." The *eyes of their understanding* were so diseased they could not see Jesus as "the Light of the world." (John 9:5) And this Jesus, who opened the eyes of those blind from birth, they refused to see for an appointment.

O JERUSALEM, JERUSALEM

Christ was not a vindictive person without reason. He was a sentimental man with a caring passion for people who He described once as "sheep without a shepherd." He was often "moved with compassion." He loved . . .

> *As Jesus approached Jerusalem and saw the city, He **wept over it** and said, "If you, even you, had only known on this day what would bring you peace—but now it is hidden from your eyes.*
>
> *The days will come upon you when your enemies will build an embankment against you and encircle you and hem you in on every side. They will dash you to the ground, you and the children within your walls. They will not leave one stone on another, because you did not recognize the time of God's coming to you.* (Luke 19:41–44)
>
> *O Jerusalem, Jerusalem, you who kill the prophets and stone those sent to you, how often **I have longed** to gather your children together, like a hen gathers her chicks under her wings, but you would not let me.*
> *Look! Your house is left to you desolate.* (Luke 13:34–35)

But murder was in the DNA of the religious right. Diabolical intrigue was in the RNA of the religious left. They were *snakes . . . a brood of vipers . . . sons of their father the Devil . . . children of Belial . . .* at heart. Even though they claimed to be purer than their ancestors who *were guilty of shedding the innocent blood of the Old Testament prophets*, the next few years would prove that they were capable of doing the same: *prophets, wise men, and teachers* would be mercilessly stoned, crucified, and tortured by them. (Matthew 23:35–34) Men like James, Stephen, Peter, and nameless families drawn out from their homes by Saul, would become victims of the Pharisees' ire. In doing so they would be *filling up the full measure of the sin of their forefathers.*

All this blood would "be on their heads." And more! Judgment for all the righteous blood that was spilled on the ground in the Old Testament would be on their heads, as well. And to leave no misunderstanding about whom Jesus was referring to, He emphasized, *This generation will be responsible for the blood . . . Yes, I tell you, this generation will be held responsible for it all.* (Luke 11:50–51; Matthew 23:36)

And with this dire prognostication, the *curtain raiser* speech ends. The (a) historical background has been laid out, (b) the main characters have been introduced, (c) an ominous mood has been set, and (d) the theme of justice . . . long time comin' was presented. It is time for the *Questionable Dialogue* to begin in earnest.

A C T   I
QUESTIONABLE DIALOGUE

THE SPIRIT OF THE LORD GOD IS UPON Me because the LORD has anointed Me to preach good tidings to the poor. He has sent Me to heal the brokenhearted, to proclaim liberty to the captives, and the opening of the prison for those bound; to proclaim the acceptable year of the LORD, and the **Day of Vengeance** of our God; to comfort all who mourn, to console those who mourn in Zion . . .

— *Isaiah 61:1–3*

THE QUESTION

MATTHEW 24 And Jesus went out, and departed from the Temple: and His disciples came *to Him* for to shew Him the buildings of the Temple. ² And Jesus said unto them, "See ye not all these things? verily I say unto you, There shall not be left here one stone upon another, that shall not be thrown down."

³ ¶ And as He sat upon the mount of Olives, the disciples came unto Him privately, saying, "Tell us, when shall these things be? and what *shall be* the sign of thy coming, and of the end of the world?"

MARK 13 And as He went out of the temple, one of His disciples saith unto Him, "Master, see what manner of stones and what buildings are here!" ² And Jesus answering said unto him, "Seest thou these great buildings? there shall not be left one stone upon another, that shall not be thrown down."

³ And as He sat upon the mount of Olives over against the temple, Peter and James and John and Andrew asked Him privately, ⁴ "Tell us, when shall these things be? and what shall be the sign when all these things shall be fulfilled?"

LUKE 21 And as some spake of the Temple, how it was adorned with goodly stones and gifts, He said, ⁶ "*As for* these things which ye behold, the days will come, in the which there shall not be left one stone upon another, that shall not be thrown down." ⁷ And they asked Him, saying, "Master, but when shall these things be? and what sign will there be when these things shall come to pass?"

WARNINGS AGAINST BEING DECEIVED

⁴ And Jesus answered and said unto them, "Take heed that no man deceive you. ⁵ For many shall come in My name, saying, 'I am Christ'; and shall deceive many. ⁶ And ye shall hear of wars and rumours of wars: see that ye be not troubled: for all *these things* must come to pass, **but the end is not yet.** ⁷ For nation shall rise against nation, and kingdom against kingdom: and there shall be famines, and pestilences, and earthquakes, in divers places. ⁸ All these are the beginning of sorrows (birth pangs).

⁵ And Jesus answering them began to say, "Take heed lest any man deceive you: ⁶ For many shall come in My name, saying, I am *Christ;* and shall deceive many. ⁷ And when ye shall hear of wars and rumours of wars, be ye not troubled: for such *things* must needs be; **but the end *shall* not *be* yet.** ⁸ For nation shall rise against nation, and kingdom against kingdom: and there shall be earthquakes in divers places, and there shall be famines and troubles: these are the beginnings of sorrows.

⁸ And He said, "Take heed **that ye be not deceived:** for many shall come in My name, saying, I am *Christ,* and the time draweth near: go ye not therefore after them. ⁹ But when ye shall hear of wars and commotions, be not terrified: for these things must first come to pass; **but the end is not by and by** (immediately)." ¹⁰ Then said He unto them, "Nation shall rise against nation, and kingdom against kingdom: ¹¹ And great earthquakes shall be in divers places, and famines, and pestilences; and fearful sights and great signs shall there be from heaven.

PERSECUTIONS PREDICTED AND INSTRUCTIONS WHAT TO DO.

⁹ "Then shall they deliver you up to be afflicted, and shall kill you: and ye shall be hated of all nations for My name's sake. ¹⁰ And then shall many be offended, and shall betray one another, and shall hate one another. ¹¹ And many false prophets shall rise, and shall deceive many. ¹² And because iniquity shall abound, the love of many shall wax cold. ¹³ But he that shall endure unto the end, the same shall be saved. ¹⁴ And this gospel of the kingdom shall be preached in all the world for a witness unto all nations; and then shall the end come.

[Note: Matthew's reference to the persecutions of the disciples is relatively brief. He omits the instructions as to premeditating, etc.

Luke omits the statement that the gospel must first be preached. His "not a hair perish," and "by your patience" (*i.e. endurance*), are the equivalent of "He that shall *endure* unto the end."]

⁹ ¶ But take heed to yourselves: for they shall deliver you up to councils; and in the synagogues ye shall be beaten: and ye shall be brought before rulers and kings for My sake, for a testimony against them. ¹⁰ And the gospel must first be published among all nations. ¹¹ But when they shall lead you, and deliver you up, take no thought beforehand what ye shall speak, neither do ye premeditate: but whatsoever shall be given you in that hour, that speak ye: for it is not ye that speak, but the Holy Ghost. ¹² Now the brother shall betray the brother to death, and the father the son; and children shall rise up against their parents, and shall cause them to be put to death. ¹³ And ye shall be hated of all men for My name's sake: but he that shall endure unto the end, the same shall be saved.

¹² But before all these, they shall lay their hands on you, and persecute you, delivering you up to the synagogues, and into prisons, being brought before kings and rulers for My name's sake. ¹³ And it shall turn to you for a testimony. ¹⁴ Settle it therefore in your hearts, not to meditate before what ye shall answer: ¹⁵ For I will give you a mouth and wisdom, which all your adversaries shall not be able to gainsay nor resist. ¹⁶ And ye shall be betrayed both by parents, and brethren, and kinsfolks, and friends; and some of you shall they cause to be put to death. ¹⁷ And ye shall be hated of all men for My name's sake. ¹⁸ But there shall not an hair of your head perish. ¹⁹ In your patience possess ye your souls.

THE DESTRUCTION OF JERSUALEM.
THE SIGN TO THE DISCIPLES — "WHEN YE SHALL SEE"

¹⁵ "When ye therefore shall see the abomination of desolation, spoken of by Daniel the prophet, stand in the holy place, (whoso readeth, let him understand:) ¹⁶ Then let them which be in Judaea flee into the mountains: ¹⁷ Let him which is on

¹⁴ ¶ "But when ye shall see the abomination of desolation, spoken of by Daniel the prophet, standing where it ought not, (let him that readeth understand,) then let them that be in Judaea flee to the mountains: ¹⁵ And let him that is on the housetop not go

²⁰ "And when ye shall see Jerusalem compassed with armies, then know that the desolation thereof is nigh. ²¹ Then let them which are in Judaea flee to the mountains; and let them which are in the midst of it depart out; and let

the housetop not come down to take any thing out of his house: [18] Neither let him which is in the field return back to take his clothes. [19] And woe unto them that are with child, and to them that give suck in those days! [20] But pray ye that your flight be not in the winter, neither on the sabbath day: [21] For then shall be great tribulation, such as was not since the beginning of the world to this time, no, nor ever shall be. [22] And except those days should be shortened, there should no flesh be saved: but for the elect's sake those days shall be shortened. [23] Then if any man shall say unto you, Lo, here is Christ, or there; believe it not. [24] For there shall arise false Christs, and false prophets, and shall shew great signs and wonders; insomuch that, if it were possible, they shall deceive the very elect. [25] Behold, I have told you before. [26] Wherefore if they shall say unto you, Behold, he is in the desert; go not forth: behold, he is in the secret chambers; believe it not. [27] For as the lightning cometh out of the east, and shineth even unto the west; so shall also the coming of the Son of Man be. . . .

down into the house, neither enter therein, to take any thing out of his house: And let him that is in the field not turn back again for to take up his garment. [17] But woe to them that are with child, and to them that give suck in those days! [18] And pray ye that your flight be not in the winter. [19] For in those days shall be affliction, such as was not from the beginning of the creation which God created unto this time, neither shall be. [20] And except that the Lord had shortened those days, no flesh should be saved: but for the elect's sake, whom He hath chosen, He hath shortened the days. [21] And then if any man shall say to you, Lo, here is Christ; or, lo, He is there; believe him not: [22] For false Christs and false prophets shall rise, and shall shew signs and wonders, to seduce, if it were possible, even the elect. [23] But take ye heed: behold, I have foretold you all things.

not them that are in the countries enter thereinto. [22] For these be the days of vengeance, that all things which are written may be fulfilled. [13] But woe unto them that are with child, and to them that give suck, in those days! for there shall be great distress in the land, and wrath upon this people. [24] And they shall fall by the edge of the sword, and shall be led away captive into all nations: and Jerusalem shall be trodden down of the Gentiles, until the times of the Gentiles be fulfilled.

[Note: The special warning to beware of false Christs and false prophets at the time of the siege of Jerusalem is omitted from Luke's account.]

AFTER THE TRIBULATION OF THOSE DAYS

[29] ¶ "Immediately after the tribulation of those days shall the sun be darkened, and the moon shall not give her light, and the stars shall

[24] ¶ "But in those days, after that tribulation, the sun shall be darkened, and the moon shall not give her light, [25] And the stars of

[25] ¶ "And there shall be signs in the sun, and in the moon, and in the stars; and upon the earth distress of nations, with perplexity; the

fall from heaven, and the powers of the heavens shall be shaken: [30] And then shall appear the sign of the Son of Man in heaven: and then shall all the tribes of the earth mourn, and they shall see the Son of Man coming in the clouds of heaven with power and great glory. [31] And He shall send His angels with a great sound of a trumpet, and they shall gather together His elect from the four winds, from one end of heaven to the other.

heaven shall fall, and the powers that are in heaven shall be shaken. [26] And then shall they see the Son of Man coming in the clouds with great power and glory. [27] And then shall He send His angels, and shall gather together His elect from the four winds, from the uttermost part of the earth to the uttermost part of heaven.

sea and the waves roaring; [26] Men's hearts failing them for fear, and for looking after those things which are coming on the earth: for the powers of heaven shall be shaken. [27] And then shall they see the Son of Man coming in a cloud with power and great glory. [28] And when these things begin to come to pass, then look up, and lift up your heads; for your redemption draweth nigh."

THE PARABLE OF THE FIG TREE

[32] "Now learn a parable of the fig tree; When his branch is yet tender, and putteth forth leaves, ye know that summer is nigh: [33] So likewise ye, when ye shall see all these things, know that it is near, even at the doors. [34] Verily I say unto you, This generation shall not pass, till all these things be fulfilled. [35] Heaven and earth shall pass away, but My words shall not pass away."

[28] "Now learn a parable of the fig tree; When her branch is yet tender, and putteth forth leaves, ye know that summer is near: [29] So ye in like manner, when ye shall see these things come to pass, know that it is nigh, even at the doors. [30] Verily I say unto you, that this generation shall not pass, till all these things be done. [31] Heaven and earth shall pass away: but My words shall not pass away."

[29] And He spake to them a parable; "Behold the fig tree, and all the trees; [30] When they now shoot forth, ye see and know of your own selves that summer is now nigh at hand. [31] So likewise ye, when ye see these things come to pass, know ye that the kingdom of God is nigh at hand. [32] Verily I say unto you, This generation shall not pass away, till all be fulfilled. Heaven and earth shall pass away: but My words shall not pass away." ◄ **KJV**

ACT I
QUESTIONABLE DIALOGUE
MATTHEW 24:1–34

IT IS TIME FOR DIALOGUE. THE BACKDROP IS THE MAGNIFICENT JEWISH TEMPLE WHICH was being remodeled with the splendor that is befitting national pride. In the foreground were the massive walls made of stones quarried with several tons each in weight. The corner towers with their imposing lights contrasted the encroachment of the evening darkness. Beyond the walls was the expansive courtyard surrounded with lecture halls and classrooms where religious instruction by the scribes and Elders was still faintly heard. Jesus and His disciples had just come from there . . . come from debating . . . come from denouncing . . . come from declaring destruction of all this!

Ever so often a whiff of the burning animal sacrifices drifted by. The stench of burning blood and offals alternated with the tantalizing aroma of roasting leg of lamb. But the only thing that concerned Jesus was the smell of holy incense mixed with *strange fire offered unto the* LORD. (Leviticus 3:12–17, 10:1–3) He walked away, heavy with sadness.

As the din of the mingling crowd inside began to fade, the disciples of Jesus came up to Him to call *His attention to this awesome Temple complex.* (24:1) Surely *this House* would never become desolate! Did not Jesus see all this remodeling, this holy edifice that was the centerpiece of Judean nationalism, this Building erected for the glory of God?

Jesus just shook His head, then pointed to the Temple, and reiterated what He had said to the crowds: *Take a look, gentlemen, look at all of this. I'm serious when I say that not one stone here will be left on another. Every one will be thrown down!* (vs. 2)

TALK TO US

Jesus sat down on a stone bench overshadowed by the gnarled olive tree orchard. The twelve disciples approached Him warily. His mood was questionable. Was He willing to talk . . . to explain . . . to clarify? *Tell us, when will all this happen . . . what will be the sign of your coming . . . and the end of the age?* (vs. 3)

Jesus answered. Alright, now we're getting somewhere. Would He finally tell us if "stones here" really meant *here*? If so, is this the end of life as we know it? Is this the end of the Second Temple era? How will we know when this traumatic turn of events is about to happen? "This generation" seemed so ominous . . . so final . . . so scary.

Whatever Jesus was about to say — and whatever He was to mean by what He said — was confined by "two book-ends". Or we might say, all the words of Jesus that were to become scripture were bounded by a front cover and a back cover with titles that read *"This Generation."* Everything mentioned in Matthew 24:4–35 was to happen within the life-time of the Apostles! No doubt about it. When Jesus made the statement, *All this will come upon this generation* (23:36; and the statement, *This generation will certainty not pass away until all these things have happened,* 24:34) He was telling the truth!

That this Olivet prophecy refers to some type of rebuilt Third Temple, thousands of years in the future, is contrafuted by the selective use of Jesus's words. He declared, "Woe to you," referring to the Pharisees in His face. He said, "Not one stone here" while staring at Herod's Temple mount. He reiterated, *"this* generation," will experience all these things — not *that* generation. And then, in the next 32 verses Jesus looked His disciples in the eye, and repeatedly said "you", emphasizing the fact that the time of the Acts of the Apostles would be what He had in mind. (15 times)

Watch out that no one deceives you (vs. 4) is a warning, though, that is applicable to all generations of Bible students. Just as some would misconstrue the application of Jesus's words in the first century, so also, there have been prophecy teachers and lecturers (and novel writers) in every decade since then who have misinterpreted and misapplied these important prophetic scriptures.

For example, some have tried to interpret *generation* as "that group of Jews who are alive, in the future, when everything is suppose to happen". "That" race of Jewish people will not die until they see the complete fulfillment of all this section of prophecy, they allege, in their life-time.

However, the Greek word used here, *genea,* translated as "generation", is used throughout the book of Matthew the evangelist as a "duration of time" (Compare Matthew 1:17; 12:41, 42, 45; Mark 8:12; Luke 11:50; Acts 13:36; Hebrews 3:10). If "race, nationality, or an aggregate of people" were intended by Jesus, the different word, *genos*, would have been used.

Again, many have not understood the use of the word, "end", and the phrase, "end of the age." (vss. 3, 5, 13, 14) They've mistakenly thought that Matthew 24:3 is a passage of scripture dealing with the "end of the world." However, the KJV translation "World" in verse 3 is not accurate; the Greek word is *aiōnos (age),* not *kosmos (world).* "The end times," "the signs of the endtime," "the last days," phrases, which are associated with the "end of the world," are *not* applicable to our present study.

Jesus was not referring to the end of the world in the first part of the Olivet Discourse, and the word, "end," must be interpreted in the context of the chapter's topic. Just as we may speak of "the end of the day," "the end of the work week," or the end of the year, so also, there are several "ends" mentioned in the Bible. The rabbis of the first century often wrote of "the present age," and "the age to come." The end of one age did not signal the end of the world. (Matthew 12:32, where Jesus employed the rabbinical phrase, cf. 1 Corinthians 10:11.) Our study will show that the destruction of Jerusalem by the Romans was the *end of the Second Temple era* . . . and the beginning of the Messianic Kingdom era (often called the Church age) which was forecast by Old Testament prophecies (Hosea 2:23; Amos 9:11–12; cf. Acts 15:14–21).

Watch out that no one deceives you! This is the first line of the Protagonist in Matthew's mysterious melodrama. And this is our "first line of defense" against being deceived by modern evangelical sensationalists who exploit our curiosities . . . our fears . . . our faith.

MATERNITY CONTRACTIONS

Many will come in My name, claiming;. "I am the Christ," and will deceive many. You will hear of wars and rumors of wars, but see to it that you are not alarmed (frightened). Those things must happen, but that is not yet the end. "Nation will rise against nation, and kingdom against kingdom"! There will be famines and earthquakes in places. But all these events are just the beginning of birth-pangs.[1] *(24:5–8; see Addendum, 'Signs of Messiah')*

Many modern antagonists proclaim these catastrophic events to be "signs of the end-times", just the opposite of what Jesus said. These are given in reference to a "beginning", not a supposed ending. And further, these alleged signs are presented as a way to alarm us and get our attention, just the opposite of what Jesus wanted to happen: *See to it that you are not alarmed (disturbed, frightened).*

---

[1]   "Birth pangs" was a rabbinical term describing the days ushering in the age of the Messiah and His kingdom. Jesus applied it to the right time.

But Jesus did inform the disciples (the you) that there would be many actors who would jump up on the stage of Jewish history in the first century. Like Shakespearean wannabes, they would strut up and down stage and speak lines that were pure fiction, in the end, signifying nothing: False Christs.

Both sacred and secular history has recorded some of these charlatans: Judas of Galilee (Acts 5:37), Simon Magus (Acts 8:9–11), Simon the Samaritan of Githon (Eusebius), Dositheus, pretending he was the Lawgiver prophesied by Moses (Origen), Theudas, who led a group to the Jordan River which he expected to divide (Josephus), and many others under the rule of Felix, who were captured and killed often (Thomas Newton).

Wars, and reports of wars filled the daily newspapers of Jerusalem, and led on the Five O'Clock news. Ancient historians such as Josephus, Seutonius, and Tacitus recorded the sallying back and forth of armies up and down the Roman Empire. Germany, Africa, Thrace, Gaul, Parthia, Armenia, Britain, Dacia all were subject to commotions, disturbances, insurrections, battles, rebellions . . . among which were the guerrilla tactics of the Judean Zealots. And keep in mind that these are not end-time signs. The end is not yet.

Nation will rise against nation would cause a Jewish member of the congregation to recall the words of Jeremiah as he described the Fall of the First Temple and the 70 years of exile in Babylon. The end of that Jewish era saw *disaster spreading from nation to nation.* (Jeremiah 25:32) The collapse of the Second Temple era would also see turmoil among nations.

Famines and earthquakes, are words that accurately picture the tenuous and fickle character of Mediterranean geography and climate. Plagues of locust that would darken the whole sky were common. Droughts affected the wheat production upon which the Roman civilization (and armies) depended. Hurrain and Bashan were considered the "bread-basket of the world." And of course, Christians suffered along with the rest during famine. (Acts 11:27–29; 1 Corinthians 16:1–5)

The whole Mediterranean landscape is dotted with ruins of cities, temples, agoras, and palaces, which were destroyed by earthquake. Solitary columns stand guardian over abandoned villages with shaken foundations.

All these cataclysmic events in verses 4–8 were to be like *birth pangs (pains) when a woman goes into labor (contractions).* This metaphor was used quite freely in the speeches and writings of the Old Testament prophets who continually spoke of pending invasions (and the fall of Jerusalem) due to the collapse of morality in Israeli culture, and the breaking of faith with the Almighty Lord their God. (Psalm 48:6; Isaiah 21:3; Jeremiah 6:24; 13:21; 22:23; 50:43, Micah 4:9)

Jerusalem, with the Temple in the foreground.

Birthing doesn't happen quickly. There are protracted periods of maternal contractions. Some last for days, some much longer. They are the signals of a coming event. The pain is now, but the end is not yet. And this is what Jesus was conveying to His disciples: It would be a while before the end of the Second Temple era would be consummated. The New Covenant era would start, but not right away. As it turned out, the transition lasted 40 years. (30 A.D. – 70 A.D.)

ACTS OF THE APOSTLES

They will deliver you to tribulation (hand you over to be persecuted) *and put to death, and you will be hated by all nations because of My name.*

At that time many will fall away (from the faith, *NIV*), *and will betray one another and hate each other. Many false prophets will arise and will mislead* (deceive) *many* (people).

Because of the increase of lawlessness, the love of many will grow cold, but he who stands firm (endures) *to the end will be saved.*

And the Gospel of the Kingdom shall be preached in all the world as a testimony to all the nations — and then the end will come. (24:9–14)

In the first section of this discourse, Jesus wore the hat of a news reporter and spoke of international affairs. Then He changed character, and put on the hat of an Archbishop and gave a "State of the Church" address. He basically gave a summary of the *Acts of the Apostles* period of Early Church history . . . in advance.

The persecution of the first disciples of Jesus is well documented: the martyrdom of Stephen (Acts 7:54–60), the murder of James (12:2), the flogging of Peter and John (4:3; 5:40), the persecution in Antioch of Pisidia (13:50), the jailing of Paul and Silas (16:22–24), etc.

Jesus had touched upon this adversity previously (Matthew 23:34, Mark 10:29–30). Just as wicked men hated the righteousness of Jesus, so they would also exercise hatred to Jesus' disciples (John 15:18–21). And no better place is this described than in Paul's own words: *I have worked much harder, been in prison more frequently, been flogged more severely, and been exposed to death again and again. Five times I received from the Jews the forty lashes minus one. Three times I was beaten with rods; once I was stoned; three times I was shipwrecked; I spent a night and a day in the open sea. I have been constantly on the move . . . I have been in danger from bandits, in danger from my own countrymen, in danger from Gentiles, in danger in the city, in danger in the country, in danger at sea, and in danger from false brothers.* (2 Corinthians 11:23–26)

All of these occasions of persecution and appearances before religious and political tribunals, we note with amazement, occurred *before* the Destruction of the Temple, and fit within the "book-ends" required by Jesus' pronouncements (23:36 and 24:34).

This tribulation (persecution, NIV) not only came from without the Church, but arose from within, as well. *Many became apostate, betrayed and hated one another. False prophets arose and mislead many. Lawlessness* (antinomianism) *increased and proportionately, charity decreased* (went cold). (24:10–12) The book of Acts and all the following Epistles are replete with instances where these acts of treason were played out on the church stage. Because it is in human nature (fallen, mutated DNA, so to speak), one minute after Pentecost, evil was at work to try to destroy the work of the Spirit! Contention over doctrine, the rise of cult leaders, teachers of demonic dogmas, betraying of the Elders, deception, prophiteering (profiteering) . . . they all turned the tranquility of the Upper Room into a spiritual rumpus room.

Examples are written down in 2 Timothy 1:15; 4:10, 16; 2 Corinthians 11:13, 2 Peter 2:1; Acts 20:29–30; 2 Timothy 2:16–17; 1 John 4:1. This last epistle, 1 John, stated that "many antichrists had already arrived on the scene." Modern pop-lecturers totally ignore this book because it tends to disparage their pet doctrine of one major Antichrist way off in the future . . . or just around the corner . . . depending on who is speculating.

A major problem in the internal workings of the Early Church was the advent of *Judaizers,* teachers who wanted to force Gentiles to observe aspects of the Mosaic Law, such as circumcision, feast days, dietary laws, etc. They, in effect, were distorting Jesus' Gospel—preaching a different Gospel (Galatians 1:6)—and imposing restrictions that, ironically, they themselves historically had never been able to fully observe. (2 Corinthians 11:13) These *false apostles, deceitful workmen, masqueraders,* who have a different Jesus, spirit, and Gospel, not only infected the Early Church with their toxic teaching, they have spawned an enduring strain of disease that even effects our modern teleprophets and radio pastors!

On one end of the spectrum of righteousness there was this restrictive observance of the Mosaic Law, but on the other end there were those engaged in "antinomianism" or *lawlessness*, that tilted the scale because of a misplaced fulcrum of "grace." They were committing all sorts of immoral sins because of their concept of "greasy grace." (Romans 6:15–23) Paul gave the example of the Corinthian believers who *had become arrogant, instead of mourning over* the report of gross perversion in their midst. (1 Corinthians 5:1–2)

He who stands firm to the end will be saved (v.13)

The end. The end of what? Some commentators have suggested that "end" refers to a completion of seven years of Great Tribulation at the last days (of planet Earth). But this approach is invalid and uncalled for since it lies outside the "book-ends" of *this (first century) generation.* (For examples of this folly, see J. N. Darby, S. I. Scofield, J. F. Walvoord, C. C. Ryrie) That interpretation is the result of preconceived schematics overlaid upon Matthew 24 (eisegesis fallacy).

Other commentators recommend the position that the "end" refers to the final consummation of the Destruction of Jerusalem in 70 A.D. That is, the "end" of the Second Temple Era by the divine instrument of God, the Roman Legion(s). We think, however, there is a better conclusion since there were many believers who died or were killed (martyred) before that ending.

Three passages of scripture clearly define for the biblical scholar what *standing firm to the end . . . saved* really is. It is important to quote them in full since "the end" is so often misdefined:

(After listing the type of corrupt people who would be in the latter days, just as Jesus did in Matthew 24, Paul continues . . .) *However, you know all about my teaching, my life-style, my purpose, faith, patience, love* **endurance***, persecutions, sufferings . . . Yet the Lord rescued me from all of them.*

In fact, everyone who wants to live a godly life in Christ Jesus will be persecuted, while evil men and impostors will go from bad to worse, deceiving and being deceived.

But as for you, **continue** *in what you have learned and have become convinced of . . . how you have known the holy Scriptures, which are able to make you wise for* **salvation** *through faith in Christ Jesus.* (2 Timothy 3:10–15)

We sent Timothy, who is our brother and God's fellow worker in spreading the Gospel of Christ, to strengthen and encourage you in the faith so that no one would be unsettled by these trials. You know quite well we were destined for them . . . We kept telling you that we would be **persecuted** *. . . For this reason, when I could stand it no longer, I sent to find out about your faith. I was afraid that in some way the tempter might have tempted you and our efforts might have been in vain.*

But Timothy has come to us from you and brought the good news about your faith and love . . . Therefore, brothers, in all our distress and persecution we were encouraged about you because of your faith. For now we really live, since you are **standing firm** *in the Lord.* (1 Thessalonians 3:2–8; see also 2 Thessalonians 1:4–10)

Remember those earlier days after you had received the light, when you **stood your ground** *in a great contest in the face of suffering. Sometimes you were publicly exposed to insult and persecution. Other times you stood side by side with those who were so treated. You sympathized with those in prison and joyfully accepted the confiscation of your property, because you knew that you yourselves had better and lasting possessions.*

So now, do not throw away your confidence; it will be richly rewarded. You need to **persevere** *so that when you have done the will of God, you will receive—what He has promised.* (Hebrews 9:32–36)

Previously, Jesus had taught the "parable of the Sower" and the need for good soil. One type of poor soil illustrated seed falling on rocky places. This represented *he who heard the Word and at once receives it with joy! But since he has no root, he lasts only a short time. When trouble or persecution comes because of the Word, he quickly falls away.* (Matthew 13:20–21) This is the opposite of "standing firm to the end." This illustrates the forfeiting of one's being "saved . . . in the end."

Because of the rampant persecution and tribulation suffered by the Early Church, the Apostles scattered verses in their comforting epistles with admonitions to stand firm. Like coaches of bruised and bleeding football players, exhausted and worn down by daunting opposition, they gave pep talks, assuring them of ultimate victory . . . if they just stood firm, and resolute, and doggedly determined. (Matthew 10:17–31; 1 Corinthians 1:21, 24; Galatians 5:1; Ephesians 6:4; Philippians 1:27; 4:1; Colossians 4:12; James 5:8; 1 Peter 5:9–10) *Encourage one another daily . . . so that none of you may be hardened by sin's deceitfulness. We have come to share in Christ* **if we hold firmly till the end** *the confidence we had at first.* (Hebrews 3:13–14; also 4:14)

It is abundantly clear that "the end" spoken by Christ is the end of one's life . . . the end of a tumultuous and rocky pilgrimage . . . but at which awards of eternal life and joy await each who has stood firm in the faith. (1 Corinthians 1:8; Hebrews 6:9–12; cf. 7:3; Revelations 2:26; contrast 2 Corinthians 11:15 *the end of evil men.*)

I NEED A WITNESS

> *This Gospel of the Kingdom shall be preached in the whole world as a testimony to all the nations, and then the End will come.* (vs. 14)

This one sentence spoken by the Master Teacher contained "a shot heard around the world", to borrow an American phrase from long ago. It reflected a "changing of the guard," to borrow a British phrase. It decisively announced the beginning of the New, and the ending of the Old. It emphatically declared the opening of the door of salvation to *all nations*, and slammed the door of exclusivity and Jewish superiority, in one fell swoop!

Previously, Jesus as declared, *The Law and the Prophets were proclaimed until John. Since that time the Gospel of the Kingdom of God is being preached.* (Luke 16:16) Out with the old, and in with the new! This Gospel had been introduced to the towns and villages of Galilee and Judea, mainly of Jewish ethnicity — but it was to take on a greater dimension: *all the nations in the whole world* (all the Gentiles) were to be included in the Kingdom. The ministers of the Church were *to testify of the salvation in Christ*, announcing to all *rulers and kings* (Mark 13:9) *this Gospel in the power of the Spirit* (Mark 13:11). And to underscore this transition, the End of the Old Covenant would come with a decisive finality. This proclamation would entail much traveling (wherever the kings and rulers governed), a lot of speeches, and several years, in order to reach the nations. But the beginning was certain . . . and the end was just as certain . . . it would come.

Later, the Apostle Paul would write to the people residing at the central capitol of the Government that ruled over many of those nations, and summarize this transition:

> *Now to Him who is able to establish you by my Gospel and the proclamation of Jesus Christ, according to the revelation of the mystery hidden for long ages past, but now revealed and made known through the prophetic writings by the command of the eternal God, so that* **all nations might believe** *and obey Him — to the only wise God be glory forever through Jesus Christ!* (Romans 16:25–27)

Of the contents of the orated *testimony* (*marturion*, Gk.) Paul explained to the academic and economic center of the ancient world, Corinth:

> *When I came to you, brothers, I did not come with eloquence or superior wisdom as I proclaimed to you the* **testimony** *about God. For I resolved to know nothing while I was with you except* **Jesus Christ and Him crucified** . . .

> *This is what we teach, not in words taught us by human wisdom, but in words taught* **by the Spirit***, expressing spiritual truths in spiritual words.* (1 Corinthians 2:1–2, 13; compare Mark 13:11, *Spirit*)

In an epistle to the young minister, Timothy, this apostle also delineated the essence of the "testimony:"

> *This is good, and pleasing to God our Savior, who wants all men to be saved and to come to a knowledge of the truth. For there is one God and one mediator between God and men, the Man Christ Jesus, who gave Himself as a ransom for all men—the testimony given in its proper time. And for this purpose I was appointed a herald and an apostle . . . and a teacher of the true faith to the Gentiles.* (1 Timothy 2:3–7)

To this, the other New Testament writers "testify" (1 John 5:11, Acts 10:34–43) Even the staunch Jewish fisherman finally admitted: *I now realize how true it is that God does not show favoritism, but accepts men from* **every** *nation who fear Him and do what is right. You know the message God sent to the people of Israel,* **telling the Gospel** *of peace through Jesus Christ . . . We are witnesses of everything He did . . . He commanded us to proclaim to the people and* **to testify** *that He is the One whom God appointed as Judge of the living and the dead. All the prophets* **testify about Him** *that everyone who believes in Him receives forgiveness of sins through His Name.*

That this awesome testimony of Jesus and this Gospel of the Kingdom traversed the **whole world** (*oikoumenē*, Gk. = inhabited earth, or area of the Roman Empire) is made evident by the claims of the Apostles. (cf. Acts 2:5; 17:6; Luke 2:1; Romans 1:8;10:18; 2 Timothy 4:17; Colossians 1:6)

We remember that the whole New Testament was written before 70 A.D., so all these claims of universal proclamation happened **before** the *End* . . . **before** the Destruction of the Temple in Jerusalem. Jesus' prophecy was accurate.[2] The "end" of Judaism with its Temple worship was to come, but not before the *testimony* of the truthfulness of the Gospel had been fully presented to the nations without favoritism?[3] The opening of one door had to happen before the other door closed behind. The movement of the Holy Spirit of Jehovah God flowing out from the Holy of Holies confinement into the free world was felt by all who were sensitive to spiri-

---

2   Note that the KJV's wording "a testimony against them" (Mark 13:9) is better translated "to them" as in the NIV, NKJV, or "before them" ESV. It referred to a presentation of the Gospel to them all with all its evidences and witnesses.

3   To "give testimony" is to testify so that persons may get knowledge of something, knowledge that will be of benefit to them. (Thayer's *Lexicon*)

tual things. The wind of the Spirit blew throughout the earth where it willed, resting upon one nation, then another, then another. (Romans 10:11–13)

Sometimes the Apostles and ministers of the Gospel of the Kingdom would be brought before rulers and kings by force, but these occasions would be within the overarching Providence of God. Luke recorded, *it shall turn to you for a testimony* (Luke 21:12). This awkward King James Version wording is better translated by the NIV as, *This will result in your being witnesses to them,* and by the NKJV as, *It will turn out for you as an occasion for testimony!* So either by bold "street preaching" or by being brought before the magistrates by street thugs, the proclamation of the Gospel would be accomplished throughout the Roman world in the first century. (For further study, do a word study on *testify (martureō,* Gk.), which is related to our word, *testimony.* Also notice Jesus's words in Acts 1:6–8, *witnesses.)*

Lest a reader mistake the meaning of "the Kingdom" message, Jesus added the adjective, *this,* when He mentioned *Gospel of the Kingdom.* He signified that He was not talking about some new type of national Kingdom for the Jews that was to be established off in the distant future. He certainly was not referring to the founding of the State of Israel "in unbelief." (God does not reward blasphemy against Jesus; John 8:42–47) Rather, Jesus had in mind all the Kingdom parables (Matthew 13), and temple teaching He had engaged in throughout His 3½ years of public ministry. *This* Kingdom was the one the disciples would recall when they went out and testified: *The Kingdom is within you* (Luke 17:21) . . . *The Kingdom of God belongs to such as are like these children* (Luke 18:16) . . . *Some who are standing here will not taste death before they see the Kingdom of God* (Luke 9:27; *come in power,* Mark 9:1) . . . *the Kingdom of God is near; repent and believe the good news* (Mark 1:15). Therefore, *The Kingdom of God is righteousness, peace, and joy, in the Holy Spirit* (Romans 14:17). The "end" of Israeli nationalism was made sure by the preaching of the Gospel to "all nations." Modern day Zionism can only be considered a political movement **outside** the biblical Kingdom of which Jesus is Lord; it has nothing to do w1th the Father or the Son. (Matthew 8:11–12; 21:42–45)

THE OLIVET DISCOURSE
PART I (23:1–24:35)

Christ's Prophecy	Jerusalem Entered by Cestius	Vespasian Attacks Judea	Daily Sacrifices Cease	Jerusalem Destroyed by Titus
30 AD	66AD	67 AD		70 AD
BEGINNING OF SORROWS			**GREAT TRIBULATION**	

Earthquake, Famine, Pestilence, Wars, Persecution, Hatred, Rumors . . .

Zealots, Siege, Murder, Horrors

Verses 4–14

15–20

Verses 21–28

29–35

1290 Days
Three years and a part

1½ mos.

1335 Days

THIS GENERATION

Matthew 23:35–36; 24:34; Hebrews 3:10

THE ABOMINATOR!

> *Therefore, when you see the abomination of desolation, which was talked about by Daniel the prophet, standing in the holy place (let him who reads understand), then those who are in Judea must flee to the mountains.* (Matthew 24:15–16)

> *When you see Jerusalem being encircled with armies, then know that her desolation has drawn near. Let those in Judea then flee to the mountains, and let those in the midst of her depart out, and those in the countries not enter into her, for the days of avenging are come so that all the things that have been written may be accomplished.* (Luke 21:20–22)

Jesus had foretold the destruction of the Temple, and it was to happen within a generation . . . within 40 years. He described many events that were to transpire within that time period, none of which were a sign of the end. The faithful disciples were to stand firm, and roll with the punches, so to speak, meanwhile, continuing to spread the word (testify) about the Gospel of the Kingdom into all the ethnic people groups . . . not just to their Jewish brethren.

But *then,* Jesus got specific. He gave *a sign of the End* that would be unmistakable. After the Gospel had spread sufficiently to both Jew and Gentile about the arrival of the new spiritual Kingdom, then the old physical kingdom was to end . . . to be beset upon by a destroying army . . . to suffer defeat at the hands of an Abominator . . . to become desolate, utterly desolate.

When Jerusalem was in the process of being encircled, it was very prudent that everyone get out as fast as they could! They had to flee because its *desolation was just around the corner (has drawn near).* The signal was observable, able to be seen by all. There was no secret handshake, no mysterious omen, no furtive action by a surreptitious cabal. The kicked-up dust from the stomping boots of soldiers . . . the clanging of shields and shiny swords . . . the neighing of war-horses . . . the barking of orders by centurions . . . collectively, this was the *sign of the end.* Foreign armies marching on holy ground was a surety of pending *desolation.*

Jesus did not say idolatrous symbols of desecration would be set up in the holy Temple; He emphasized *desolation (erēmōsis,* Gk.) Desecration does not destroy, nor *tear down stone by stone;* it only profanes. But desolation does level edifices considered sacred. The encircling armies "fit that bill." They would get the job done of carrying out *the Day of Vengeance.* (Isaiah 61:3, Luke 21:22)

The plural word, armies, is appropriate. There were at least four different Legions of Roman soldiers which eventually encircled and attacked the city of Jerusalem. And these Legions were comprised of mercenaries (non-Romans) from different nations throughout the conquered territory of the Roman Empire . . . as well as, the pagan Roman heathens!

Cestius, Vespasian, and Titus, the names of Roman generals would soon become familiar, household names in Jerusalem. They would strike terror in the hearts of its residents. They would be indelibly etched into its history.

A REVOLTING MATTER

Time should be taken to explore the reason why the Roman Legions left Syria and came *en force* into the holy land (Galilee, Samaria, Judea, Perea) with a vengeance. To be sure, it was a God thing (providential), but we can ascertain the historical intrigue and course of events that facilitated the fulfillment of the *Days of Vengeance* of our God.

Ever since the time of the Maccabees, the Jewish people had desperately tried to free themselves from foreign domination. The memories of the cruel oppression under the Seleucids and Ptolemies were always kept fresh in their minds by the stories told around the evening fireplaces. Every village and clan could relate a story about the murder or theft they had endured.

Now the Romans, with headquarters in far away Italia, dictated their daily lives. This subjugated people could find no national pride in that. The thought of it grated them like a mouth full of sand on teeth. The lack of "equal opportunity", exorbitant taxation, quartering of soldiers, political corruption, collusion with foreign powers, poverty . . . and the presence of idolatrous ensigns bandied about by the Romans . . . all were germs that infested the heart and liver of Jewry. They were sick of it all.

In response, nationalists whipped up the fervor of revolt. In the country, bands of robbers, highway men, bushwhackers, and extortionists ran wild. In the city, there arose organized companies of assassins and mafioso: Sicarii, the high priest "guards", terrorists (Acts 21:38).

Along with armed revolutionaries, there were the unarmed false prophets, who just as effectively aroused the spirit of patriotism in the crowds to the point of rebellion. For example, one Egyptian prophet led 30,000 men from the wilderness to the Mount of Olives, in the days when Felix was procurator (prefect). Paul was mistaken for one of his ilk.

The social condition of this time was restless . . . dissatisfied . . . hopeless. The people could put no faith in the High Priest — who for decades was appointed by the secular rulers. The Herodians and the Sadducees and the Pharisees all vied for dominance and favor and power . . . and money. The economy was always at the mercy of the weather, as were the crops at the mercy of the pests (think locusts).

The barbarities and atrocities the people suffered was excelled only by their cries of agony and lament. Josephus, the Jewish historian, recorded one occasion when soldiers crucified about 3600 after plundering them. It is suggested that the procurator, Florus, (after Felix and Festus), tried to goad the Jews into a revolt so that his own acts of plunder and tyranny could be covered up. (ruled, 65–70 A.D.)

Knowing the futility of fighting against the super-power of Rome, King Herod Agrippa II is recorded to have given a most passionate speech to try to quell the fervor and restrain the Jews from the madness of revolting. It had mixed reviews! And little success. In fact right afterwards the priests were persuaded to stop receiving any gifts or sacrifices from "foreigners" . . . including sacrifices for Caesar. This act sparked the "War with Rome". The dry kindling of social uneasiness caught fire. The sweltering heat of oppression has prepared the conflagration of rebellion.

The city of Jerusalem became divided into factions: One advocated immediate revolt . . . "to arms!" Another sought to restrain the seditious crowds, but failing that, they had the troops of Florus and Agrippa brought in to reestablish order. Just the opposite effect ensued: civil war in which Jews killed one another in far greater numbers than the soldiers!

Roman garrisons — one located in the fortress of Antonia, near the Temple mount — were besieged, overran, and the men either slain unmercifully or dispersed. Even those who surrendered instead of fighting, were not spared, but treacherously killed.

The Roman authorities did not take all this lying down; in the city of Caesarea, over 20,000 Jews were killed in one hour, and it was emptied of all its Jewish inhabitants. And in a "tit for tat", the whole Jewish nation laid waste to villages of Syria, burning some to the ground. And then the Syrians responded in kind:

> *The Syrians were even with the Jews in the multitude of the men they slew. The disorders in all Syria were terrible. Every city was divided into two armies, and the preservation of the one party was in the destruction of the other. So the daytime was spent in shedding of blood, and the night in fear, which was, of the two, the more terrible.*
>
> *It was common to see cities filled with dead bodies, still lying unburied; those of old men mingled with infants, all scattered about together. Women also lay among them without any covering. You might then see the whole province full of inexpressible calamities. (Josephus, II.17)*

In city after city, Jew fought against Jew. In Scythopolis alone, over 13,000 were slain at one time. In Alexandria, the home of a Jewish ghetto for centuries, they were incited to revolt, but were all destroyed with abandon: Houses were plundered and then set on fire by the Romans . . . no mercy was shown to infants or aged . . . until 50,000 of them lay dead in heaps.

Then, the Roman general, Cestius Gallus, entered the bloody stage, and there began another Act of Shakespearean quality. The scene was set for the entrance of Providence.

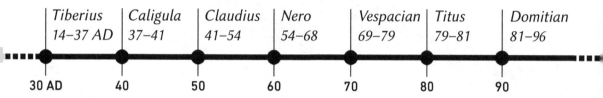

EMPERORS OF THE ROMAN EMPIRE

Tiberius	Caligula	Claudius	Nero	Vespacian	Titus	Domitian
14–37 AD	37–41	41–54	54–68	69–79	79–81	81–96

30 AD   40   50   60   70   80   90

STANDING ARMY

We were informed by Christ that *the abomination of desolation, a term used in the Septuagint, and not the ancient Hebrew, would stand in the holy place.* The parallel synoptic account of Luke revealed that this was a reference to Roman armies marching into the land of Israel. (Luke 21 :20–21)

The word, *stand,* is quite common when referring to militaries. Today, we say that a country has a "standing army." And even way back in ancient history, this word is used of the rise of authorities and rulers backed by their armies:

> *A king of fierce countenance . . . shall stand up* (Daniel, 8:23,25). *A mighty king shall stand up, that shall rule with great dominion . . . and when he shall stand up . . .* (11:3,4). *Another will stand in his estate, and shall come with an army* (11:7).

> *A king shall be stirred up to battle with a very great and mighty army; but he shall not stand* (11:25).

> *The kings of the earth stood up and the rulers were gathered together against the Lord* (Acts 4:26).

The location mentioned, *the holy place (topos,* Gk.), is a reference to the land of Israel, in general. Today, we call it the "holy land." In the first century, "Jerusalem was the holy city, Canaan the holy land, the Mt. Moriah, which lay about Jerusalem, for its nearness to the Temple, was thought, in a particular manner holy ground." (Matthew Henry, *Commentary on the Whole Bible,* vol. 5, p. 352)

It does not refer to the large, 30-acre Temple enclosure (complex, *hieron,* Gk. Matthew 12:6; Mark 13:3), nor to the inner sanctums: The Holy Place and the Holy of Holies (*naos,* Gk. Matthew 23:16; 27:40). And because of this, no one can interpret the "abomination" as merely "idols" placed within the Temple. The majority of people could not have seen such idols as a *sign.* Only the priests were allowed into the inner sanctums, and the majority of people would not be spending every day in the temple complex, so that idols placed there would be inadequate for warning the disciples and believers throughout the city of Jerusalem. An advancing army could indeed, rather, be seen . . . and heard . . . and feared.

"Furthermore, the setting up of an idol in the sanctuary is a thing which could not be done until the city and temple were taken by the enemy, which would be at the end of the siege. Hence it could not possibly serve as a sign to the disciples to save themselves from the horrors of the siege by timely flight." (Philip Mauro, *The Seventy Weeks,* p. 231)

To be sure, the Old Testament considered idols to be an abomination unto the Lord. But so were a lot of other things . . . people . . . habits. So we are not locked into interpreting "the abomination" as just an idol, or even a Roman ensign, which was also considered an abomination to the Jews.

The scenario, advocated in recent times (since 1830) by Darbyites (Plymouth Brethren), and their acolytes (Scofield, Chafer, Walvoord, Ryrie, Lindsey, LaHaye, Watson, Jenkins, *et al.)* that all this refers to the setting up of an idol in a rebuilt Temple (3rd Temple) during the days of a future antichrist by covenant with (Messiah rejecting) Jews . . . is pure silliness and folly . . . ludicrous, if it weren't so tragic in deceiving both Jews (to hope in another salvation), and Christians (who are exploited by greedy prophiteers). Such nonsense is forbidden by the verbiage that Jesus used, and by the time-context book-ends He designated.

Even if these popular, end-time book writers wish to misinterpret the word, this generation, as "Jewish race" instead of "contemporary men" standing in front of Jesus while He was speaking, they still cannot ignore the very plain declarations of Jesus in other passages:

> *Therefore, I tell* **you** *that the Kingdom of God will be taken away from* **you** *and given to a people who will produce its fruit. He who falls on this stone will be broken, but he on whom it falls will be crushed.*
>
> *When the chief priests and the Pharisees heard Jesus' parables,* **they knew He was talking about them**. (Matthew 21:43–45)

> *As the* **crowds** *increased, Jesus said,* This *is a wicked generation. It asks for a miraculous sign, but none will be given it except the sign of Jonah.* (Luke 11:29)

> *O Jerusalem, Jerusalem,* **you** *who kill the prophets and stone those sent to you, how often I have longed to gather your children together as a hen gathers her chicks under her wings, but* **you** *were not willing. Look!* **Your house** *is left to you desolate.* (Luke 13:34)

> *As Jesus approached Jerusalem and saw the city, He wept over it and said, If* **you**, *even you had only known on this day what would bring* **you** *peace—but now it is hidden from* **your eyes**.
>
> *The days will come upon* **you** *when your enemies will build an embankment against you and encircle you and hem you in on every side. They will dash* **you** *to the ground, you and the children within your walls. They will not leave one stone on another because* **you** *did not recognize the time of God's coming to you.* (Luke 19:41–44)

There can be no doubt, to the honest exegete, that Jesus's warnings and invectives were directed to men of His day who were standing right in front of Him! "That generation" of contemporaries would experience the desolation brought by the abomination of Rome. No idol in a rebuilt temple—which profanes and desecrates, *not* desolates—was ever intended by Jesus's prophecy. A "standing army" can, *and did*, bring desolation to Jerusalem (in 70 A.D.). There is no future required fulfillment. To insist on some future event would be teaching contrary to Jesus . . . against Christ . . . antichrist.

DAYS OF VENGEANCE

The denunciations spoken by Jesus may seem excessive and cruel. But we must keep in mind that Jerusalem was a capitol of corruption, a cauldron of chaos and crime, and was to be a cup of trembling. (Cf. Isaiah 51:17–20)

There was no excuse for their unbelief . . . their failure to repent from gross wickedness . . . their rejection of the Messiah, their Messiah. They all had seen the miraculous signs (healings, exorcisms, deliverances) never before demonstrated to such a degree in history. They had opportunity to "see the light" but they willingly turned a blind eye, all the while claiming to be seeing guides. God, the very God of Abraham, their revered forefather, was in their midst, and they spit on Him! (Matthew 11:20–24; 26:67)

It wasn't like they never had a chance. It wasn't like they didn't know. It wasn't like they were never told. But they decided to *fill up the measure of the sin of their forefathers* until their cup ran to overflowing with the blood of the Lamb of God. (Matthew 27:25)

They all had been warned by John the Baptizer: *You brood of vipers! Who has warned you to flee from the coming wrath? . . . the ax is already at the root of the trees, and every tree that does not produce good fruit is to be cut down and thrown into the fire.* (Luke 3:7–9) And before that, Moses had warned the Israelites about the conditional nature of their Covenant with God. He listed blessings, **and** He enumerated curses if they turned their back on the LORD.

> *The LORD shall bring a nation against thee from far, from the end of the earth, as swift as the eagle flieth; a nation whose tongue thou shalt not understand; a nation of fierce countenance, which shall not regard the elderly, nor show favor to the young . . .*
>
> *He shall besiege thee in all thy gates until thy high and fenced walls wherein thou trusted, come down . . .*

And thou shalt eat the fruit of thine own body, the flesh of thy sons and daughters, which the LORD thy God hath given thee, in the siege and in the straitness wherewith thine enemies shall distress thee . . .

The tender and delicate woman among you, who would not venture to set the sole of her foot upon the ground for delicateness and tenderness, her eye shall be evil toward . . . her young . . . for she shall eat them for want of all things, secretly in the siege and straitness wherewith thine enemies shall distress thee in thy gates. (Deuteronomy 28:49–59)

The rebellious and stiffnecked people were to be plucked from off their land and scattered from one end of the earth to the other. These predictions would become an accurate description of what was to befall the residents of Jerusalem during their siege. (Some commentators contend that this is more of an accurate portrayal of what happened in 70 A.D., than anything that took place at the capture by Nebuchadnezzar when the first Temple was destroyed.)

The evangelist, Luke, wrote: *These are the Days of Vengeance, that all things which are written may be fulfilled.* (Luke 21:22) Those writings would include the Law (Deuteronomy 28), and the Prophets (Daniel 9–12), and even the Historical Books (1 Kings 9:1–9).

SPOKEN BY DANIEL

The appellation that Jesus used overwhelmingly more than any other was the title, *Son of Man.* He used it because it emphasized His receiving a Kingdom from the Father as described in Daniel 7. The prophesying of Daniel paved the way for Christians to comprehend the mission of Jesus in declaring that the *Kingdom was at hand.* (Luke 8:1; 9:26–27) As Son of Man, Daniel certified Jesus as the King of Israel. (John 18:36–37; 19:12, 19–22) Thus, Pilate hung up the sign, *Jesus of Nazareth, King of the Jews (I.N.R.I.).*

Jesus was also familiar with the other major prophecies of Daniel. He was aware that some of them pointed directly to the coming judgment on the Second Temple. This is why He directed the disciple's attention to Daniel when He mentioned the enigmatic phrase, *the abomination of desolation* (LXX).

. . . the Anointed One will be cut off and will have nothing (or, will be cut off, but not for Himself). The people of the ruler who will come will destroy the city and the sanctuary.

The end will come like a flood; war will continue until the end and desolations have been decreed.

> *He will confirm a covenant with many for one heptad* (seven years) *and in the middle of the heptad he will put an end to sacrifice and offering.*
>
> *And on a wing of the temple, he will set up an abomination that causes desolation* (the abomination of desolation, LXX), *until the end that is decreed is poured out on the desolated city.* (9:26–27, New International Version)
>
> *. . . Messiah shall be cut off, but not for Himself; and the people of the prince that shall come shall destroy the city and the sanctuary.*
>
> *The end thereof shall be with a flood, and unto the end of the war desolations are determined.*
>
> *And He shall confirm the covenant with many for one week, and in the midst of the week He shall cause the sacrifice and the oblation to cease,*
>
> *And for the overspreading of abominations he shall make it desolate, even until the consummation, and that determined, shall be poured upon the desolate.* (King James Version)

Most respected scholars see a definite reference to the crucifixion of Christ, the Anointed One, after His 3½ years of ministry; and that by the shedding of His blood, He established the New Covenant. But that those responsible for His death, the city of Jerusalem's rulers, would precipitate judgment for their evil act, and the capitol would be destroyed.

In the KJV, words like "flood" and "overspreading" are ones normally used to describe metaphorically, encroaching hostile armies'. (Psalm 18:4; Isaiah 59:19; Jeremiah 46:7–9; Nahum 1:1, 8; Daniel 11:10–11)

FLEE, MAN, FLEE!

> *Let those who are in Judea flee to the mountains. Let no one on the roof of his house go down to take anything out of the house. Let no one in the field go back to get his cloak. How dreadful it will be in those days for pregnant women and nursing mothers! Pray that your flight will not take place in winter or on the Sabbath.* (Matthew 24:16–20)

If there ever was a time to remember Lot's wife, then was the time. (Luke 17:32) When the Roman's entered the holy land — which in reality, had become quite unholy — there was no time to equivocate . . . no time to vacillate . . . no time to be indecisive! The Roman soldiers did not "mess around", and neither should the disciples. The Jewish rebels had become so obnoxious, the military had become fed up, and showed no mercy to anyone. Jewish life had become cheap, and the soldiers paid little attention to any cries for mercy. Radical *zealotes* were constantly engaged in guerrilla warfare, attacking without warning, so the Romans "fired first, then asked questions later"! The iron-clad boots stomped on village and town, hamlet and house, up and down the countryside.

The disciples had asked for a *sign* of when the destruction of the Temple would occur. This was it. The desolators were the designators. Up to this time the new-born Early Church council had their headquarters in Jerusalem, but then was the time to relocate . . . and fast.

Perhaps these verses contain some hyperbole, but they did because of the urgency of the matter. The instructions apply to the culture of first century Judea, and the warnings were something they could understand. Homes, back then, had flat *rooftops* where a lot of the daily chores were done, or at night, where the family slept during the hot months. The cloak is a reference to the outer coat that a laborer would take off while working in the field. *Sabbath day* was a strictly observed day of the week in which no work was allowed (certainly, no moving vans), and on which travel was restricted to the Pharisaical designation of about ¾ of a mile.

To complicate matters, the radical, nationalistic Zealots *(cananites* in Heb.; *zealot* in Eng. Matthew 10:4) would attack any of their own countrymen whom they thought were compromising with the Romans, or who even were slack in observing Mosaic Law. Galilean villages were not spared the fanaticism of these people. Anyone fleeing on the Sabbath would have been slain with no questions asked! "Not standing up to the Romans", to them, would have been considered an act of treason worthy of death. Living, or fleeing, in Judea, with the Romans on your left, and the Zealots on your right, was like being between a rock and a hard place. But fleeing was the only viable option. Thus . . . pray . . . pray . . . *pray.*

Luke, the evangelist, presented a dilemma for his readers: *When you see (the sign of) Jerusalem being encircled* (surrounded) *by armies, flee!* (Luke 21:20–21) How can a person (family) flee if he is surrounded? Would not all the escape routes be cut off? Wouldn't it be too late to flee? What did Luke really mean by this perplexing "sign"? This seemed like "cutting it too close" for practical advice.

Fortunately, we are not left to wonder the answers to these questions. Historians recorded the advance of the Tenth Legion under general Cestius Gallus in the fall of 66 A.D. as a response to the rebellion in Judea that Gessius Florus, the local procurator, was unable to quell. He came down from Syria and forged a swath all the way to Jerusalem where he started a siege. No doubt this startled the Church at Jerusalem, and brought to mind the olivet Discourse which spoke of a *sign to flee.*

But, for what some commentators call an inexplicable reason, Cestius packed up his army bags and retreated. A biblical geographer, however, reckoned that drought and lack of water for such a large army, was the underlying cause for departure back to the flowing rivers of Syria. For whatever reason, though, the Roman army left, giving the Christians a chance to flee the city, and head for the mountains . . . *post haste!* . . . with abandon.

Do not let anyone on the roof of his house go down to take anything out of the house. (Matt. 24:17)

After camping near the city for three days, Cestius had begun his attacking, and was so successful that the fearful citizens in Jerusalem were about to surrender and open the gates in hopes of saving the city and Temple. But instead, the general withdrew his troops and departed. And not willing to leave matters alone, the rebels and Zealots chased after them, inflicting a lot of damage through guerrilla warfare, suddenly striking and then vanishing into the countryside, only to strike again unawares. (Josephus, *Wars of the Jews*, II,15–19)

> We learn from ecclesiastical histories, that at this juncture all who believed in Christ departed Jerusalem, and removed to Pella and other places beyond the river Jordan; so that they all marvelously escaped the general shipwreck of their countrymen; and we do not read anywhere that so much as one of them perished in the destruction of Jerusalem. (Bishop Thomas Newton, *Dissertations on the Prophecies*, 1754, p. 389)

> It is very remarkable that not a single Christian perished in the destruction of Jerusalem though there were many there when Cestius Gallus invested the city. (Adam Clarke, *Commentary,* Vol. I, p. 228; see also Eusebius, *Ecclesiastical History*, Bk. 3, ch. 5)

The timely withdrawal of the Tenth Legion, and its limping back to Syria did indeed give opportunities for the Jerusalem Church to pack their bags and head for the hills. But just as importantly, if Cestius had ended the Jewish wars right then, the city and Temple would have been spared, negating the prophecy about "stone upon stone being torn down." The Jewish historian noted, *it was, I suppose, owing to the aversion God already had towards the city and the sanctuary that he was hindered from putting an end to the war that very day.* (Josephus, *Wars*, II. 19:6)

The die was cast. Wars had been determined; desolation had been decreed. (Daniel 9:26, Matthew 23:38) Much more was yet to come . . . upon those left behind . . . tribulation like you would not believe!

AND I MEAN TROUBLE

> *For then there shall be great* **tribulation** *such as was not since the beginning of the world to this time, no, nor ever shall be. And unless those days should be shortened, there should no flesh be saved; but for the elect's sake those days shall be shortened.* (Matthew 24:21–22)

> *For in those days there will be* **affliction** *such as was not from the beginning of the creation which God created, unto this time, neither shall be . . .* (Mark 13:19

> *For these be the days of* **vengeance**, *that all things which are written may be fulfilled . . . And they shall fall by the edge of the sword, and shall be led away captive into all nations; and Jerusalem shall be trodden down by the Gentiles until the times of the Gentiles be fulfilled.* (Luke 21:22, 24)

Jesus, who already had referred to Daniel, now quotes from one of his prophecies: *There will be a time of distress* (trouble, KJV) *such as has not happened from the beginning of nations until then. But at that time your people—everyone whose name is found written in the book—will be delivered.* (Daniel 12:1) We have already seen how His people were miraculously spared and escaped to the mountains of Perea. Now we are given a summary of the plight of those left behind in Judea.

The coming days are described as being filled with *tribulation, affliction, and vengeance.* The first two words are the same in Greek, *"thlipsis",* and it is a generic word that simply means "pressing, oppression, distress, straits, affliction, or tribulation." *Great Tribulation* is not to be taken as a proper name of a specific period of time, like many modernists tweak it to be. Tribulation and distress are the same straits that Christians of all ages (eras) are to endure because of their faith. (Hebrews 10:33 *persecutions;* Colossians 1:24 *afflictions*) These verses in the Olivet Discourse do not refer to some future end-time event, but the context clearly limits them to the destruction of Jerusalem in 70 A.D. However, the tribulation that the Jews have brought on themselves is here of grand proportions! Self-inflicted sorrows often too great for words.

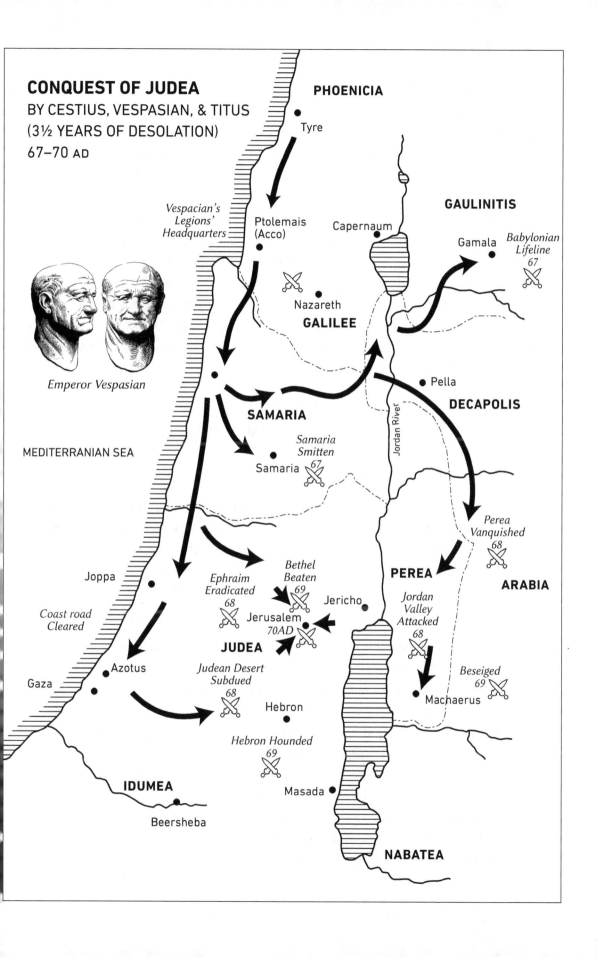

CONQUEST OF JUDEA
BY CESTIUS, VESPASIAN, & TITUS
(3½ YEARS OF DESOLATION)
67–70 AD

PHOENICIA

Tyre

GAULINITIS

Vespacian's Legions' Headquarters

Ptolemais (Acco)

Capernaum

Gamala

Babylonian Lifeline
67

Nazareth

GALILEE

Emperor Vespasian

SAMARIA

Samaria Smitten
67

Samaria

MEDITERRANIAN SEA

Pella

Jordan River

DECAPOLIS

Perea Vanquished
68

Joppa

Ephraim Eradicated
68

Bethel Beaten
69

Jericho

PEREA

ARABIA

Coast road Cleared

Jerusalem
70AD

JUDEA

Jordan Valley Attacked
68

Azotus

Judean Desert Subdued
68

Hebron

Beseiged
69

Gaza

Machaerus

Hebron Hounded
69

Masada

IDUMEA

Beersheba

NABATEA

FLAVIUS JOSEPHUS

We are indebted to the histories of Flavius Josephus for enlightenment concerning the tremendous affliction the Jews suffered at the end of the Second Temple Era. He was a general put in charge of Galilee at the outbreak of the Roman invasion (b. 37 – d. 100). At the battle of Jotapata he was captured on July of 67 A.D. but his life was spared.

He eventually became friends of the Roman generals, and became an interpreter, and mediator for them during the battles throughout Palestine. He took notes of the conflict, and published two monumental works which provide historians with great detail about the Jewish Wars, as well as ancient history. Nearly 400 pages of painstaking detail are written about the fall of Jerusalem and the terrible horror experienced there. Stephen Spielberg's spectacular movies pale in comparison to the drama described by Josephus. The ink that sprawled across his parchment was laced with blood and soldier sweat.

* * * * *

ACCOUNT OF GENERAL JOSEPHUS

In the introduction of his *Wars of the Jews:*—

"It had come to pass that our city Jerusalem had arrived at a higher degree of felicity than any other city under the Roman government, and yet at last fell into the sorest of calamities again. Accordingly it appears to me that *the misfortunate of all men from the beginning of the world, if they be compared to those of the Jews, are not so considerable as they were.*"

"It is impossible to give every instance of the iniquity of these men. I shall therefore speak my mind here, at once briefly:—that *neither did any other city suffer such miseries, nor did any age ever breed a generation more fruitful in wickedness than this was, from the beginning of the world.*" [This forcibly brings to mind the Lord's own words.] "Finally they brought the Hebrew nation into contempt, that they might themselves appear comparatively less impious with regard to strangers. They confessed, what was true, that they were the scum, and the spurious and abortive offspring of our nation, while they overthrew the city themselves, and forced the Romans, whether they would or no, to gain a melancholy reputation by acting gloriously against them; and did almost draw that fire upon the temple which they seemed to think came too slowly." (V. 10:5)

"For," says Josephus, "they returned to their former madness, and separated one from another, and fought it out and they *did everything that the besiegers could desire them to do.* For they never suffered from the Romans anything worse than they made each other suffer; nor was there any misery endured by the city which after what these men did, could be esteemed new. It was most of all unhappy *before it was overthrown;* and those that took it did it a kindness. For I venture to say that *the sedition destroyed the city,* and the Romans *destroyed the sedition.* This was a much harder thing to do than to *destroy the walls.* So that we may justly ascribe our misfortunes *to our own people.*" (V. 6:2)

"Now this vast multitude was indeed collected out of remote places, but the entire nation was now shut up by fate as in prison, and the Roman army encompassed the city when it was crowded with inhabitants. Accordingly the multitude of those that perished therein exceeded all the destructions that either men or God ever brought upon the world." (VI. 9:4)

"But," says Josephus, "the Syrians were even with the Jews in the multitude of the men they slew. The disorders in all Syria were terrible. Every city was divided into two armies and the preservation of the one party was in the destruction of the other. So the daytime was spent in shedding of blood, and the night in fear, which was, of the two, the more terrible . . .

"It was then common to see cities filled with dead bodies still lying unburied; those of old men mingled with infants all scattered about together. Women also lay among them without any covering. You might then see the whole province full of inexpressible calamities." (II. 18:1 & 2)

"Then," says Josephus, "did the famine widen its progress and devour the people by whole houses and families. The upper rooms were full of women and children dying by famine and the lanes of the city were full of the dead bodies of the aged. The children also and the young men wandered about the marketplaces like shadows, all swelled with the famine, and fell down dead, wheresoever their misery seized them." (V. 12:3)

"Thus did the miseries of Jerusalem grow worse and worse every day. . . . And indeed the multitude of carcases that lay in heaps, one upon another, was a horrible sight, and produced a pestilential stench which was a hindrance to those that would make sallies out of the city and fight the enemy" (VI. 1:1).

"The number of those that perished by famine in the city was prodigious, and their miseries were unspeakable. For if so much as the shadow of any kind of food did anywhere appear, a war was commenced presently, and the dearest friends fell a fighting one another about it."

"A false prophet was the occasion of the destruction of those people, he having made a public proclamation that very day that *God commanded them to get upon the temple and that they should receive miraculous signs of their deliverance.* There was then a large number of false prophets suborned by the tyrants to impose on the people, who announced to them *that they should wait for deliverance from God."* (VI. 5:2)

"But as for that house, God had for certain long ago doomed it to the fire; and now that fatal day was come, according to the revolution of ages. It was the tenth day of the month Ab, *the day upon which it was formerly burnt by the king of Babylon."* (VI. 4:5)

"While the holy house was on fire everything was plundered that came to hand, and ten thousand of those were slain. Nor was there commiseration of any age, or any reverence of gravity; but children, old men, profane persons, and priests were all slain in the same manner. . . . Moreover, many, when they saw the fire, exerted their utmost strength, and did break out into groans and outcries. Perea also did return the echo, as well as the mountains round about Jerusalem, and augmented the force of the noise.

"Yet was the misery itself more terrible than this disorder. For one would have thought that the hill itself, on which the temple stood, was seething hot, as if full of fire on every part, that the blood was more in quantity than the fire, and that the slain were more in numbers than they who slew them. For the ground did nowhere appear visible because of the dead bodies that lay upon it" (VI. 5:1).

"I should not mistake if I said that the death of Ananus was the beginning of the destruction of the city, and that from this very day may be dated the overthrow of her wall, and the ruin of her affairs; that being the day whereon they saw their high priest and the procurer of their preservation, slain in the midst of their city. . . . And I cannot but think it was because God had doomed this city to destruction, as a polluted city, and was resolved to purge His sanctuary with fire, that He cut off these, their great defenders while those that a little before had worn the sacred garments and presided over the public worship, were cast out naked to be the food of dogs and wild beasts. . . .

"Now after these were slain the Zealots and the Idumeans fell upon the people as upon a flock of profane animals, and cut their throats." (IV. 5:3)

"Along all the roads also vast numbers of dead bodies lay in heaps; and many who at first were zealous to desert the city chose rather to perish there; for the hopes of burial made death in their own city appear less terrible to them. But those zealots came at last to that degree of barbarity as not to bestow a burial either on those slain in the city or on those that lay along the roads; as if . . . at the same time that they defiled men with their wicked actions they would pollute the Deity itself also, they left the dead bodies to putrefy under the sun." (IV. 6:3).

About this time above 15,000 fugitive Jews were killed by the Romans, "and the number of those that were forced to leap into the Jordan was prodigious. . . . The whole country through which they fled was filled with slaughter, and Jordan could not be passed over, by reason of the dead bodies that were in it" (IV. 8:5, 6).

"The noise of those that were fighting was incessant, both by day and by night; but the lamentations of those that mourned exceeded the noise of the fighting. Nor was there ever any occasion for them to leave off their lamentations, because their calamities came perpetually, one upon another. . . . But as for the seditious bands themselves, they fought against each other while trampling upon the dead bodies which lay heaped one upon another, and being filled with a mad rage from those dead bodies under their feet, they became the more fierce. They, moreover, were still inventing pernicious things against each other; and when they had resolved upon anything, they executed it without mercy, and omitted no method of torment or of barbarity" (V. 2:5).

"And now Titus gave orders to his soldiers that were with him to dig up the foundations of the tower of Antonia, and make a ready passage for his army to come up, while he himself had Josephus brought to him; for he had been informed that, on that very day, which was *the seventeenth day of Panemus, the sacrifice called 'the daily sacrifice' had failed, and had not been offered to God* for want of men to offer it; and that *the people were grievously troubled at it.*" *(Wars,* VI. 2:1.).

* * * * *

It is greatly recommended that the serious student of prophecy obtain a copy of Josephus's works *(The Jewish Wars)* and read for himself the detailed fulfillment of Jesus's prophecy concerning the unspeakable distress that occurred during the time of *Divine vengeance.* (Isaiah 61:2)

The humiliation of the Legion under general Cestius reached the ears of Nero, who then ordered General Vespasian to take over, and crush the revolt. Vespasian then began his military crusade in the spring of A.D. 67, with the X and XII Legions under his command, and the XV Legion led by his son, Titus.

They entered Palestine from the north, marching down to Askelon along the coast, *where* 18,000 were killed, and according to Josephus, *Galilee was all over filled with fire and blood; nor was it exempt from any kind of misery or calamity.* (III 4:1) The stubborn resistance of the Jews infuriated the Romans, and so they spared no one, elderly or child, man or woman.

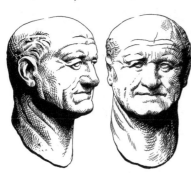

THE EMPEROR VESPASIAN.
Born A.D. 9; died A.D. 79.

Jotapata fell, Joppa was captured, then Tiberias and Taricheae on the shores of the Sea of Galilee (Lake Gennesaret). Thirty thousand from Taricheae were sold into slavery.

In A.D. 68, Vespasian went farther south and cleared the coastal road to Azotus, then he vanquished Perea and the Greek cities that the Jewish rebels had taken. The western Judean Desert was conquered; Samaria ransacked; and the Jordon Valley smitten, with Jericho and the Qumram Community by the Dead Sea destroyed. All this reminds us that Jesus's warning was not just that those in Jerusalem flee, but that those in Judea flee to the mountains, for the abomination that desolates (Daniel 12:11) described an army that would march the length and breadth of the holy place (holy land) reeking havoc and destruction. Those who think "an idol was the topic of Jesus's warning fail to take into account that Judea was vanquished for over three years before Jerusalem and the Temple were besieged. Those who stayed in Judea would have been massacred if they had looked for some setting up of an idol in the Temple, instead of fleeing at the opportune time—at the retreat of Cestius.

In A.D. 69, the area around Bethel in the north, and the region of Hebron in the south, were overcome. But because of political unrest in Rome, Vespasian left, and placed his son in charge of the on-going fighting. (In the space of 18 months, four Emperors had come to a violent end: Nero drove a dagger into his throat; Galba was run down by horsemen; Otho stabbed himself in the breast; Vitellius was killed by slow torture and then dragged by a hook into the Tiber. (See Seutonius.) Vespasian eventually became emperor.

In A.D. 70, Titus began his siege of the capitol. Jerusalem was relentlessly attacked from May to August, when the Temple was finally burned to the ground. A total of 1290 days of conquest completed the *Days of Vengeance*. But the slaughter in the territory throughout Israel (Judea) was only half the drama. What happened inside the walls of Jerusalem was breathtakingly haunting.

CAPITAL CRIMES

Just as there were civil wars in every city, so Jerusalem suffered indescribable disorder and social disaster. If there were no Romans to fight, they fought each other! Bitter contesting between those who sought rebellion, and those who were for peaceful coexistence with the Romans, was just the beginning of troubles.

The basest of men were being appointed to the office of High Priest, and the sanctuary was profaned daily. If a venerable and worthy man, such as Ananius, were high priest, it was of no benefit for he would be slain forthwith.

The riches of the aristocracy were a false security. Torture was inflicted upon the nobles and citizenry of a better sort who did not go along with the demands of the Zealots who had taken control of the city. They were then slain, and none even dared to bury them for fear of the rebels. Twelve thousand of the more eminent inhabitants perished.

The Zealots led by one named John had reeked havoc in the villages of Judea, keeping one step ahead of the Romans, until they had ultimately sought refuge inside Jerusalem. They brought with them a band of blood-thirsty Idumeans who slew young and old as if it was second nature, until the outer Temple area over-flowed with blood from the slaughter of 8,500 in *one day*. Josephus related: *After those who wore the sacred garments were cast out naked to be the food of dogs and wild beasts . . . the Zealots and Idumeans fell upon the people as upon a flock of pro-fane animals, and cut their throats . . .*

Also Josephus noted, About this time above 15,000 fugitive Jews were killed by the Romans, and the number of those that were forced to keep into the Jordan was prodigious . . . The whole country through which they fled was filled with slaughter, and Jordan could not be passed over, by reason of the dead bodies that were in it (IV. 8:5, 6).

Because of the atrocities and wanton murders of the Zealots, the people put a false hope in another tyrant named Simon, hoping he would overthrow the power of John. From then on, the warfare within the city became more intense and inces-sant . . . more deadly. Now there were three factions instead of two.

BREAD OF SORROWS

When anyone exerts a lot, works hard, or fights intensely, he needs a supply of protein to rebuild his strength. Food is important. But where does one find food when a city is surrounded with a siege wall?

The "Desolation" of Jerusalem.

This is the dilemma the factions soon came to face . . . let alone, the common folk . . . the pilgrims who had come and over-populated the city because of the Passover Festival . . . and the children and mothers who were with child (Matthew 24:19). Where is the food for all these people?

Needless to say, famine's stranglehold began to squeeze the throats of the citizenry. As the siege drew on, food became more scarce. Many of the granaries and food supplies had been destroyed in the fighting. Those men kept what food there was for themselves, and seemed to take great delight in seeing the others suffer.

Due to the need for food, some starving Jews went out during the night into the surrounding valleys in search for sustenance. These were caught by the Romans, tortured, and crucified in the sight of those on the walls of Jerusalem. We are told that 500 every day were treated like this. The number of them became so great, the Romans couldn't find enough crosses for the victims, so several men were nailed to the same cross! (V. 11:1, 2)

The Roman Legions had surrounded the city and set up a siege wall: the Twelfth (xii) and Fifteenth (xv) Legions were encamped in the northwest, the Fifth (v) Legion in the south, and the Tenth (x) Legion on the east side. No supplies entered, and no fugitives were allowed to leave.

> "Then did the famine widen its progress and devour the people by whole houses and families. The upper rooms were full of women and children dying by starvation, and the lanes of the city were full of dead bodies of the aged. The children also and the young men wandered about the marketplace like shadows, all swelled with the famine, and fell down dead, wherever their misery seized them." (V. 12:3)

> "If so much as the shadow of any kind of food did anywhere appear a war was commenced presently, and the dearest friends fell fighting one another about it . . . Children pulled the very morsel that their fathers were eating, out of their very mouths, and what was still more to be pitied, so did the mothers do to their infants, and when those that were almost dead were perishing under their hands, they were not ashamed to take from them the very last drops that might preserve their lives . . .
>
> "The seditious . . . also invented terrible methods of torment to discover where any food was, and they were these: To stop up the passages of the private parts of the miserable wretches, and to drive sharp stakes up their fundamentals!" (V. 10:3)

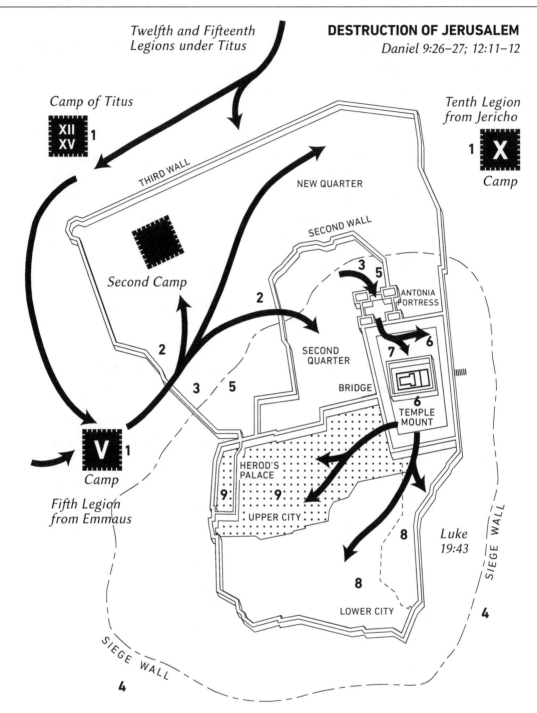

DESTRUCTION OF JERUSALEM
Daniel 9:26–27; 12:11–12

Twelfth and Fifteenth Legions under Titus

Camp of Titus

XII XV 1

Tenth Legion from Jericho

1 **X**

Camp

THIRD WALL

NEW QUARTER

SECOND WALL

Second Camp

3 5

ANTONIA FORTRESS

2

2

SECOND QUARTER

7 6

BRIDGE

3 5

V 1

Camp

6 TEMPLE MOUNT

Fifth Legion from Emmaus

HEROD'S PALACE

9 9

UPPER CITY

8

Luke 19:43

SIEGE WALL

8

LOWER CITY

4

SIEGE WALL

4

1 Titus, with the XV and XII Legions arrived from the North; V Legion from Emmaus; and X Legion from Jericho. **2** Third wall breached, May 25th, and second wall, May 30th. **3** Attack on towers north of Herod's palace, and Antonia fortress, but unsuccessful, June 16th. **4** Siege dike built around Jerusalem. **5** Renewed assault, July 20–22, takes Antonia, but not the palace. **6** August 6th, the sacrifice ceased; Temple porticoes burned Aug. 15th–17th. **7** Temple entered and burned the 9th of Ab (Aug. 28th). **8** Lower city captured, Aug. 30th. **9** After a month more, the upper city and Herod's palace finally taken; and resistance ceased; the city was leveled!

The cannibalism that went on is reminiscent of the prophecy of Moses who warned the Jews who ever thought of "breaking faith" with the LORD: *Because of the suffering that your enemy will inflict on you during the siege, you will eat the fruit of the womb, the flesh of the sons and daughters the Lord your God has given you . . . The most gentle and sensitive woman among you—so feminine and petite that she would not venture to touch the ground with the sole of her foot—will begrudge the husband she loves and her own son or daughter . . . for she intends to eat them secretly during the siege and in the distress that your enemy will inflict on you in your cities.* (Deuteronomy 28:53ff; VI 3.4) God's word is sure; He does not lie.

While Jesus was being led away to be crucified, Jesus saw that there were a number of women who mourned and wailed for him. Through his own pain and agony He mustered the strength to say, *Daughters of Jerusalem, do not weep for me; weep for yourselves and for your children. For the time will come when you will say, "Blessed are the barren women!" . . . Then they will say to the mountains, "Fall on us, and to the hills, Cover us"* (quoting Hosea 10:8) *For if men do these things when the tree is green, what will happen when it is dry?* (Luke 23:27–31) Truer words were never spoken. The heart-wrenching agony was unbearable.

CLOSE THE CURTAIN

> *And they shall fall by the edge of the sword, and shall be led away captive into all nations; and Jerusalem shall be trodden down by the nations, until the times of the nations is fulfilled.* (Luke 24:24)
>
> *And except the Lord had shortened those days, no flesh would be saved; but for the elect's sake, whom He has chosen, He has shortened the days.* (Mark 13:20)
>
> *And except those days should be shortened, there should no flesh be saved; but for the elect's sake those days shall be shortened.* (Matthew 24:22)

Have you ever seen a movie, or a play, that was so gross, unprofessional, or obnoxious, that you couldn't wait for the curtain to close? You just couldn't wait for your agony to end? Sitting through it was a waste of time . . . a drain on your emotions . . . an insult to your intelligence.

Such was the case as the general Titus watched Jerusalem devour itself. For even the Romans were shocked at the atrocities that happened there. It is reported that Titus even swore, with God as His witness, that he was not responsible for the tyranny that enveloped Jerusalem and that sealed its doom more than anything the Roman armies could have done. Josephus commented on this:

Pray ye that your flight be not . . . on the Sabbath day.

They never suffered anything that was worse from the Romans than they made each other suffer; nor was there any misery endured by the city after these men's actions that could be esteemed new . . . For I venture to say that the sedition destroyed the city, and the Romans destroyed the sedition. This was a much harder thing to do than to destroy the walls. So that we may justly ascribe our misfortunes to **our own people.**

These historian's words echo the prophecy of Daniel who foresaw: **The people of the ruler** (prince, KJV) *who will come will destroy the city and the sanctuary.* (Daniel 9:26) The Prince, being Jesus; and the people being the Jewish race (not the disciples) who "received Him not" but also "did unto Him" what they wished: Crucifixion!

Josephus commenting upon the vile conduct of all concerned, wrote: *I suppose that had the Romans* **delayed their coming** *against these villains, the city would either have been swallowed up by the ground opening upon them, or been overflowed by water, or else been destroyed by such thunder as the country of Sodom perished by, for it had brought forth a generation of men much more atheistical than those that suffered such punishments; for by their madness it was that all the people came to be destroyed.* (V 13.6) Perhaps he was recalling the lament of Isaiah: *Unless the Lord Almighty had left us some survivors, we would have become like Sodom.* (Isaiah 1:9, compare 13:19)

But the scriptural fact remained, *Unless the Lord had shortened those days, no flesh would be saved.* (Matthew 24:22, Mark 13:20) Not just Jerusalem, but the whole territory of Judea was being laid waste, and that endangered even those Christians (the elect) who had fled earlier.

Had the civil wars been allowed to continue indefinitely, *no flesh would have survived.* (Matthew 24:22; Mark 13:20) Not even the "elect", the Christian believers, would have made it out unscathed. The tyranny from within the nation, and the warfare from without, would have decimated the population all around Judea, eventually reaching the outskirts of Perea where the Christian disciples were hiding out.

The Roman soldiers had breached the three walls of Jerusalem, and advanced on the Temple itself. They burned its porticoes which surrounded it, and then focused their attack on the Temple. There is on-going debate about who started the fires. The general had hope to spare it, possibly as a standing trophy of his conquest. But either the rabid rebels set fire to it so that would not happen, or the soldiers got out of hand and in their fury put it ablaze.

Either way, the fire melted the gilded doors and golden temple instruments that seeped down between the newly remodeled stone-work. We wouldn't want to accuse the soldiers of greed . . . but they did rip apart all the stones to get at the gold! Stone by stone . . . which brings to mind something said by Someone forty years earlier. (Matthew 24:2) Someone who knew whereof He spoke . . . Someone who knew human nature . . . Someone who knew the limitation God would place on wickedness.

Then the Legionaires overtook the Lower City, and headed for the Upper City where Herod's stronghold was. This was the last of the holdouts of the Jewish defenders . . .No progress was made against it and its very strong towers for a month of fighting. But *one and a half months* (45 days) *later,* after the "daily sacrifice had ceased, mysteriously this last citadel of resistance surrendered!

The fortress was well supplied with water and food, and its bulwarks were insurmountable. But for some inexplicable reason they opened their gates and gave up. Inexplicable, that is, unless you consider the prophetic and divine Providence of God, whose Word does not "fall to the ground" but accomplishes that which He wills. (Isaiah 55:11) *The days were shortened.* Although the rebels could have lasted another year or so, they surrendered without a struggle.

> " . . . they fell upon their face, and greatly lamented their own mad conduct; and their nerves were so terribly loosed, that they could not flee away. And here, one may chiefly reflect on the power of God exercised upon these wicked wretches, and on the good fortune of the Romans;
>
> "For these tyrants did not wholly deprive themselves of the security they had in their power, and come down from those very towers of their own accord, wherein they could have never been taken by force, nor in deed by any other way than by famine . . .
>
> "Three of those towers were too strong for all mechanical engines what-soever . . . So they now left these towers of themselves, or rather they were ejected out of them by God himself." (Josephus, *Wars,* VI, 8:4b-5)

The general, Titus, added, *We have certainly had God for our assistant in this war, and it was no other than God that ejected the Jews out of their fortifications, for what could the hands of men, or any machine do towards overthrowing these towers.* (Ibid, 9.1)

TIMES OF THE GENTILES

The phrase found in Luke 21, *the times of the Gentiles (ethnics,* Gk.) has been bandied about by thousands of prophecy teachers in every generation. One does not have to listen long to televangelists or radio preachers before this phrase is appealed to for understanding their view of eschatology (the study of "end-time" events).

We hear it. We hear it often. But do we hear it correctly interpreted? Does it really refer to end-time or future events? Does it describe the condition of the Israelis for the last two thousand years? Did the "times" end with the rebirth of the nation of Israel in the Mideast? Just how should we interpret this phrase?

KEYS TO UNDERSTANDING

It is not to be doubted that if we go to the scriptures themselves, first, instead of trying to glean an understanding by reading the latest evangelical novel about the end-times, or watching apocalyptic-centered movies, then we will be on the right track. Understanding prophetic events comes from our examination of the Bible verses themselves for ourselves!

This takes time and effort. But it is certainly worth it. What one thinks about the end-times—and what one ought to be doing in the present—affects one's actions . . . for good or for evil. Beliefs can bring us despair and discouragement . . . or they can inspire us on and encourage Christian charity in every day management of life. They can act like an overdose of suppressants, or like a good cup of steaming hot aromatic coffee like grandma used to percolate on the old wood stove! Invigorating and refreshing!

First, then, let us notice the *time context* of the passage of scripture where this phrase, *times of the Gentiles*, is mentioned. In verse 9 of this chapter 21 of Luke, Jesus said that "the end will not come right away." And then later, Jesus emphatically stated, "this generation will certainly not pass away until **all these things** have happened" (vs. 32). So we can conclude that the events of chapter 21 were to happen between 30 A.D. and 70 A.D. the forty-year time of a generation (compare Numbers 32:13; Hebrews 3:9–10).

So then, when Jesus said the words, *Jerusalem shall be trampled on,* He was referring to an event that was to happen by the time 70 A.D. rolled around. It could not refer to the long era of time between the first century and the twenty-first century! It also was not a reference to the oppression of Jewry throughout modern history . . . supposedly ending in 1948 when Israel became a nation. Nor is the trampling description of some future event during the alleged end-times (i.e. end of the world).

Was the city of Jerusalem "trampled on" during the generation beginning right after Jesus' sermon? History resounds with an absolute "Yes!" The Romans sent four or five Legions of soldiers into Judea to quell the Zealot guerrilla warfare that was questioning the authority of the Empire. The general Vespasian began destroying the villages of Galilee, Joppa, and the coast in 67 A.D.

THE TIMES OF THE GENTILES

When you hear of wars and revolutions, do not be frightened. These things must happen first, but the end will not come right away . . . When you see Jerusalem being surrounded by armies, you will know that its desolation is near . . . Jerusalem will be trampled on by the nations until the **times of the Gentiles (nations)** *are fulfilled "I tell you the truth, this generation will certainly not pass away until all these things have happened." (Luke 21:9, 20, 24, 32)*

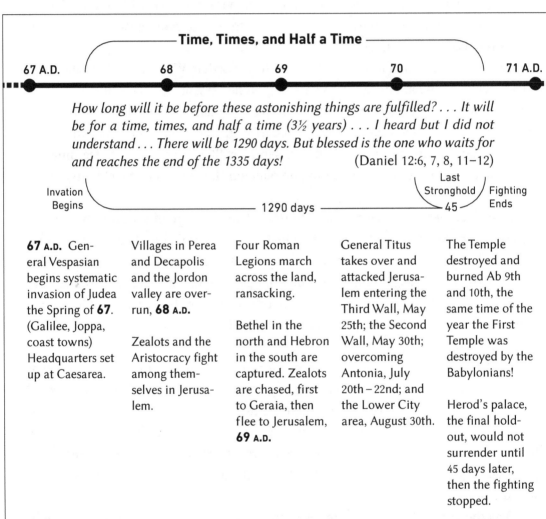

Time, Times, and Half a Time

67 A.D.   68   69   70   71 A.D.

How long will it be before these astonishing things are fulfilled? . . . It will be for a time, times, and half a time (3½ years) . . . I heard but I did not understand . . . There will be 1290 days. But blessed is the one who waits for and reaches the end of the 1335 days! (Daniel 12:6, 7, 8, 11–12)

Invation Begins

Last Stronghold / Fighting Ends

1290 days — 45

67 A.D. General Vespasian begins systematic invasion of Judea the Spring of **67**. (Galilee, Joppa, coast towns) Headquarters set up at Caesarea.

Villages in Perea and Decapolis and the Jordon valley are overrun, **68 A.D.**

Zealots and the Aristocracy fight among themselves in Jerusalem.

Four Roman Legions march across the land, ransacking.

Bethel in the north and Hebron in the south are captured. Zealots are chased, first to Geraia, then flee to Jerusalem, **69 A.D.**

General Titus takes over and attacked Jerusalem entering the Third Wall, May 25th; the Second Wall, May 30th; overcoming Antonia, July 20th – 22nd; and the Lower City area, August 30th.

The Temple destroyed and burned Ab 9th and 10th, the same time of the year the First Temple was destroyed by the Babylonians!

Herod's palace, the final holdout, would not surrender until 45 days later, then the fighting stopped.

So when you see standing in the holy place the abomination that causes desolation, spoken of through the prophet Daniel—let the reader understand—then . . . flee. (Matthew 24:15–16)

The next year, 68 A.D., the Roman Legions marched through Perea and the Decapolis, and down the Jordan valley, stomping on all who opposed the Emperor. The next year, 69 A.D., Bethel in the north, and Hebron in the south were captured. The Zealot rebels were slowly being driven back and fled to Gerasa, Herodium, and the hills . . . eventually ending up in the capitol city, Jerusalem . . . where they caused unbearable havoc among the residents there. Not only did they put a strangle hold upon the ruling aristocracy, but the Zealots began to fight among themselves until the streets ran with blood.

Then in 70 A.D., the son of general Vespasian, Titus, took over and besieged Jerusalem. He built a siege wall, barricading the people so they could neither leave or enter the city . . . nor could food supplies be available for the starving residents. Methodically, Titus attacked the walls until he gained entry up to the Temple itself. On the same day that the First Temple was destroyed by the Babylonians, this Second one was burned! Each stone was ripped from its walls and foundations . . . according to the accurate prophecy of Jesus (Matthew 24:2).

The whole city lay in ruins except for Herod's palace with its insurmountable towers of defense. The besieged stronghold had enough food stored in it for perhaps years if they wanted to hold out that long. Titus remarked that the stones of the palace were so thick and huge that his war engines could not penetrate them.

But mysteriously, after 45 days (1½ months) the gates flew open, and the people surrendered on their own! Amazingly, this was prophesied by Daniel four and a half centuries earlier (Daniel 12:11–12, Matthew 24:15–6): *There will be 1290 days* (of trampling), *but blessed is the one who waits and reaches the end of the 1335 days.* Jerusalem was indeed "trampled on" by the Gentiles (nations) until their time was up. There is no need to look for another interpretation of this phrase. Any event in the future has nothing to do with this accurate prophecy of Jesus . . . and Daniel. [Note: the Roman armies were made of Romans **and** many mercenaries from different nations . . . so the plural, Gentiles (nations), is an appropriate word.]

PLAYING PRANKS

An example of the attempt to rip this verse out of its time constraints and extend it to an indefinite length of time is given by H. A. Ironside, in his speculative book, *The Great Parenthesis:*

> *. . . the times of the Gentiles' covers the entire period during which the nation of the Jews, the city of Jerusalem, and the land of Palestine are under Gentile domination. This began with Nebuchadnezzar's conquest of Palestine and will end at the Revelation of the Lord Jesus Christ from heaven at the close of the Great Tribulation.* (p. 84)

The book bank-rolled by the Darbyites (the Plymouth Brethren), the *Scofield Study Bible,* set forth the basis for this type of teaching in its footnotes. It has led many an expositor down a rabbit trail, or a wild goose chase, depending on your prey of choice. But Luke's verse is not mentioning a "ruling over" Judea, but a "trampling down" of Jerusalem . . . for a specific length of time . . . a military thumping for a short while . . . a *desolation* by those abominable Roman thugs until the end of the Second Temple Era.

A synoptic comparison highlights this point. In those parallel verses, Matthew and Mark wrote of *days that were shortened.* Not, we repeat, not an indefinite period of time of thousands of years. Shortened days. And to pull the "times of the Gentiles" phrase out of its setting (context), and to stretch them into a long period of time, or a *Gentile Age,* or even a supposed *Church Age,* is contrived fabrication with an unscriptural demeanor. It is, as Philip Mauro quipped, *playing pranks with prophecy.*

SPIRITUAL QUACKS

> *Then if anyone says to you, 'Look, here is the Christ' or 'There!' do not believe it. For false christs and false prophets will rise and show great signs and wonders to deceive, if possible, even the elect. Behold, I have already warned you.*
>
> *Therefore if they say to you, 'Look, He is in the desert!' do not go out; or 'Look, He is in the inner rooms!' do not believe it.*
>
> *For as the lightning comes from the east and flashes to the west, so also will the coming of the Son of Man be.*
>
> *For wherever the carcass is, there the eagles will be gathered together.* (Matthew 24:23–29; also Mark 13:21–23)

The most conniving scum on the face of the earth are those who would take advantage of people who are experiencing a tragedy of any sort. Those who would exploit the adverse situation of a distressed soul are to be loathed. Men who commit such acts of opportunism are a blight on the skin of this green earth.

However, worse than them, are spiritual charlatans who deceive and lead men astray. Wolves who wrap themselves in evangelical robes and say, "Thus saith the Lord," when God has not spoken. Weasels who climb into pastoral pulpits and defraud the congregation of brothers and sisters.

Such was the dilemma facing the citizens of Judea in the Old Testament era of Jeremiah:

> *I have heard what the prophets say who prophesy lies in My Name. They say, 'I had a dream!' How long will this continue in the hearts of these lying prophets who prophesy the delusions of their own minds? . . .*

> *Let the prophet who has a dream tell his dream, but let the one who has My word speak it faithfully. For what has straw to do with grain?, declares the LORD . . .*
>
> *Therefore, declares the LORD, I am against the prophets who steal from each other words supposedly from me. Yes, declares the LORD, I am against the prophets who wag their own tongues and yet declare, 'the LORD declares.' Indeed, I am against those who prophesy false dreams . . . They tell them and lead My people astray with their reckless lies, yet I did not send or appoint them. They do not benefit these people in the least, declares the LORD.* (Jeremiah 24:25–32)

And such was the dire straits of the people besieged inside the walls of Jerusalem in 70 A.D. False prophets roamed the streets at random.

Desperate people will grasp at any straw if they suppose there is the littlest bit of help in it. Jesus knew how fragile victim's emotions could be, and how gullible the sorrowing soul can become. He realized how, insult upon injury, credulous the worried mind was. The down-trodden heart will cling to the smallest sign of hope.

Behold, *I have already warned you before,* Jesus exclaimed to His confused and bewildered disciples. Yes, just a few moments earlier in His *questionable dialogue,* He had warned about false prophets. But even before that, way back when He had delivered His lecture at the Seminar on the Mount, Jesus had said, *Watch out for false prophets. They come in sheep's clothing, but inwardly they are ferocious wolves . . . Many will say to me on 'that Day', "Lord, Lord, did we not prophesy in your name, and in your name drive out demons and perform many miracles?" Then I will tell them plainly, I never knew you. Away from me, you evildoers!* (Matthew 7:15–23)

In the first part of the Olivet Discourse Jesus dealt with prophets who would deceive in the time frame before the siege, the period laid out in the Acts of the Apostles. Now, Jesus warned about those who would be deceivers during the time of the siege. A worse sort of scoundrel.

No doubt, the parents of famished children would look wistfully at the sky, remembering when Hezekiah prayed for divine intervention as the armies of Assyria under Sennacherib approached Jerusalem, how God answered favorably. (2 Kings 19:14–37) They hoped the same would occur during the terrible tribulation they were enduring.

But false prophets would come out from the woodworks and take advantage of the people for their own gains . . . their own greed . . . their own glory. Josephus recorded the fact that before the siege, the procurator Felix executed many of those impostors daily. *(Antiquities* XX. 8:5, 6) And that during the siege the false prophets continued to ply their trade:

> Now there was then a great number of false prophets suborned by the tyrants to impose upon the people, who denounced this to them, that they should wait for deliverance from God; and this was in order to keep them from deserting, and that they might be buoyed up above the fear and care by such hopes.
>
> . . . thus were the miserable people persuaded by these deceivers . . . while they did not heed, nor give credence to the signs that were so evident that did so plainly foretell their future desolation. (*Wars*, VI. 5: 2–3)

Josephus gave a specific example of the great calamity that occurred when the people neglected to follow the wisdom of Christ:

> The soldiers also came to the rest of the cloisters that were in the outer temple, where the women and children, and a great mixed multitude of the people, fled, in number about 6,000. But before Caesar had determined anything about these people, or given the commander any orders, relating to them, the soldiers were in such a rage that they set that cloister on fire; by which means it came to pass that some of those were destroyed by throwing themselves down headlong, and some were burnt in the cloisters themselves.
>
> Nor did any one of them escape with his life. A false prophet was the occasion of these people's destruction, who had made a public proclamation in the city that very day, that God commanded them to get upon the temple, and that there they would receive miraculous signs of their deliverance. (VI. 5.2)

Twice, Jesus warned, *Believe it not!*, very emphatically. The desolation of Jerusalem had been "decreed" . . . his disciples were not to anticipate any of the previous Old Testament-type deliverances by the coming of God to their rescue. Neither the return of the Messiah nor the Messenger of Light of the Qumram sect was going to show up and chase away the Romans.

SECRET, RAPT COMING?

The first century disciples were specifically warned about any proclamation that claimed the Coming of Christ would be shrouded in secrecy. A secret type of return for believers (the Elect, the Church comprised of Jew and Gentile) was out of the question. In fact, this teaching of Christ was in response to the very question the disciples asked at the beginning of the Olivet Discourse: *What will be the sign of your coming?* (24:2)

Any Coming of Christ, any return of the Lord, would not be a secret one! Only false prophets (and prophecy conference lecturers, or television pastors) would teach that . . . out of their own imagination . . . or from dipping into each other's cup. (See Jeremiah 24.) Any *secret rapture* scenario would be that coming from the mouth of a false prophet.

No sign would be necessary when Christ would return. No announcement would be necessary to herald His Coming. No one would ever have to be told about it. The unique aspect of it would be its *self-manifestation*. Because *just as lightning that comes from the east is visible even in the west, so will be the Coming (parousia,* Gk.) *of the Son of Man.* (24:27) When the Christ of eschatology returns, no prophet will be necessary to announce it! His glorious return will be flashed across the heavens for all to see. It will be conspicuous for all to see everywhere.

The Second Coming of Christ is revealed to be in contrast to the type of coming in judgement on Jerusalem. Signs were given to "flee to the hills" , but any mani-fested sign at the Second Coming would be ludicrous. Fleeing would be out of the question at the Second Coming. So any sign to flee would be quite unnecessary. Up to verse 27 there had been no mention of the Second Coming; all those visible signs and omens of coming disaster had nothing to do with Christ's return at the end of the world . . . they applied only to the 'Abomination that makes Desolate,' The con-quering armies of Rome, and the end of the Second Temple Era.

That modern telepastors and prophecy lecturers would list the signs attending the Fall of Jerusalem and the conditions Jesus called "birth pangs", as *signs of the end-times* just before the Second Coming, is unconscionable, and if marketing of products is involved, unscrupulous.

Note that Christ's mentioning the Coming of the Son of Man (Second Coming of Christ) at this juncture of the Discourse does not mean that He expected it to follow: Immediately after the siege of Jerusalem with all its distress and affliction. He is merely **contrasting** the false concepts of the Coming of Christ by the wicked prophets, with the eventual Coming of Christ, *whenever it happens in the future* in its true form: *openly, self-manifesting* . . . as visible as bolt of lightning on a Sam Snead golf course in the middle of a hot day in July under a wide Kansas sky!

That the eventual Second Coming of Christ at the end of the world is to be *overt* . . . public . . . without concealment . . . is confirmed by a plethora of other New Testament statements. Notably is Paul's written description in the first letter to the Thessalonican church:

> *The Lord Himself will come down from heaven with a loud command (shout, NKJV), with the voice of the archangel, and with the trumpet of God, and the dead in Christ will rise first.* (1 Thessalonians 4:16)

And undoubtedly, the similarity with the description of the meeting of Israel and God at Mount Sinai, was on the mind of the Apostle:

> *On the morning of the third day, there was thunder and lightning, with a thick cloud over the mountain, and a very loud trumpet blast.* (Exodus 19:16; also 20:18; compare Zechariah 9:14)

When the Lord returns to earth, it will be in the same manner in which he left when He ascended; He will descend down from the skies . . . and not emerge out from some desert . . . nor walk out from a cloister. (Acts 1:11) Anyone who teaches contrary, first or twenty-first century, is a false teacher . . . even if they wrap themselves in evangelical clothes or fundamental robes.

CARCASSES AND CARRION

> *Wherever there is a carcass, there the vultures* (eagles, NKJV) *will gather.* (24:28)

Jesus ended this section of prophecy with a proverb that is quite graphic as well as straightforward. The simplest of minds would understand that it was no compliment. When applied to a culture—and in this case, the Jewish society—it would be a metaphor of people rotten to the core! It would prefigure moral and spiritual decay beyond remedy, and illustrate a finality.

Such was the condition of the Jewish nation to whom Jesus applied this: there was no justice in the court system, with widows and orphans ripped off and cast into the street; the priestly caste was involved in covetousness and greed; the aristocracy ignored the plight of the poor; the political scene was rife with factions at each other's throat . . . literally! Murder and assassinations were commonplace; bandits roamed the hillside, and Zealots dealt treacherously with fellow countrymen. Villages were pillaged, homes burned, and villas ransacked. And, oh yes, prophets stoned to death.

The plight of the inhabitants of Jerusalem was horrendous! Famine and pestilence plagued them by day, and fear and distress haunted them at night. Odors of cooking food, or rumors of hidden scraps of food, attracted desperate friends, relatives, and robbers, like flies on some rotting carcass.

On top of this was the heavy toll of a blood-letting civil war. There were the Zealots and Idumeans led by John, the rival gang of ruffians under Simon, the corrupt high priests, and the rich aristocracy . . . all vying for control of what was left of this beset society. Dead bodies lay unburied in the streets, and other corpses were thrown over the Jerusalem walls by the thousands.

Those beleaguered souls who tried to escape were either killed by the Zealots within the city, or suffered the fate of crucifixion by the Romans outside the decaying civilization. Desolation was decreed by God, and it was carried out to the max. (Daniel 9:26; Matthew 24:2)

The *false prophets deceived* their society by offering a false hope: "Their iniquities were not really so bad, such that God would overlook them and provide deliverance from desolation, like He had done for Hezekiah and the ancient city of Jerusalem." "God would never let the 'holy city' become desolate . . . and especially, never let the 'holy Temple' become a pile of stones."

Those were false assurances, for the nation was deserving of Divine judgment. The dazzling robes, the blue tassels, the priestly mitres, the shepherd's staffs, and the scrolls, were all external accouterments that concealed (poorly) a bone-dead spirituality and putrefying lawlessness inside their souls. (23:27-28) Like new suits on a corpse in a coffin, all their outward appearances belied their deadness toward God. According to Jesus' imagery, they were now merely *bird bait*.

The Greek word, *aetos*, is usually translated as "eagle", but may be referring here to the *vultur pernopterus* (vulture), which resembles an eagle. But "eagle" is a fitting word that was used in the Jewish literature to picture foreign armies that would act as God instruments, punishing sinful nations.

> *The LORD shall bring a nation against thee from far, from the end of the earth, as swift as the* **eagle** *flieth; a nation whose tongue thou shalt not understand.* (Deuteronomy 28:49)

> *He shall come as an* **eagle** *against the House of the Lord because they have transgressed My Covenant, and trespassed against My Law.* (Hosea 8:1)

> *Their horses also are swifter than the leopards, and are more fierce than the evening wolves; and their horsemen shall spread themselves, and their horsemen shall come from far; they shall fly as the* **eagle that hasteth to eat**. (Habakkuk 1:8)

The "eagle" was represented on many of the Roman Legion's standards, and this significance is not to be lost when reading of Jesus's use of this proverb. Those military ensigns may have been an abomination to the self-righteous priests, but they were to be an accurate representative of how abominable the priests themselves were to their God. In God's eyes, they had become spiritually putrid and loathsome . . . moral carrion . . . to be devoured. Their prophets' reassurances, notwithstanding!

Beyond the figurative, there is the literal aspect of Jesus' prophecy. During the merciful putting of an end to the corruption of the First Temple society, Jeremiah prophesied: *The carcasses of this people will become food for the birds of the air and the beasts of the earth, and there will be no one to frighten them away.* (Jeremiah 7:33, also 19:7) Even though they put hope in their national symbol, the holy Temple's presence, the consequence of their iniquity was death and destruction. Their slain bodies became carrion, literally, for the birds.

So also with the Second Temple society: Over a million defenders were slain (by the Zealots and the Romans), with many of them just dumped into the surrounding valleys, unburied, according to Josephus. (VI. 9:3, 4) Carrion!

ASTRONOMICAL EXTRAVAGANZAS

> *Immediately after the tribulation of those days, the sun shall be darkened, and the moon shall not give her light, and the stars shall fall from heaven, and the powers of the heavens shall be shaken.* (Matthew 24:29; also, Mark 13:24)

> *And there shall be signs in the sun, and in the moon and in the stars; and upon the earth distress of nations with perplexity; the sea and the waves roaring; men's hearts failing them for fear, and for looking after those things which are coming on the earth; for the powers of heaven shall be shaken.* (Luke 21:25)

A prequel to *Star Wars?* Or a sequel to the movie, *Armageddon?* Is this passage of scripture a preview of a Carl Sagan "Cosmos" docudrama? Is this a meteorologist's once-in-a-lifetime dream forecast? How about it being the description of an ecoterrorists maddening plot?

A modern interpreter's imagination could really go wild at the reading of these verses! In fact, a lot of prophecy teachers have not put the brakes on as their fanciful interpretations have taken off and sky-rocketed. They have stepped on the gas pedal of adrenaline with Saturn booster proportions.

Whatever the meaning is, the able exegete is still bound to interpret these verses within the curtain raising and the curtain dropping laid out by Jesus: *All this will come upon this generation* (23:36; 24:34). And since the previous verses dealt with the destruction of the Second Temple edifice, the "immediately after" designation limits any fulfillment to the first century. These celestial disturbances are not precursors of Christ's Second Coming at the end of the world for the teaching of Jesus absolutely forbids that interpretation, as well. We are debarred by the Lord's plain statements from taking these commotions to be physical signs, visible to the eye, that are to herald His end-time Coming: No one knows about that day or hour, not even the angels in heaven, nor the Son, but only the Father. (Mark 13:32). (If Jesus didn't know "when", He certainly could not give signs of "when" it will occur!)

SANE AND SENSIBLE

To derive a sane and sensible interpretation of these astronomy-drenched verses, a person must "get in the skin" of the original Speaker and into the minds of His disciples. The actors on the Olivet stage were all Hebrews (except One who was only Hebrew on his mother's side); and they were well versed in the Hebrew literature, history, and vernacular. They were familiar with figures of speech germane to prophetic dialogue. They understood the terms pertinent to the theology of the first century.

These actors did not speak in the vernacular of Shakespearean britons; nor were they conversant in the language of Hollywood movie stars. Modern English was not their first language (nor was modern Spanish their second language). The figures of speech used in the twenty-first century would be quite foreign to them.

The use of the word, immediately (*eutheōs,* Gk.), clearly mandates an interpretation of an event hard on the heels of the Destruction of Jerusalem and all the tribulation (KJV; distress, NIV) of those days. This same word was used when a leper *stretched forth his hand and was* **immediately** *healed* (Matthew 8:3) . . . And when Jesus, called the fishermen to be His disciples, they **immediately** *left their nets, and followed Jesus* (Matthew 4:20, 22; see also Galatians 1:6, James 1:24 and Revelation 4:2).

Even though the verbiage of the scriptures at hand lend themselves to dramatic scenes of apocalyptic proportion, there is no warrant for all the speculative, end-time scenarios that modern prophecy novelists and movie script writers extract from these verses. *Immediately* does not allow the separation of these events from the Jewish drama in 70 A.D. . . . especially not a huge gap of over two thousand years! To list these phenomena as signs at the climax of the so-called Church age, or even at the end of some Great Tribulation of the Jews in the future, would be a forced interpretation based on a preconceived bias, largely influenced by the Jesuits and the Darbyites (both heretical sects).[4]

It would even violate the futurists' (Dispensationalists') own rule of interpretation, which they call, "The Golden Rule of Biblical Interpretation . . . *(When the plain sense of Scripture makes common sense, seek no other sense, but take every word at its primary, literal meaning unless the facts of the immediate context clearly indicate otherwise*—Tim LaHaye, *No Fear of the Storm,* 1992, p. 240) The plain sense of Jesus' "book-ends" ('this generation') and the use of "you standing here" in the plain sense, and the accurate description of the Fall of Jerusalem (destruction of the Temple in

---

4   The pervasive End-time prophecy interpretations which teach just the opposite of what Jesus spoke, illustrate the psychological phenomena mentioned by William James, "If you tell a lie often enough, people will believe the lie; and the greater the lie, the greater the deception!"

70 A.D.), all together referring to the first century, *make common sense.* And then the employment of the word, *immediately,* would dictate that those events described, also happened in the first century. We should *seek no other sense.*

ENLIGHTEN US

So, how are we to interpret these astronomical phenomena mentioned by Jesus . . . which were to happen in the first century? What do they really mean? And did they occur when Jesus said they would occur?

A survey of the Old Testament literature, the Hebrew writings, give a clear and unmistakable answer. Remember, Jesus was talking to Hebrews, not modern English literature university majors; so looking back at the original language of the Bible characters is appropriate . . . apropo . . . necessary. Here is what they reveal: *These very same words* are used repeatedly in a figurative (symbolic) sense to describe the collapse of a government and its governed society. These cosmic phrases are common prophetic language used at the important vortex of an ancient nation when they are consumed by a dark hole of God . . . judgment. This is how the disciples would comprehend them.

For example, when God was about to arouse the Medes and Persians to go and destroy Babylon for all its pride and wickedness, He had Isaiah write:

> *Behold, the day of the LORD is coming, cruel, with fury and burning anger, to make the land a desolation; and He will exterminate its sinners from it.*
> *For the stars of heaven and their constellations will not show their light; the rising sun will be darkened, and the moon will not reflect its light.*
> *I will punish the world for its evil, the wicked for their sins; I will put an end to the arrogance of the haughty and will humble the pride of the ruthless.*
> (Isaiah 13:9–11)

The beginning of the 13th chapter opens with "the burden of Babylon . . ." which was a large, magnificent metropolis, once feared by nations all around the ancient Mideast. So if the fall of the government of a pagan, unenlightened city can be described in such astronomical terms, certainly it's quite appropriate for Jesus to use this imagery to forecast the down fall of a government that had the privilege of obtaining the Law of God, and the consolation of the Prophets, and *the Light of the world (Messiah Jesus)* in their midst.

SIGNS OF THE TIMES

FIRST COMING

YES

Jesus

ADVENT SIGNS:
Daniel 9:25;
Isaiah 9:6;
Micah 5:2;
Luke 2:12

MIRACULOUS / MESSIANIC SIGNS:
Isaiah 35:4-6;
John 7:31;
John 5:30-47;   Matthew 12:38-45
John 20:30-31;

Christmas

c. 4 BC

JUDGMENT SIGNS:
Luke 12:54-57;
Luke 21:25-32;
Matthew 24:1-35;
Luke 13:34-35

Easter

30 AD ◄ **"This Generation"** ► **70 AD**

Matthew 23:35-38
Mark 13:30

67-70 AD
"Times of the Gentiles"
Luke 19:43-44;
Luke 21:20-24;
Daniel 9:26-27;
Daniel 12:11-12

SECOND COMING

NO

Jesus as High Priest

NO SIGNS!
Mark 13:32-37;
Matthew 24:36-25:13;
Luke 17:26-30;
Acts 1:7;
1 Thessalonians 5:1-3

? AD

No warnings.
Stay alert.
Occupy until …

"No one knows about that day
or hour, not even the angels in
heaven, nor the Son, only the
Father. Be on guard! Be alert!
You do not know when that
time will come." (Mk 13:32–33)

The *First Coming* of Jesus Christ was accompanied by many signs
and "infallible proofs" so that the Israelis, and the world, would
definitely know who the Messiah (Savior) is. But the *Second Coming*
of Jesus needs no identification, just consummation: A wrapping up
of history, and an accountability of every person for their conduct in
the Kingdom of God in the days of that history.

The Jews had turned a blind eye to their Messiah. Those Pharisees who boasted in being "guides of the blind *(hoi polloi)*" were to have even what light they had become darkness. Recall the words of Jesus: *If your eyes are bad, your whole body will be full of darkness. If then the light within you is darkness, how great is that darkness!* (Matthew 6:23) Collectively then, the whole national government (and priestly system) would be without a sun and moon to shine on them: How great would be their darkness of despair and desolation.

This same stellar imagery was used by God to predict the collapse of the First Temple Era:

> *Woe to you who long for the Day of the LORD. For what purpose will the day of the LORD be to you? It will be darkness and not light . . .*
>
> *It will come about in that day, declares the Lord GOD, that I will make the sun go down at noon and make the earth dark in broad daylight.* (Amos 5:18; 8:9)

And continuing the same type of metaphoric meteorological missive, even the prophet Ezekiel lambasted the mighty Pharaonic dynasty of Egypt with:

> *When I extinguish you (snuff you out, NIV), I will cover the heavens and darken their stars; I will cover the sun with a cloud, and the moon will not reflect light. All the shining lights in the heavens I will darken above you; I will set darkness over your land, declares the sovereign LORD.*
>
> *I will trouble the hearts of many peoples when I bring about your destruction among the nations . . . I will cause many peoples to be appalled at you, and their kings will shudder with horror . . .* (Ezekiel 32:7–10)

Notice Ezekiel's reference to the "troubling of hearts, etc." and then just look at the way the evangelist, Luke, picks up on this same idea: *On the earth, nations will be in anguish and perplexity at the roaring and tossing of the sea. Men will faint from terror, apprehensive of what is coming on the world . . .* (Luke 21:25–26) These same demeanors were mentioned in the previous prophecy of Isaiah:

> *Wail, for the day of the LORD is near; it will come like destruction from the Almighty (Shaddai). Because of this, all hands will go limp, every man's heart will melt. Terror will seize them, pain and anguish will grip them . . . they will look aghast at each other . . .* (Isaiah 13:6–8)

The pending destruction of Edom, and its capitol, Bozrah, were also pictured in terms similar to that used by Jesus concerning Jerusalem:

All the stars of the heavens will be dissolved and the sky rolled up like a scroll; all the starry host will fall like withered leaves from the vine, like shriveled figs from the fig tree . . .

God will stretch out over Edom the measuring line of chaos and the plumb line of desolation. Her nobles will have nothing there to be called a kingdom, and her princes will vanish away. Thorns will overrun her citadels, nettles and brambles her strongholds. (Isaiah 34:4, 11–13)

And there are many more Old Testament references to "light" representing times of blessing, and "darkness" referring to destruction brought on by wickedness. (Isaiah 59:9–10; Habakkuk 3:11; Joel 2:10; Psalm 37:6; Jeremiah 4:23, 28) Especially noteworthy is the wording of Micah: *Night will overcome you . . . Therefore because of you, Zion will be plowed like a field, Jerusalem will become a heap of rubble, and the Temple hill a mound overgrown with thickets.* (Micah 3:6, 12)

It can be concluded that with utmost certainty that Jesus' references to the shakeup of the heavens is a direct application of Old Testament imagery to the utter collapse of the Judaean economy, the eradication of the priesthood with its animal sacrifices, and the complete overthrow of whatever government was left in Jerusalem.

He was emphasizing that the disciples were not to expect a recovery from the Roman invasion. They were not to look for a resurgence of the society after its Divine judgment took place. *Immediately after* the last Roman arrow was shot, the enlightened observer would look around and find nothing of the Israeli government there that could be called a kingdom. The physical Temple hill, that once housed the Presence of the Shekinah Glory of the Almighty, would merely be a mound, with no need **ever** to rise up again. (Hebrews 7:18–19; 9:8–11; 12:22) As the Apostles would later teach, a better, spiritual Tabernacle would take its place where people of all nations could enter into the Presence of God, not just one Jewish priest!

This point is underscored by the quotation of Joel by Peter on the Day of Pentecost (Joel 2:28–32; Acts 2:14–21). With the birth of the Church there would be an ending, death of the old theocracy and Mosaic system.

In a previous generation, the biblical scholar, Milton S. Terry had lamented in his monumental work, *Biblical Hermeneutics,* that far too many exegetes and commentators on biblical doctrine, had assumed as a principle not to be questioned, that such highly wrought language that was clearly taken almost *verbatim* from Old Testament prophecies of judgment on nations and kingdoms which long ago had perished, must now be understood and taken *literally.* If he were alive today, he would be heart-broken to see that such absurdity has a stranglehold upon the pastoral throats of evangelical denominations. And that the tide of silliness does not seem to be any time soon abating.

The reason for the proliferation of error in interpreting scriptures of a prophetic sort, he gave as: *Too little study of Old Testament ideas of judgment, and apocalyptic language and style, would seem to be the main reason for this one-sided exegesis. It will require more than 'assertion' to convince thoughtful men that the figurative language of Isaiah and Daniel, admitted on all hands to be such in those ancient prophets, is to be literally interpreted when used by Jesus and Paul.* (p. 466) The modern dilemma, one would note, is that there is a lack of those "thoughtful men" who resorted to primary research. Instead, pastors, who by the way, claim to be students of prophecy, are merely dipping into the cups of propheteers (reading books, novels, and watching fictitious movies), and not doing original, personal word studies on their own initiative. (Compare Jeremiah 23:30–32)

THE CLOUDED ONE

> *And then shall appear the sign, "the Son of Man in heaven" and then shall all the tribes of the earth mourn, and they shall see the Son of Man coming in the clouds of heaven with power and great glory.* (Matthew 24:30; Mark 13:26; Luke 21:27)

"And *then* a sign shall appear", or as the NIV translates, *at that time*, which brings forth a clearer understanding. "Then" does **not** mean an adverb announcing something to happen a long time later. It means "at the time when the things under consideration were taking place (of a concomitant event)" (See Thayer, *Lexicon*, p. 629) It could be translated, *thereupon*, that is, "When the thing under consideration had been said or done."

For example, this word, *tote* (Gk.), is used beginning the sentences of a conversation when two people are dialoguing back and forth with no measurable time lapse in between. (Matthew 25:34–46) It is used by Matthew when he immediately applies an Old Testament prophecy to a New Testament "in progress" event or fulfillment. (Matthew 2:17)

At the time when "the sun was darkened, the stars falling, etc" . . . when the Jewish economy and culture was collapsing, this sign was also appearing: *The Son of Man in heaven.* And it is important to not misread this statement of Jesus; He did **not** say, "then shall appear in heaven the Son of Man" but rather, "then shall appear the sign . . . *"In heaven"* defines the locality of "the Son of Man", not of the sign. "A sign was not to appear in the heaven, but the destruction of Jerusalem was to indicate the rule of the Son of Man in heaven." (Marcellus Kik, Matthew XXIV, p. 79)

The fall of Jerusalem "signified" the rise of a new Authority. As the Britons would shout, "The king is dead; Long live the (new) king!" Marcellus Kik informed Bible students: "One must note that the verse speaks of a *sign* and not of the personal appearance of Christ Himself. If Christ had referred to His visible coming in the heavens, He would have said; 'And then shall appear the Son of Man in heaven.' But He prophesied the appearance of a *sign* of the Son of Man who dwells in heaven." (Kik, p. 79)

The old had to pass away in proportion to the institution of the new. If Judaism's temple rites and regulations had remained in power, and held sway over the mentality of the culture, it would have been a tremendous hindrance to the spreading of the Gospel . . . the gathering together of the Elect *from the four winds* (24:31) The Church was not to be a Judaism junior!

The Apostle Paul made it clear *that the Jews' transgression (leading to desolation) means riches for the world, and their loss means riches for the nations (Gentiles) . . . Their rejection (results in) is the reconciliation of the world.* (Romans 11:12, 15) The shaking of the heavens over Judea was a "kick-start" for the Christian Church — which, we must insist, is comprised of Jew and Gentile without distinction . . . without favoritism. The Jews who believe are not to be part of the desolation, but are a "remnant" enjoying the fulfillment of all that the prophets said would happen under the Messiah's reign. Jewry is not abandoned; the door of salvation is wide open to all who place faith in Jesus, "to the Jew first, then the nations."

How do we know that Jesus, the Son of Man, is in heaven? First, we have the vision of Stephen the martyr. While he was being stoned, full of the Holy Spirit, he looked up to heaven and saw the glory of God, and said, *Look! I see heaven open and the Son of Man* (Jesus) *standing at the right hand of God.* (Acts 7:55–56)

And secondly, we have the apostolic revelation repeated over and over again: *God has raised this Jesus to life . . . Exalted to the right hand of God, He has received from the Father the promised Holy Spirit . . . For David did not ascend to heaven, and yet he prophesied, 'The Lord said to my Lord, sit at my right hand until I make your enemies a footstool for your feet!' Therefore, let all Israel be assured of this: God has made this Jesus . . . both Lord and Christ.* (Acts 2:32–36. Study Acts 5:31; Romans 8:34; Ephesians 1:20; Colossians 3:1; Hebrews 1:3, 13; 8:1; 10:12; 12:2; 1 Pet. 3:22)

Thirdly, we have the testimony of Jesus Himself. Speaking to the chief priests and elders of the Sanhedrin, just before His crucifixion, Jesus declared, *I say to all of you, in the future you will see the Son of Man sitting at the right hand of the Mighty One and coming on the clouds of heaven.* (Matthew 26:64)

REMORSE REGRET REPENT

The ascension and enthronement of Jesus (Mark 16:19) would result in *all the tribes of the land mourning* (Matthew 24:30; *nations of the earth,* NIV, but *'phulai tēs gēs'* better refers to the locality of this prophecy: *the tribes of the land of Judea.*) Some would mourn because of the consequence of crucifying (piercing) Christ; others would mourn out of true repentance when approached with the message of salvation through that same crucified Christ. Some wail because of desolation; others, of deliverance.

> *And all the people that came together to that sight, beholding the things which were done, smote their breasts, and returned* (Luke 23:48; *koptō* in Matthew means to *"beat one's breasts")*
>
> *Now when they heard this, they were pricked in their heart, and said to Peter and to the rest of the apostles, "Men and brethren, what shall we do?"* (Acts 2:37)

There is an interesting passage of verses along this line given by the prophet Zechariah, who wrote several references to the coming Messiah which are quoted in the New Testament:

> *I will pour out on the House of David and the inhabitants of Jerusalem a spirit of grace and supplication. They will look on Me, the One they have pierced, and they will* **mourn** *for Him as one mourns for an only child, and grieve bitterly for Him as one grieves for a firstborn son.*
>
> *On that day, the weeping in Jerusalem will be great, like the weeping of Hadad Rimmon on the plain of Megiddo. The land will* **mourn, each clan** *by itself, with their wives by themselves; the clan of the house of David and their wives . . . and all the rest of the clans and their wives. On that day a fountain will be opened to the house of David and the inhabitants of Jerusalem,* **to cleanse them from sin** *and impurity.*
>
> *. . . I will remove both the prophets and the spirit of impurity from the land. And if anyone still prophesies, his father and mother . . . will say to him, 'You must die because you have told lies in the LORD's name. . . . On that day* **every prophet will be ashamed** *of his prophetic vision . . .*
>
> *Strike the shepherd, and the sheep will be scattered, and I will turn my hand against the little ones. In the whole land, declares the LORD, two-thirds will be struck down and perish, yet one third will be left in it . . .* (Zechariah 12:10–13:8)

Several of these verses are applied to Christ's first Coming by the New Testament authors. (John 19:37; Matthew 26:31) On the one hand, there is mourning by all the "tribes of the land",[5] and sorrowing because of all who perished. But there is salvation and cleansing from sin for all those who mourn in repentance . . . precisely what Jesus confirmed in the Olivet Discourse. False prophets are also singled out as one of the problems of Judea by Zachariah.

BACK TO DANIEL

They will see the Son of Man coming on the clouds of the sky, with power and great glory. (24:30)

The third phrase of verse 30 still refers to events in the first century, and lay within the time constraints decreed by Jesus. This phrase does not make a "hop, skip, and jump" thousands of years later to the Second Advent. Many modern commentators are tempted to do just that. While begrudgingly admitting that Matthew 24 deals some with the 70 A.D. destruction of the Temple, they assign this verse (and the Tribulation before it) to the end-times for the Great Judgment. They are quick to accuse the historical commentators of forcefully attempting to turn these verses into symbolic interpretations. They think that the traditional exegetes pushed the historical perspective too far by forcing them into a first century straitjacket. They just can't believe in any interpretation that isn't as literal as they would like.

However, as noted before, the Bible is not a twenty-first century English legal dossier limited to strict, literal verbiage. It is Hebrew, filled with historical *and* poetic literature, literal and figurative imagery, physical *and* spiritual connotations. And those who wish to put all the prophecies into a literal straitjacket are doing a disservice to the Kingdom of God.[6] They are dissing the way that Jesus and the Apostles interpreted the Old Testament, and imposing the tradition of men upon the Bible, thereby making "the Word of God of none effect."

A true minister of the Gospel simply cannot ignore the culture and habits of ancient Israel. As a rule of hermeneutics, he has to take into consideration all the figures of speech, idioms,, and shop talk, of the natives. To depart from this rule opens the biblical student to all forms of confusion and sometimes even heresy!

---

5   The Greek word, *phylē*, is translated 31 times in the N.T. 29 of which it is rendered "tribe" and only once as "nation", by the NIV. The Matthew verse, it seems, should therefore, also be translated with "tribe" (clan).

6   A close examination of the writings of modern pop-propheteers shows that even they are *not* consistent in their literalism application . . . and that many times when they insist upon a literalism their commentary leads to absurd conclusions!

So what does this phrase mean? For an answer to that we must do what Jesus instructed: *read and understand Daniel.* Much of Jesus' teaching was based on His understanding of Daniel's prophesying about the Messiah. *Son of Man,* a title from Daniel, was the most-used self-designation of Jesus. (In the epistles of Enoch, this title was applied to the Messiah, and by the first century, the people equated the two: John 12:34)

The whole history of the Second Temple Era was given prophetically in chapters 10–12. And the desolation of the Temple given in detail in chapters 9 and 12. Christ's crucifixion was foretold in chapter 9, as well (9:26–27). Jesus was quite familiar with all of these, like the back of His hand . . . His nail-scarred hand.

In the seventh chapter we come to our topic at hand. So to really understand and interpret correctly, 24:30 of Matthew it is mandatory that we read that chapter.

* * * * *

ANANI: THE SON OF MAN

The first century rabbis considered the Messiah to be the Anani: the Clouded One. And the Jewish literature leading up to the time of Christ portrayed the Messiah as "The Son of Man." (John 12:34; Matthew 26:64)

"In the first year of Belshazzar king of Babylon, Daniel had a dream, and visions passed through his mind as he was lying on his bed. He wrote down the substance of his dream.

Daniel said: 'In my vision at night I looked, and there before me were the four winds of heaven churning up the great sea. Four great beasts, each different from the others, came up out of the sea.

'The first was like a lion, and it had the wings of an eagle. I watched until its wings were torn off and it was lifted from the ground so that it stood on two feet like a man, and the heart of a man was given to it.

'And there before me was a second beast, which looked like a bear. It was raised up on one of its sides, and it had three ribs in its mouth between its teeth. It was told, "Get up and eat your fill of flesh!"

'After that, I looked, and there before me was another beast, one that looked like a leopard. And on its back it had four wings like those of a bird. This beast had four heads, and it was given authority to rule.

'After that, in my vision at night I looked, and there before me was a fourth beast—terrifying and frightening and very powerful. It had large iron

teeth; it crushed and devoured its victims and trampled underfoot whatever was left. It was different from all the former beasts, and it had ten horns.

'While I was thinking about the horns, there before me was another horn, a little one, which came up among them; and three of the first horns were uprooted before it. This horn had eyes like the eyes of a man and a mouth that spoke boastfully.

'As I looked, thrones were set in place, and the Ancient of Days took His seat. His clothing was as white as snow; the hair of His head was white like wool. His throne was flaming with fire, and its wheels were all ablaze. A river of fire was flowing, coming out from before Him. Thousands upon thousands attended Him; ten thousand times ten thousand stood before Him. The court was seated, and the books were opened.

'Then I continued to watch because of the boastful words the horn was speaking. I kept looking until the beast was slain and its body destroyed and thrown into the blazing fire. (The other beasts had been stripped of their authority, but were allowed to live for a period of time.)

'In my vision at night I looked, and there before me was one like a Son of Man, coming with the clouds of heaven. He approached the Ancient of Days and was led into His presence. He was given authority, glory and sovereign power; all peoples, nations and men of every language worshiped Him. His dominion is an everlasting dominion that will not pass away, and His kingdom is one that will never be destroyed.

'I, Daniel, was troubled in spirit, and the visions that passed through my mind disturbed me. I approached one of those standing there and asked him the true meaning of all this.

'So he told me and gave me the interpretation of these things: "The four great beasts are four kingdoms that will rise from the earth. But the saints of the Most High will receive the kingdom and will possess it forever—yes, for ever and ever."

'Then I wanted to know the true meaning of the fourth beast, which was different from all the others and most terrifying, with its iron teeth and bronze claws—the beast that crushed and devoured its victims and trampled underfoot whatever was left. I also wanted to know about the ten horns on its head and about the other horn that came up, before which three of them fell—the horn that looked more imposing than the others and that had eyes and a mouth that spoke boastfully. As I watched, this horn was waging war against the saints and defeating them, until the Ancient of Days came and

pronounced judgment in favor of the saints of the Most High, and the time came when they possessed the kingdom.

"He gave me this explanation: 'The fourth beast is a fourth kingdom that will appear on earth. It will be different from all the other kingdoms and will devour the whole earth, trampling it down and crushing it. The ten horns are ten kings who will come from this kingdom. After them another king will arise, different from the earlier ones; he will subdue three kings. He will speak against the Most High and oppress his saints and try to change the set times and the laws. The saints will be handed over to him for a time, times and half a time.

"'But the court will sit, and his power will be taken away and completely destroyed forever. Then the sovereignty, power and greatness of the kingdoms under the whole heaven will be handed over to the saints, the people of the Most High. His kingdom will be an everlasting kingdom, and all rulers will worship and obey him.'

"This is the end of the matter. I, Daniel, was deeply troubled by my thoughts, and my face turned pale, but I kept the matter to myself."   ◄ NIV

* * * * *

Over 80 times the title, *Son of Man*, appears in the New Testament. Jesus used it to describe Himself, almost exclusively.[7] There is no doubt that Jesus wanted to identify with this event portrayed in the seventh chapter of Daniel (vss. 13–14). "He" was the Messiah who would receive *authority, glory, and sovereign power.* Along with those, He would also be the recipient of dominion and a Kingdom.

The *saints of the Most High* (v. 22; *people of the Most High*, vs. 27) were to share in that Kingdom, as well! In fact it would be *handed over* to them, but not until they had suffered at the hands of the Roman military for *time, times, and half a time* (3½ years). [The fourth beast of this prophecy, by nearly all commentators, is a symbol of the Roman Empire.] (vs. 25) Daniel — and the saints — are assured that the Kingdom will be an everlasting Kingdom.

What of great importance to our study are the use of the words, "coming with the clouds of heaven." The "Son of Man" approached the Ancient of Days (God Almighty), "coming with clouds." To help us understand this imagery it is beneficial

---

7   The term used for the Messiah was *bar enosh* (Chald.), and is also used as such in the Book of Enoch, Talmud, etc. The term for 'son of man' in Ezekiel is different: *Ben adam* (Heb.); it just signified human descent.

to see how much "clouds" are used in the Old Testament (Taanach) to signify the glorious Presence of God (Divinity).

> *And the LORD went before them by day in a pillar of a* **cloud**, *to lead them the way.* (Exodus 13:21)

> *And the LORD said unto Moses, Lo, I come unto thee in a thick* **cloud** *that the people may hear when I speak with thee.* (Exod. 19:9)

> *And the LORD said unto Moses, 'Speak to Aaron your brother that he come not at all times into the holy place . . . that he die not, for I will appear in the* **cloud** *upon the mercy seat.* (Leviticus 16:2)

> *And it came to pass when the priests came out of the holy place that the* **cloud** *filled the House of the LORD so that the priests could not stand to minister because of the cloud; for the glory of the LORD filled the House of the LORD.* (1 Kings 8:10–11)

> *The LORD has His way in the whirlwind and in the storm, and the clouds are the dust of His feet. (Nahum 1:3b)*

In the New Testament as well, clouds accompanied the manifestation of God. During the "transfiguration" of Jesus, Deity spoke from the cloud. (Matthew 17:5; Luke 9:34–35)

So when someone comes "with the clouds" we would expect Him to be super-human, a resplendent personality bespeaking divinity. He comes sublimely, with majesty. Some of the rabbis called the Messiah, *Anani* (Heb. for *cloud)*, "the Clouded One". (Edersheim, *Life and Times*, Vol. I, p. 179)

EIGHT DANIEL ALLUSIONS

10:23 Preach this message 'the Kingdom of heaven is near . . .' When you are persecuted in one place, flee to another . . . You will not finish going through the cities of Israel before the Son of Man comes.

16:28 Some who are standing here will not taste death before they see the Son of Man coming in His kingdom.

28.18 Having come, Jesus said, All authority in heaven and earth has been given to Me . . . Go make disciples of all nations.

26:64 You (priests) will see the Son of Man sitting at the right hand of the Mighty One.

19:28 When the Son of Man sits on His glorious throne, you who have followed me will also sit on twelve thrones.

24:30 The Son of Man will appear . . . all the nations mourn.

They will see the Son of Man coming on the clouds of the sky, with great power and great glory.

16:27 The Son of Man is going to come in His Father's glory with His angels . . . He will reward each person according to what he has done.

25:31 The Son of Man comes in His glory . . . all the angels with Him, He will sit on His throne . . . All the nations will be gathered before Him . . . He will separate the people . . . sheep and goats.

Jesus continually drew prophetic imagery from the prophet, Daniel, and from chapter seven in this case, where the Son of Man received a Kingdom from the Ancient One, and then shares that Kingdom with the saints. Every use of the word, *coming*, is the common Greek word, *erchomai*, not the eschatologically charged word, *parousia*.

The main point is the reigning of Jesus Christ (coronation and enthronement at the right hand of God) after His resurrection and ascension into heaven . . . and His on-going demonstration of the authority given Him in the affairs of mankind's history: e.g., destruction of the Temple, spread of the Gospel, dispensing of Charismatic gifts, and the empowerment of His ministers to govern the Church (comprised of both Jew and Gentile) . . . ultimately culminating in the Final Judgment of all nations. (Compare Ephesians 2:4–6)

Only by ignoring the Old Testament imagery, can these verses be ripped out of the present *age* and plopped down in a futuristic melee of international cabals and alleged (fabricated) end-time signs.

So what do we see in all of this imagery that will help us understand Jesus' prophecy on the Mount of Olives? Simply this: Daniel came to see that during the Roman Empire's existence a divine Being was to ascend to the Heavenly Almighty God and receive untold power and authority in the form of a Kingdom with great dominion that would last forever. And this awesome Kingdom would be shared (conveyed) to a holy people after a 3½ year struggle with the Romans, in particular, a "stout" Roman who had replaced 3 other rulers, and who was different from the others.

LOOK WHAT I SEE!

Stop the press! Hold the phone, Gertie! This is breaking news. You'll never guess what I see. Fantastic announcement: "All that was foretold by the angel to Daniel has come to pass with amazing detail!"

It was during the days of the Roman Empire that the Anani/Messiah came. He came and prophesied that very soon the Kingdom of God would appear . . . it was at hand . . . but that it would not come with physical observation . . . it would take spiritual insight to behold it . . . that it would suffer violence.

This Messiah/Anani claimed to be the "Son of Man" who was to receive the Kingdom from the Ancient of Days! In fact, after His demise . . . and fantastic resurrection from the dead . . . He claimed to have been given *all power in heaven and earth. His disciples even claimed that God set Him at His own right hand in the heavenly places, far above all principality, and power, and might, and dominion . . . . . even every name that is named, not only in this world, but also in that which is to come* (Ephesians 1:20–23).

This Son of Man conveyed His Kingdom to His disciples so they could share in His power to heal and deliver and redeem. (Luke 22:29) But it was through much tribulation that they would enter into this Kingdom. In fact, a Roman general who was stout (bull-necked) in appearance . . . who was not in the Julio-Claudian line, but began the Flavian dynasty . . . who took the place of three rulers . . . ransacked the land of the holy people for 3½ years. But the Kingdom of God prospered, and spread throughout the earth. Those who survived indeed *saw the Son of Man come on the clouds of the sky with power and great glory!* And still , today, they see His power manifest.

And the rest is history . . . church history. The times were 'a changing.

With the background of Daniel 7 it is easy to see how Matthew 24:30's last phrase could be fulfilled. When we stick to Hebrew literature's figures of speech, instead of being engulfed with modern English connotations, we can see what Jesus really meant on the Mountain that day.

But more than our *"comparing scripture with scripture"* to arrive at the truth, we also have Jesus's own interpretation of what He said . . . and that should make any interpretation final. Some examples:

After the episode of Peter's confession at Caesarea-Philippi, Jesus began to reveal His coming crucifixion. He ended His announcement with an exhortation to remain faithful, for at the end of the world *the Son of Man is going to come in His Father's glory with His angels, and He will reward each person according to what he has done.* (Matthew 16 :27)

Then Jesus really got their attention by adding: *I tell you the truth, some who are standing here will not taste of death before they** see** the Son of Man coming in His kingdom!* (16:28; *"come with power"* Mark 9:1) This is a definite application of Daniel 7 to a fulfillment in the first century. It implies to the disciples, "not right away", but it will happen within this generation. (It also reveals that there are several "comings" of Christ!)

Then also, at the Last Supper, Jesus informed His disciples: *I confer on you a Kingdom, just as My Father conferred one on Me, so that you may eat and drink at My table in My Kingdom, and sit on thrones, judging the twelve Tribes of Israel.* (Luke 22:29–30) The picture here is exactly like the one in Daniel 7 where there were "thrones" (plural) in the Presence of Deity, and the Kingdom was given to the Son. Those expositors who are familiar with Daniel (and obey Christ's admonition "to let him understand") cannot but help see the hand-in-glove application / fulfillment. (Recall Luke 12:32)

And certainly, we cannot overlook the time when Jesus spoke to the Sanhedrin during their trial on that fateful evening: *I say to all of you, In the future you will** see** the Son of Man sitting at the right hand of the Mighty One and coming on the clouds of heaven.* (Matthew 26:64)

At that time, the Pharisees and elders of the Sanhedrin just could not see how that person standing in front of them was "the Messiah, the Son of God." The *eyes of their understanding* were blinded, and could not see Divinity incarnated in a lad from Nazareth of Galilee. (Ephesians 1:18; compare Isaiah 6:10) It would take a desolation of biblical proportions, and the destruction of their Temple with all its sacrifices, before they could see their mistake . . . before they could see that they crucified their only hope of salvation. (See 2 Corinthians 3:12–16)

And, tragically, prophecy expositors of the modernistic ilk (Jesuits and Darbyites, a.k.a. Dispensensationalists) also just cannot *see* the detailed and fantastic fulfillment of Jesus' Mount Olivet prophecy. Even though Jesus declared that the people living in the first century *would see* what He said come to pass, the commentators running around in evangelical robes won't accept His words as true!

Through the Spirit the prophets of old *saw Jesus' day* and rejoiced! (John 12:41; Acts 2:31; John 8:56) They were not blinded by a veil of literalism that restricted prophecies to a physical fulfillment and constricted any hopes by a national (earthly) aspiration. They looked for a better country, a heavenly one, and therefore God has prepared a city for them, the heavenly Jerusalem. (Hebrews 11:16; 12:22) By faith they did not receive the promises, but *saw them* and welcomed them from a distance. Such spiritual eyesight is commendable, and *therefore God is not ashamed to be called their God!*

To be sure, there is a future "Day of the LORD" at the end of the world, when Jesus will return without the warning of any signs, and judge the living and the dead. He will, also, come then with ten thousand of His angels, and *with the clouds of heaven (splendor of majesty)*. But even Jesus admitted that there were "several" comings "in the clouds" (mainly in judgment of nations in history) in the mean time. (Matthew 16:27–28) And this is what we, too, ought to teach . . . ought to *see* . . . with the eyes of our understanding.

PREACH THE GOSPEL

> *And Jesus will send His messengers* (anggelous, Gk.) *with great sounding of a trumpet, and they shall gather together His elect from the four winds, from one end of the heavens to the other.* (24:31)

If we follow the rules of hermeneutics (interpretation), and we remember to recognize the figures of speech used by the Hebrews in the first century, then we will see that this verse is just another way of stating the "Great Commission". *All authority in heaven and on earth has been given to Me. Therefore go and make disciples of all nations . . .* (Matthew 28:18–19)

The word often translated as "angels" is the common word for **messengers**. John the Baptist was a messenger (Matthew 11:10), as were his disciples Luke 7:24, 27). Jesus sent messengers (Luke 9:52). Paul's thorn in the flesh was a "messenger from Satan" (2 Corinthians 12:7). And Rahab of old entertained messengers (James 2:25). To translate this Greek word here, *anggelous*, as "messenger" is in line with biblical usage.

They shall gather together (those scattered) revealed the intent of the preaching of the Gospel of the Kingdom in the mind of Christ. . . . *As the high priest that year, he prophesied that Jesus would die for the Jewish nation, and not only for that nation but also for the* **scattered** *children of God, to* **bring them together** *and make them one.* (John 11:51–52; see also Isaiah 56:8, *"I will gather still others . . . "*)

Where are the "elect" whom Christ is very much interested in gathering? Are they just the believers in Judea? To whom did Jesus send His disciples (messengers) with the Gospel? Just to the local Jews? The final directive Jesus gave just before His ascension was *to receive power when the Holy Spirit comes on you, and you will be My witnesses in Jerusalem, and in all Judea and Samaria, and to the **ends of the earth**.* (Acts 1:8) This is in line with Isaiah's prophecy: *In that day the Root of Jesse will stand as a banner for the peoples; the nations will rally to Him . . . He will raise a banner for the nations and **gather** the exiles of Israel; He will assemble the **scattered** people of Judah from the **four corners of the earth**.* (Isaiah 11:10, 12)

Quoting from Psalms 19:4, the Apostle Paul spoke of the worldwide aspect of the preaching of the Gospel: *'How beautiful are the feet of those who bring good news! . . . Did they not hear? Of course they did: 'Their voice has gone out into all the earth, their words to the **ends of the world**.'* (Romans 10:15, 18) And again he emphasized to the Ephesian Christians the awesome privilege they had in hearing the Gospel: *You who are Gentiles . . . remember that at that time you were **separate** from Christ . . . But now in Christ Jesus you who once were far away have been **brought near** through the blood of Christ.*

The impetuous Apostle Peter even calmed down to exhort *God's **elect** . . . scattered throughout (Asia Minor) . . .* (1 Peter 1:1) And this recalls the expressed intent of Jesus that people far and wide should be saved: *I say to you that many will come from the east and the west, and will take their places at the feast with Abraham . . . in the Kingdom of Heaven.* (Matt. 8:11; Luke included, *"north and south"*, Luke 13:29.)

The words of Isaiah that echoed in the ears of Charles Spurgeon, resulting in his discipleship and eventual ministry, summarize the great universality of the Gospel message presented in Matthew's chapter:

> **Gather together** *and come, assemble, you fugitives from the nations . . . There is no God apart from Me, a righteous God and a Savior; there is none but Me.*
>
> *Turn to Me and be saved, all you **ends of the earth**; for I am God, and there is no other.* (Isaiah 45:20, 22; see also Psalm 22:27–28)

But what of "the trumpet's great sound"? Isn't that associated with the Second Advent at the end of the world? *. . . we will all be changed—in a moment* (a flash, NIV), *in the twinkling of an eye, at the last trumpet. For the trumpet will sound, the dead will be raised imperishable, and we shall be changed.* (1 Corinthians 15:51–52; also 1 Thessalonians 4:16)

In both of these verses the sounding of the trumpet of God announces the resurrection from the dead and the Coming of the Lord. And because of this, many commentators in recent times consider our Matthew passage to be a description of that occasion. However, that would be a superficial response to the reading of the Bible.

Notice that Paul wrote, *"the last"* trumpet! That reflected the historical truth that there were many other "blasts" of the trumpet previously. A word study will reveal that in Israeli history trumpet blowing played a varied and important role. As far as literal blowing of a metal trumpet (or ram's horn), it was to be blown at a festival appropriately known as "the Feast (holiday) of Trumpets." (Leviticus 23:24; Numbers 29:1)

A literal trumpet was also blown at the announcement of the "Year of Jubilee" when mortgaged property was restored to the former owners, and indentured servants were freed. Also, when soldiers were to be mustered a trumpet was blown; when Israel was to congregate at the Tent of Meeting, or when the elders were to appear there, certain trumpet signals were given. (Numbers 10:5; Judges 3:27) At the coronation of a king also. (1 Kings 1:34) At watch-towers, the sound of a trumpet was to herald advancing enemy troops. (Ezekie1 33:1–4)

In addition, both literally *and figuratively*, a trumpet blast was to summon Israel to repentance and to return to the LORD they had forsaken by their wickedness or idolatry. Figuratively, it announced God's rising up against the enemies of His people:

> *The LORD will appear over them; His arrow will flash like lightning. The Sovereign LORD will* **sound the trumpet***; He will march in the storms of the south . . .* (Zechariah 9:14)

> *In that day the LORD will thresh from the flowing River to the Wadi of Egypt, and you, O Israelites, will be gathered up one by one. And in that day a* **trumpet** *will sound. Those who were perishing in Assyria and those who were exiled in Egypt will come and worship the LORD on the holy mountain in Jerusalem.* (Isaiah 27:12–3)

No sensible commentator will insist that a literal trumpet was blown in Assyria or Egypt. It was a figure of speech denoting that God was about to deliver the people.

> *Blow the trumpet in Zion; sound the alarm on My holy hill. Let all who live in the land tremble, for the day of the LORD is coming. It is close at hand—a day of darkness and gloom, a day of clouds and blackness . . .*
>
> *Rend your heart and not your garments. Return to the LORD your God, for He is gracious and compassionate. . . . Blow the trumpet in Zion, declare a holy fast, call a sacred assembly. Gather the people, consecrate the assembly . . .* (Joel 2:1–2, 13–15)

*Shout it aloud, do not hold back. Raise your voice like a trumpet. Declare to
My people their rebellion, and to the house of Jacob their sins.* (Isaiah 58:1)

In the same figurative way, the ministers (messengers) of the Gospel were to
prophesy Jesus, lift up their voices in unison like a trumpet, and announce the fantastic, long awaited, Year of Jubilee . . . the year of the favor of our God (Isaiah 61:2;
Luke 4:19) . . . the year of deliverance from the slavery of sin . . . for all people *from
one end of the heavens to the other!*

We know from reading the book of Acts of the Apostles that the new-born
Church was constantly attacked by *Judaizers* who wanted to limit it to the rituals of the old Mosaic Laws . . . and worse, the idiosyncrasies of the Pharisees and
scribes. The world-wide mission of the Kingdom of God could not be fully realized
as long as the Temple stood on Mount Zion with animals bleating and Levitical
priests mumbling about.

But with the destruction of the old way of doing religion, and the recognition
that Christ was exalted and coronated as King of Kings, and the giving of the Holy
Spirit from the Father (a definite sign of Jesus being in the Heavens; Acts 2:33), the
Church was free to proclaim the Gospel of salvation, and gather His elect together.

Matthew 24:31 uses symbolism and imagery that is similar to other "comings".
Notable is the final Coming, the Second Advent at the end of the world. But it must
be repeated that similar doesn't always mean "same."

For example, if we were to describe the coming of Queen Elizabeth with her
entourage of horsemen, gilded carriage, and royal trumpeters, when she visited one
of her nation's territories, say for instance, the Bahamas. And then we were to
describe her visit to Canada with her entourage of horsemen, gilded carriage, and
royal trumpeters, we would of necessity use the same language . . . but there are two
different events being reported!

So also it is when we see the Comings of the LORD in the Bible. The one that we
all now look forward to, though, is the last one, with the blowing of *the last trumpet* . . . which Jesus had warned, will come unannounced . . . without any signs. That
Day will be totally different from the Destruction of Jerusalem which had many
prophetic signs and omens.

REDEMPTION

*And when these things begin to come to pass, then look up, and lift up your
heads, for your redemption draweth nigh.* (Luke 21:28)

Luke, who wrote more for the Gentile audience, has thus far interpreted key passages in Matthew, and shed light on the figures of speech that the Hebrew audiences of Matthew and Mark would naturally understand, but which the Gentiles would be unfamiliar with. In verse 28, he continued that trend, and reworded those Hebraic references to "messengers, trumpets, and gathering the elect".

This parallel (synoptic) verse introduced a new word that packs a wallop, and powerfully summarizes the preaching of the Gospel of the Kingdom to all the earth, that Matthew recorded. Jesus declared that He would assemble together all the 'elect' (cf. Romans 8:29–30) from every nation. Now Luke encouraged people by referring them to the efficacious means whereby they all could be gathered into the glorious Kingdom of God: *Redemption . . . awesome redemption . . . amazingly gracious redemption!*

This word, redemption *(apolutrōsis,* Gk.), is defined as "the releasing of a person effected by the payment of a ransom" An indentured servant could be released from his indebtedness by a family member buying out the remaining debt; a kidnapped person could be ransomed by a friend; a slave could be freed by a purchase price given to a slave-owner. This is what it *literally* means. This is the "physical" meaning.

However, metaphorically, that is, in a non-literal sense, to the Christian theologian (and laity) it means "deliverance, effective through the death of Christ, from the wrath of a holy and just God, and from the earned (merited) penalty of sin."

> *You know that it was not with perishable things such as silver or gold that you were* **redeemed** *from the empty way of life handed down to you from your ancestors, but with the precious blood of Christ, a lamb without blemish or defect.* (1 Peter 1:18–19)

This was a major theme in the Apostle Paul's letters as well: Romans 3:24; Ephesians 1:7; Colossians 1:14; and Hebrews 9:15. The clarion trumpet call to people everywhere *(to the four winds)* was the face-brightening, headlifting, news of "amazing grace." Forgiveness of sins because the penalty was paid by Someone else. Hope because of Help from a Transcendent Source.

The cultural concept of a literal, physical ransoming was *spiritualized* by the inspired New Testament men of God. So, it must be emphasized, the staunchest "literalist" interpreter of prophecy in modern times (unduly influenced by the Darbyites and Jesuits) must acquiesce to the idea that *spiritualizing is legitimate . . .* or else he has no salvation from the wrath of God. He must be "redeemed" in a non-literal, spiritual sense . . . or else!

To the Pharisee watching the Five O'Clock news, the Desolation of Jerusalem and the Destruction of the Temple (stone by stone) was disheartening; but to the spiritual Jews and to the rest of the world of sinners, it meant redemption in the fullest sense! Salvation had drawn nigh!

THIS BUD'S FOR YOU

> *Learn this lesson from the fig tree: As soon as its branches get tender and its leaves come out, you know that summer is near. Even so, when you see all these things, you know that it is near, right at the door.* (Matthew 24:32–33; Mark 13:28–29)

> *And He spoke unto them a parable: Behold a fig tree, and all the trees, when they now shoot forth, you see and know of your own selves that summer is now near at hand.*
>
> *So likewise, you, when you see these things come to pass, know ye that the Kingdom of God is near at hand.* (Luke 21:29–31)

How do we know that the cold and dreary Winter is done and gone? It's the appearance of Spring-time buds. And how do we know that sunny Summer days are just around the corner? It's the appearance of Spring-time buds . . . on all the trees . . . fig, pomegranate, olive, apple, lemon, date, etc.

With this annual phenomena, Jesus drew a parable from nature. Just as there are signs, and one in particular (the budding of leaves), to announce the nearness of Summer, so also the firm establishment of the Kingdom of God was to be considered next on God's agenda, after *all those things* Jesus had just enumerated to the disciples transpired. The indisputable reign of Jesus was to be manifest. Christians around the world could sing with accuracy, the chorus of Jack Hayford's creativity, *Majesty, we worship your Majesty!* And of His Kingdom there would be no end, we remember Daniel informing us in his prophecy. (Daniel 7:14)

How would the disciples know this? After all, they had asked for a "sign" of the end of the age (Second Temple Era). The answer was in the historical accomplishment of *all these things.* What *things?* Whatever they were, they had to have happened within the time frame of that *generation.*

A review of all the scriptures that use this phrase would be a good way to know what Jesus was referring to by saying, all these things .

> *Upon you (Pharisees and scribes) will come (the guilt) of all the righteous blood that has been shed on earth . . . I tell you the truth,* **all these things** *will come upon this generation.* (Matthew 23:35–36)

> *Do you not see all these things? Jesus asked. I tell you the truth, not one stone here will be left on another.* (24:2) *The disciples came to Jesus privately. Tell us, they asked, when will* **these things** *happen . . . ?* (24:3)

> *You will hear of wars and rumors of wars, but see to it that you are not alarmed.* **All these things** *must happen, but the end is still to come.* (24:6)

> *I tell you the truth, this generation will certainly not pass away until* **all these things** *have happened.* (24:34)

The phrase, *all these things*, can only refer to the punishment of the Pharisees, the international intrigue leading up to the invasion of Judea, the spiritual corruption in Judaism and the effect of divisive sects within the Early Church, the abortive surrounding of Jerusalem by Cestius, the eventual desolation of the Temple by Titus, the advance of the Gospel beyond the constraints of the Mosaic Law, the utter collapse of Jewish government, and the recognition of the majesty of Christ at the right hand of God.

When you see all these things coming to pass, then you know the Kingdom of God at hand (near) . . . so near that it is knocking at the door! The use of all this terminology precludes any idea that Jesus is referring to the Second Advent at the end of the world. And even more evident — contrary to the misconceptions of modern telepastors who relish in talking about end-time signs — "these things" do **not** refer to any alleged "budding again" of the nation of Israel at the end of the world. (Notice that Luke envisioned "all the trees" budding, not just a fig tree.) *These things* are **not** the end-time cosmic portents and unprecedented catastrophes signaling the close of the last age of earthly existence, that modern novels and fictitious movies portray for evangelical audiences.

The *budding leaves* signal the start of Summer, not the end of Summer when the harvest takes place (the Fall)! According to Jesus's words, there are no spectacular events or signs of the times at the Second Advent. His topic here is of the beginning of the Kingdom Age (with local churches as its local embassies). When Jerusalem's Temple is totally gone, the transition period is over, and the Kingdom of God is in full swing, so to speak.

Hear the knock at the door, disciples? Guess who? Guess what? It is the manifestation of Jesus Christ (the Son of Man) reigning in His Kingdom, which is a Kingdom planted in the springtime of earth as a *small mustard seed* which grows into a very large tree so that the birds of the air can take refuge in its branches. (Matthew 13:31–32) It will proliferate.

But first, we must shed our winter Mackinaw coats, remove our snow blinders, and sit under the fig tree . . . and observe the budding leaves . . . and meditate on the new regime taking over . . . the Kingdom of God . . . whose citizens are *elect . . . gathered together from one end of the heavens to the other.*

YOUR LIVING FAMILY

> *I tell you the truth, this generation will certainly not pass away until all these things have happened (shall have taken place).* (24:34)

In this verse we have the back "book end" that *with certainty* put a time-context on all the things that Jesus prophesied. This forbids any / every expositor from ripping all these events out of the first century and plopping them down at the end of the world. No end-time "Great Tribulation", no Secret Rapture, no restoration of the Jewish nation, no Antichrist, etc.

And the modern day "literalists" have no justification for *allegorizing* any of these verses to posit end-time "oil crisis" (Walvoord), or stock market crash, or Mideast conflict, or atomic cruise missiles, or a shower of meteorites. The "imaginations gone wild" of futurists has been a blight on the exegetical health of the church. Their refusal to let Jesus set the time frame is a preposterous stance that leaves modern propheteers on poor footing.

By not showing appreciation for Hebrew literary devices (vernacular, idioms, figures of speech, etc.), or by a prejudice for the traditions of men (or some man), or by neologism (giving a new meaning to a word), modernists have variously interpreted the phrase that Jesus used repeatedly: *This generation.*

1. The "generation" Jesus mentioned was to be the end-time people living during the *last days* of planet Earth at the Second Coming. An indefinite space of time in the future.
2. The generation which began with the establishment of the nation of modern Israel in 1948. (Hal Lindsey and his colleagues)
3. The First Century right then, in which Jesus expected to come again soon *(parousia):* His Second Coming would be to that generation, literally.
4. "Generation" is to be considered a "race of people" or a "nation of the Jews" who would not cease to be until all the signs were fulfilled. *(Scofield Reference Bible)*
5. "This very generation" in which we (the prophecy teacher and his contemporaries) now live because of the present existence of all the "signs" of the end-times! [Of course, when this interpretation fails, the next prophecy teacher of the next generation "picks up the ball" and runs with the same message for his time period . . . ad infinitum. They all ignore the fact that the failure rate for this type of application is 100% throughout history!]

In analyzing these interpretations we can quickly dismiss number "1.". It makes no sense to say "the generation that will experience these things will not pass away until it experiences all these things." It is a meaningless tautology, and adds nothing to the discussion.

Number "2." was commonly advocated by Dispensational date-setters during the 1900s. Expectations were heightened by the Zionists before WWII, and they sky-rocketed with the establishment of (non-Messianic) Israel as a nation in 1948. But this interpretation has been shown to have been made by false teachers because of *the test of time* (Deuteronomy 18:21–22), and can be dismissed as nonsense. Forty years have come and gone, and all the doomsday predictions have not transpired (the Great Tribulation, the Covenant of Antichrist with the Jews, the Secret Rapture of the Church, etc.) Many die-hard Dispensationalists have done a lot of back-peddling in their reprints of books . . . and others have simply (and wisely) left that camp of erroneous exegesis, disillusioned.

The third group of exegetes relied heavily on other passages of scripture that seemed to point to a "soon return" of Jesus. Some in the first century church, as well as modern liberal commentators, believed Christ had already come! (2 Thessalonians 2:1–2) If not literally, then mystically. As Paul had to set them straight then, so also, the modernists need drastic correcting. Jesus was not prophesying a literal Coming in His generation.

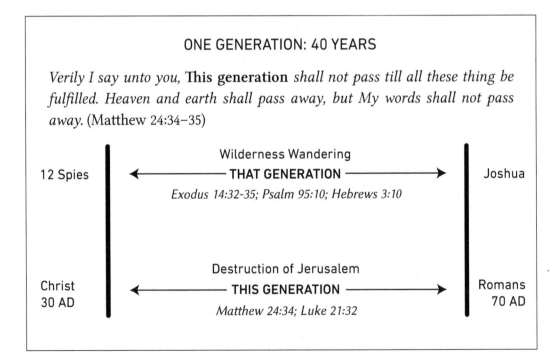

ONE GENERATION: 40 YEARS

Verily I say unto you, **This generation** *shall not pass till all these thing be fulfilled. Heaven and earth shall pass away, but My words shall not pass away.* (Matthew 24:34–35)

	Wilderness Wandering	
12 Spies	◄———— THAT GENERATION ————►	Joshua
	Exodus 14:32-35; Psalm 95:10; Hebrews 3:10	

	Destruction of Jerusalem	
Christ 30 AD	◄———— THIS GENERATION ————►	Romans 70 AD
	Matthew 24:34; Luke 21:32	

The fourth group of interpreters who try to define "generation" as simply "a race, a people, a stock, or an ethnic clan" fail to do a Greek word study. If they did, they would discover that the word employed by Jesus is *genea*, not *genos*. While *genea* refers to contemporaries, *genos* is used for "race." So Jesus was **not** talking about a race "not passing away", but a contemporary living collection of Pharisaical families "not passing away" before all the things prophesied would take place. The religious leaders that He was staring in the face, would experience the decreed desolation of Judea with all its horrors and devastation.

Not to be outdone by the "futurists", there are ubiquitous prophecy lecturers who assuredly declare that their present generation is the one Jesus referred to because, they avow, all the *signs of the times* are evident in society and in the news! These are the *end times* just before the imminent Rapture of the Church (pretribers), or just before the Covenant of Antichrist and the Jews (midtribers), so this fifth group reveals.

Most members of church congregations have never studied the history of the Church, and are ignorant of the weed crop of propheteers that have arisen in every decade in the past. A new batch of prognosticators seem to breed every year in the petri dish of seminaries, or rise from the toxic swamp of uneducated pastorism. The historical fact that all their predecessors have a failure rate of 100% doesn't seem to deter them from rushing headlong into the same garbage dump of discarded prophesies and disingenuous prophets.

We cannot but note that the selling of books on the Last Days (eschatology) is *big business*. End-time hysteria has fueled the publishing industry more than mesquite bushes in a Southern California dry summer brush fire, licking up home after home in its conflagration. There's big bucks in playing to the curiosities, fears, and sincere questions of new believers. To be sure, money, more than truth, keeps this train moving down the tracks.

YOU THERE, SIR

To clear up just whom Jesus was referring to in His Olivet Discourse, consider the use of the word, "you." In Matthew 23, *Jesus said to the crowds and to His disciples . . .* and then continued to give warnings for the next twelve verses. Then beginning in verse thirteen, Jesus addressed the *teachers of the Law and Pharisees* with "you". And he employed this word forty-seven times! There is absolutely no doubt or misunderstanding as to whom Jesus is talking; *the men living in the first century.* Men in the same room in the Temple.

And notice that Jesus summarized His invective against the hypocrisy of the religious leaders with the precise statement: *I tell* **you** *the truth, all this (desolation) will come upon this generation . . . Look,* **your** *House is left to* **you** *desolate.* (23:36, 38)

In the next chapter, we are informed that Jesus was walking with **His disciples** when He announced: *Do you not see all these things (Temple buildings)? Not one stone here will be left on another.* (24:1–2) And when they arrived at the Mount of Olives, **the disciples** came to Him . . . (24:3) In the next thirty verses Jesus again employed the word, "you" twelve times. There is no doubt to whom Jesus is talking: *Disciples living in the first century.*

This chapter also closed with Jesus warning them: *I tell you the truth, this generation will certainly not pass away until all these things are fulfilled (shall have taken place).* (24:34) There is absolutely no way any honest interpreter of scripture could ever teach that the time period in which all these things were to happen is off into the future . . . or even in the present (twenty-first century). Those who pride themselves in being "literalists" and who follow the alleged "Golden Rule of Interpretation", should never be guilty of ripping these scriptures out of their first century setting. If they do, as some have done, no doubt Jesus would address them in the same way He spoke to the Pharisees: *Woe to you, teachers . . . you hypocrites!* Such "futurism" is wholly without merit.

In both summaries, Jesus said *this generation,* not *that generation,* indicating a present one, and not another of a different time zone. Turning "this" to mean a future era is highly irregular, illogical, and immaterial. If Jesus had wished to point to a future era He was literate enough and savvy enough to use "that" as an adjective instead of "this." And that He would repeat this same sentence at the end of each dialogue is quite telling.

These are not the first times that Jesus spoke of "this generation." Throughout the Gospels, Jesus spoke this phrase and directed it at the people then living. (Matthew 11:16; 12:41, 42, 45; Mark 8:12; Luke 7:31; 11:30, 31, 32; 17:25) Every occurrence of this phrase referred to the lifespan of those living at that time,

While a consistent and straight forward approach to understanding this fantastic — and accurately detailed — Olivet prophecy of Jesus, showing its historical fulfillment in the cataclysmic events of the horrendous desolation of Jerusalem and its Temple, many modernists just can't seem to get past the figurative language of the Hebrew people. It is an insurmountable stumbling block to the Anglo-Saxon mind set.

But careful attention paid to the prophetic language of the Old Testament is quite sufficient to remove that obstacle. As Marcellus Kik has noted: *There is not a single figure employed whose use has not been already sanctioned and its meaning determined in the Old Testament.* (Matthew Twenty-four, p. 98)

The characters of the Old order had to exit. Their scenery and backdrop were removed from the stage of history. Many of the actors had forgotten their God-scripted lines, and tried to fake it, in spite of the side prompters' corrective words. In fact, the theater itself had caught fire and was demolished.

But not to worry! It was time for faithful characters who would stick to their lines, to come front and center. Their dialogue would contain good News about the King of splendor, coming in the clouds of heaven, establishing His reign in the loyal hearts of men around the world. Act II would not be a tragedy of the Elizabethan theater, but would be quite *climacteric* with a grand finale that is out of this world! After a brief intermission, it is to that that we turn our attention.

ADDENDA

(A) SIGNS OF MESSIAH

The religious thought of Intertestamental Judaism, and of rabbinical schools during the time of Christ, included ideas concerning the signs that would announce the arrival of Messiah. Although there was variation of belief between the competing schools, several points stand out. First, there was the preliminary ministry of "Elijah." This prophetic forerunner would prepare the way for the coming Messiah. This would be accomplished by issuing a call for Israel to repent. Through humility and holiness, there would be peace on earth, and a way for the LORD to restore all things.

> *See, I will send you the prophet Elijah before that great and dreadful day of the LORD comes.* (Malachi 4:5; see Sirach 48:10)

> *The disciples asked Jesus, "Why then do the teachers of the Law say that Elijah must come first?"*
> *Jesus replied, "To be sure, Elijah comes and will restore all things. But I tell you, Elijah has already come, and they did not recognize him, but have done to him everything they wished . . ." Then the disciples understood that He was talking to them about John the Baptizer.* (Matthew 17:10–13; Mark 9:11–13)

The message of John the Baptist (i.e. "Elijah") was written out by the prophet Isaiah, and later, Malachi:

> *Comfort ye, comfort ye My people, says your God. Speak tenderly to Jerusalem, and proclaim to her that her hard service has been completed, that her sin has been paid for . . .*

> *A voice of one calling: "In the desert prepare the way of the LORD; make straight in the wilderness a highway for our God. Every valley shall be raised up, every mountain and hill made low . . . and the glory of the LORD will be revealed, and all mankind together will see it." (Isaiah 40:1–5, cf. Matthew 3:1–12; 11:7–19; Luke 3:2–6)*

> *See, I will send My messenger, who will prepare the way before Me. Then suddenly the Lord whom you seek will come to His temple: the messenger of the covenant whom you desire, will come, says the LORD Almighty.*
>
> *But who can endure the day of His coming? Who can stand when He appears? For He will be like a refiner's fire or a launderer's soap. He will sit as a refiner and purifier of silver; He will purify the Levites and refine them like gold and silver . . . So I will come near to you for judgment; I will be quick to testify against . . . those who oppress the widows and the fatherless, and deprive aliens of justice, but do not fear me . . . (Malachi 3:1–5; Luke 3:7–20)*

John's boldness and faithfulness to God's message eventually got him arrested and imprisoned . . . and beheaded. But he did introduce Israel to Messiah Jesus: "Behold, the Lamb of God, who takes away the sin of the world!" (John 1:29, 36)

BIRTH PANGS

Secondly, the age of the Messiah was to be introduced by the *"birth pangs"* of troublous times. What Jesus referred to in the Olivet Discourse was common vernacular in rabbinical schools. (24:8) The final age was to be preceded by a special period of affliction and trouble, the woes of the Messiah. (Babylonian Talmud, Sanhedrin 97a, Sibylline Oracles 3:635–61; 2 Baruch 25)

The term *birth pangs* (ōdines, Gk.) was used in the Old Testament to describe God's judgment on corrupt societies or pagan nations. It described the sudden and definite display of the wrath of God so that righteousness and justice could be restored in the earth. (Isaiah 13:8; 26:17; 66:7–9; Jeremiah 4:31; 6:24; 13:21; 22:23; 49:22; 50:43; Hosea 13:13; Micah 4:9–10) By the first century B.C., it had become a technical term in rabbinical literature.

> *. . . this shall be a time of salvation for the people of God . . . the battle of destructions for the sons of darkness. And it shall be a time of tribulation for the people which God shall redeem; of all its afflictions none shall be as this, from its sudden beginning until its end in eternal redemption. (War Scroll, 1 QM1; see also 1 Enoch 1:3–8)*

Julius Scott, Jr. summarized their expectation, saying that "the times will change, and there will be threatening signs in the cosmic order, between nations, between individuals, and in the spiritual realm; sin and wickedness will run rampant and rule the earth . . . animosities and hostilities will increase." (Sibylline Oracles 3:796–808; 2 Baruch 26–29; 48:38; 2 Esdras 4:52 – 5:13; 6:20–24; 9:1–6; Testament of Moses 10)

It was appropriate for Jesus to lift this phrase, and apply it to the transition period between 30 and 70 A.D. . . . . the time when Jesus first announced the "Kingdom is near" and when the old Mosaic / Levitical era was to come to an end (destruction of the Temple). As we studied, that period was marked by international conflict, on the one hand, and internal religious conflict on the other hand. The *birth pangs (contractions)* would cease finally, when the Church was born, delivered from the womb of Judaism . . . but there would be *postpartum blues (mourning)* by those who had pierced the Messiah, if we may carry the metaphor a little farther.

ADDITIONAL SIGNS

In addition to the general "signs of the times" at the advent of the Messiah, the rabbis expected more specific signs. They expected miracles sometimes of an outrageous or silly nature, and sometimes of a practical kind. John the Baptizer's request would be an example of a practical kind. The response of Jesus was to take a look at the signs being performed among the crowds:

> *Go back and report to John what you hear and see: The blind receive sight, the lame walk, those who have leprosy are cured, the deaf hear, the dead are raised, and the Gospel is preached to the poor* (Matthew 11:4–5)

These miracles were convincing to John because they were such that Isaiah prophesied. (Isaiah 29:18–19; 35:5–6; *Be strong, do not fear, your God will come . . .*) And they were proofs to the people in Judea, as well: "When the Messiah comes, will He do more signs than this Man has done?" (John 7:31)

The works (miracles) that the Father has given Me to complete, the very works that I am doing, testify on My behalf that the Father has sent Me! (John 5:36; 10:24– 25; 14:11) And Peter echoed this on the Day of Pentecost when he said that *Jesus was attested by deeds of power, wonders, and signs that God did through Him.* (Acts 2:22). It was because the residents of some villages did not accept the signs as proof of His Messiahship, that He did not hesitate to pronounce curses on them. (John 12:37–41; Matthew 11:20–24)

BOWELS OF THE EARTH

There was one "sign" that the Rabbis of the various schools weren't expecting, that Jesus did offer as an harbinger of the Messianic reign:

> *A wicked and adulterous generation asks for a miraculous sign! But none will be given to it except the 'sign of the prophet Jonah'. For as Jonah was three days and three nights in the belly of a huge fish, so the Son of Man will be three days and three nights in the heart of the earth.* (Matthew 12:39–40)

By this mysterious reference, Jesus announced His death. But a dying Messiah was not on the agenda of the rabbis. On another time Jesus said *"Destroy this temple, and I will raise it again in three days!"* (John 2:19, compare Matthew 26:61) And by this, He signified that He would be raised from the dead. But this was beyond the comprehension of both the Pharisees, and His own disciples. (Luke 18:31–34; Matthew 16:21–23; John 2:20, 22)

And yet this "death and resurrection" was the epitome of proofs for anyone claiming to be the prophesied Messiah! Who has ever conquered death? Who ever could but a true—and Divine—Messiah? To this Jesus appealed, and it was to this that Peter referred in his famous oratory at Pentecost. (Acts 2:22–36) Peter even alleged that this notable sign was prophesied by none other than the Psalmist, David! (Psalm 16:8–11)

Some men are blind, and restored sight would be convincing to them that Jesus was Messiah. Some people are lame, and walking again would help them believe in Jesus. Many have skin diseases, and cleanliness would be a sign for them to accept Jesus.

But not everyone is blind, lame, or diseased. Those miracles would not impress them as much. However, the common denominator of all mankind is *death*. Everyone is mortal, and will die. So if someone could conquer this ubiquitous malady, that Person would deserve worship from everyone! He would be worthy of all praise and adoration.

That would be the ultimate *sign* of a true Messiah. It would be hard to argue with an empty tomb. An ascended Messiah lends great evidence to a reigning Messiah in this age.

(B) TIME TO FLEE

When you see Jerusalem being surrounded by armies, you will know that its desolation is near. Then let those who are in Judea flee to the mountains, let those in the city get out, and let those in the country not enter the city. (Luke 21:20–21)

The days will come when your enemies will build an embankment (siege wall) *against you and encircle you and hem you in on every side. They will dash you to the ground, you and the children with in your walls. They will not leave one stone on another, because you did not recognize the time of God's coming to you.* (Luke 19:43–44)

Due to the rioting instigated by the Zealots who wanted total freedom from the occupation of Rome, the chief priest and the local procurator were concerned that it was about to go too far out of hand. They requested that Cestius Gallus come down from Syria with his Roman Legion and quell the disturbances. They did not want Judea to arouse the full fury of Rome in retaliation to the Zealots' arrogant defiance.

Cestius arrive and attacked Jerusalem from the 15th to 22nd of Tishri (October 1st – 8th) ; and then the troops entered the city November 17the (Hyperberetaeus 30th = the 30th of Elul). But for an inexplicable reason, the general up and retreated from the area, and began to return to Syria. Some say it was divine providence: If the city "fell without a fight" then the Temple would not have been destroyed according to Jesus' prophecy . . . and Daniel's prophecy about a desolation lasting 3½ years would also not have been fulfilled.

But it did serve an important purpose. A whole bucket full of biblical commentators see this act of the general as "the sign" whereby the Christians would be warned to flee to safety. (Luke 21:20–21) They recall that the desolation that was about to transpire was not just the destruction of Jerusalem, but the whole land of Judea was to experience a massive invasion by the Roman Legions with vengeful violence. Thus Luke recorded Jesus as saying, *flee Judea, as well as the city of Jerusalem.*

Because the retreating general Cestius Gallus was mercilessly attacked by the guerrilla warfare of the Zealots, resulting in great loss of Roman life, the general, Titus Flavius Vespasianus (Vespasian) headed on down to Judea with a vengeance. In February he came with the 10th, 12th, and eventually 15th Legions of veteran soldiers . . . and they came a'stomping with boots of iron and fists of bronze (See Daniel 7:7).

In the Spring of 67 A.D. they conquered major cities of Galilee, and then headed down the coast as far as Joppa, subduing it.

In the spring of 68, Perea perished on the eastern border of Judea, and another campaign saw the western Judean desert destroyed. Later that year the armies marched across Samaria, across to the Jordon valley all the way to Qumran on the northeastern shore of the Dead Sea, leaving devastation in their wake.

In 69 A.D., Vespasian left his headquarters at Caesarea on the coast, and set off on a campaign through the territory of Ephraim and Benjamin. But in July he was called back to Rome to become *Emperor!*

He turned the *abomination that makes desolate* over to his son, who had been stationed in Egypt with another Legion there. The two Zealot leaders, Simon Ben Gioras, and John of Gischala, (who by the way, were at each other's throats vying for the position of "top bully") were forcedly evicted from their strongholds and eventually ended up finding refuge in the city of Jerusalem. Along their paths, villages were laid bare, especially if there was any hint of compromise or allegiance with the Romans. The Israeli people suffered at the hands of those within *and* without the Law. Inside the city of Jerusalem, there was fighting between the aristocracy, the Band of Simon's Zealots and the Gang of John's (who were also joined by the ruffians from Idumea). Blood ran in rivers down the streets of that holy city . . . including the blood of the pious high priest . . . including the blood of anyone who thought of leaving the city.

In the Spring of 70 A.D. Titus approached Jerusalem, and began his attack (May 20th). Unbelieving Jews who had not heeded Jesus's warning, had flocked to the city to observe the Passover, so the city was teeming with crowds of pilgrims — millions of people. The Tenth Legion came from Jericho and set camp on the eastern hills of Olivet; the Fifth Legion approached from the southwest; the Twelfth and Fifteenth Legions directly under Titus invaded from the North. Jerusalem was surrounded, and the military noose was soon to strangle the whole enclosure of people . . . like a pack of wolves surrounding a herd of defenseless sheep. With fangs showing and drooling tongues hanging from their insatiable mouths, the Romans, fed up with the obstinance of the Israelis, went for the kill.

On May 25th, the outer 3rd wall that had protected the Jewish marketplace, was breeched. Then on May 30th, the 2nd wall was opened up. In July a siege-wall was erected around what was left of the bottled up city, and it prevented anyone from supplying the people with food or arms . . . and it kept anyone from escaping unnoticed.

Those who managed to escape the watchful eyes of the Zealot, and got over the wall, were faced with being eviscerated or crucified by the Romans! Rumor had it that the Jews were trying to abscond with money by swallowing it.

On August 6th (the 17th of Tamoz) the sacrifices ceased; on August 15th – 17th, the porticoes were burned; and on August 28th (the 9th of Ab) the Temple itself was burned . . . the same day the First Temple was destroyed by the Babylonians in 586 B.C. The lower city was captured a couple days later, and then the upper city where Herod's Palace was located, was attacked. It did not fall for another month and a half . . . fulfilling Daniel's prophecy of 12:11–12.

ALTERNATIVE VIEW

There are a few commentators who do not subscribe to the advance of Cestius Gallus as the Legion mentioned by Luke, who would *surround the city*, which would serve as a sign *to flee post haste*. They contend that that escape could have been done on a slow mule!

They suggest that anyone could have escaped the city of Jerusalem because the "siege wall" was not erected until July of A.D. 70. The words of "haste" apply to Titus's attack instead of Cestius' . . . with better sense, they argue. Jesus had asked the disciples to pray that the attack would not happen in winter; Cestius approached the city in November, and Titus in the summer around May.

This alternative view, however, does not seem to take into account the ferocity of the rampage of the Roman Legions throughout Judea for years on end. Nor does it consider the tyranny of the Zealots against their own countrymen in the villages and hillsides of Israel. Escaping death during that time would have been a feat in itself, long before Jerusalem proper was attacked by Titus.

They also ignore the statements of Jesus that referred, not just to the city of Jerusalem, but to the whole region of Judea: *Let those in Judea flee to the mountains* (24:16). Right after Cestius's engagement, the whole of Judea was a dangerous place to be. The compassion and mercy of the Roman soldiers had worn as thin as the ice on Lake Michigan in July.

Nor do the commentators consider the fact that the whole area surrounding the city was swarming with soldiers during the final siege, not just the places near the walled capitol. The Romans caught everyone who tried to leave and crucified them in sight of the city . . . some times two or three to a cross! The birth pangs of wars and rumors of wars (23:8) — after the Christians had left the womb of Judaism — turned into *post-partum blues*. The wailing and gnashing of teeth kept the Roman soldiers awake at night, and made them the more grumpy in the morning. The depression of the pilgrims within the city was incurable because their situation was indeed hopeless. The stench from the unburied thousands of dead corpses would make even a Gestapo internment camp guard consider it revolting and repulsive. And they couldn't leave.

As the early historian, Eusebius Pamphilius, noted, if it weren't for the warning of Jesus that prompted the Christians to flee to Pella, across the Jordon River in Perea . . . and if *those days of fighting had not been shortened, no life would have been saved.* (24:22) Not even the "elect" would have survived. *(Ecclesiastical History,* Bk. 3, ch. 5; also see, Edersheim, *Life and Times of Jesus the Messiah,* p. 448)

The Roman general, Cestius Gallus' retreat was indeed quite providential! And the warning of Jesus was quite providential! And the destruction of the Second Temple era was providential because it removed the major obstacle to the establishment of the Kingdom of God throughout the earth, with local churches as its embassies of hope and redemption.

(C) PEOPLE OF THE PRINCE

In Daniel's prophecy of Seventy Weeks located in chapter nine, we find an interesting phrase: *The* **people of the Prince** *who will come will destroy the city and the sanctuary. The end will come like a flood; war will continue until the end, and desolations have been decreed!* (vs. 26)

Undoubtedly this verse is a prophetic reference to the destruction of Jerusalem, and the end of the Second Temple Era. Both Jewish and Protestant commentators agree on this. The time context given by the angel prohibits any other interpretation: *Seventy weeks* (heptads, Heb.) *are determined upon thy people.* (vs. 24) This corresponds to 490 years, and beginning with the decree of Cyrus, we find the ending to be in the first century A.D.

But who is the *Prince who will come?* And who are the people that will partake in doing the destroying of the city and Temple? Whoever they are, these words portray them as capable and able of devastating the land of Judea to the bitter end.

Basically, there are two possibilities, both of which would fit the details of the actual Fall of Jerusalem; (a) the Prince is Jesus, and His people are the stubborn and vicious Jews who ransacked the territory mercilessly, precipitously causing its total annihilation (i.e. the Zealots); and (b) the son of the Roman emperor, Titus, who was the general in charge of the Roman Legions that eventually surrounded Jerusalem and put an end to the rebellious madness of the Jews. His military would be considered the "people" of the Prince.

JESUS, THE PRINCE

Of the many titles given to Jesus, one that stands out in the New Testament is that of *Prince*. We find it in four references:

> *You disowned the Holy and Righteous One . . . you killed the* **Prince** *of Life, but God raised Him from the dead.* (Acts 3:14–15)

> *God exalted Him to His own right hand as* **Prince** *and Savior that He might give repentance and forgiveness of sins to Israel.* (Acts 5:31)

> *In bringing many sons to glory, it was fitting that God . . . should make the* **Prince** *of their salvation perfect through suffering.* (Hebrews 2:10)

> *Let us fix our eyes on Jesus, the* **Prince** *and finisher* (completer) *of our faith, who for the joy set before Him endured the cross, scorning its shame, and sat down at the right hand of the throne of God.* (Hebrews 12:2)

These verses seem to confirm that Jesus really is "Messiah, the Prince" as stated in Daniel 9:25.

In all four instances where *Prince (archēgon,* Gk.) occur, it also mentions Christ's suffering, and refer to His death on the cross. This ties in with Gabriel's announcement in the book of Daniel, where Christ the Anointed One, *is cut off and will have nothing* (or, *cut off, but not for Himself).*

"Viewing these scriptures together, we see in them God's fourfold objective in sending forth His Son in the likeness of man, and in anointing Him with the Holy Ghost and with power. It was (1) that He might be the Prince of life, thus to meet the deepest need of His perishing people, for He came 'that they might have life'; (2) that He might also be the Prince and Savior, empowered to grant repentance and forgiveness of sins; (3) that He might be the Prince or Leader of the salvation of God's many sons, to bring them all safely home to glory; and (4) that He might be the Leader as well as the Finisher of that faith whereby God's people are to run . . . with endurance the race which is set before them." (Philip Mauro, *Seventy Weeks,* p. 68)

In accepting the application of this title to Jesus, the people who destroyed the "city and sanctuary" would refer to the rebellious Zealots who terrorized all of Judea, and then when forced to retreat to Jerusalem, reeked extreme havoc on all the inhabitants there! Flavius Josephus recorded all the pandemonium, the fury, the bloodfest, that the differing factions of the rebels unleashed upon the city. The pleasure with which these animals inflicted suffering on the rest was much more than the stuff that Shakespearean or Spielbergian dramas are made of. It was a tragedy that was off the charts. It was not "drops of blood" that were shed; it was puddles, yea, lakes of blood, that flowed in the final days of that city. There was no room to bury all the slain, such that the Zealots resorted to merely throwing them over the city wall. The stench of the piled heaps made even the staunchest veteran Roman soldier vomit, and curse in disgust.

"The people of the Prince" filled up the sin of their forefathers, not only by crucifying the Anointed One, but by murdering their own countrymen with abandon. So that the guilt, and judgment, *for all the blood that was shed from Abel to the time of the priest, Zechariah, who was murdered between the temple and the altar (i.e. from Genesis to the last book in the Hebrew Bible, 2 Chronicles)* would fall on them. (Matthew 23:35) The Zealots would become victims of their own treachery; they would self-destruct.

TITUS, THE PRINCE

The other possible application of this title would refer to the general, Titus. His father had begun the 3½ year conquest of Judea, but was called back to Rome by the military leaders there to help set things in order. Four emperors were killed in an 18-month period! Would he come and be the next emperor? (Quite an invitation!)

Vespasian did eventually become the next emperor of Rome and reigned until A.D. 79. His son, Titus, then, would in a sense, be a *Prince*. He would be next in line for the crown when his father died . . . with the blessing of the S.P.Q.R., of course . . . and the military's approval.

The *people* of the Prince, then, would be the massive, marching Roman military. His soldiers would be the agents of destruction. They would indeed, be the *Abomination that makes Desolate* (Daniel 12:11). And, as a matter of historical fact, the Roman soldiers did facilitate the "end."

The Legions of Titus did surround the city and put a siege wall up to prevent any escapees from fleeing without punishment. Titus's men did breach the three city walls and subdue the defenders within. They then ransacked the Temple Mount, eventually burning it to the ground. In search for any remaining gold that had melted off the gilded doors and walls, they did remove each stone, just as Jesus had prophesied! (Matthew 24:2) And then, those poor souls who were still alive, were taken by Titus' military and *led away captive to all nations,* and sold as slaves. (Luke 21 :24) The boots of Titus's men were the ones that *trampled on Jerusalem for the full time designated* (by Daniel's prophecy, 12:11–12).

So, a commentator, may have justification for applying "the people of the Prince" to the Roman armies . . . just as other commentators apply their exegesis to the Zealots whose hands were drenched with blood. Either way, Gabriel's foresight was fulfilled . . . in 70 A.D. . . . to the max . . . unto the End.

SOME FUTURE PRINCE? NOT

Since 1830, a new and novel interpretation of Daniel's prophecies has been proffered. Through fictitious novels and apocalyptic movies, it has been introduced to thousands of unsuspecting brothers and sisters in the evangelical Church. This highly speculative and heretical approach to the prophetic writings has infiltrated much of Christendom's Bible colleges and seminaries, whose students (alumni) become unwitting hawkers of its scheme of things.

Most of the modern believers who have read the books of men like Scofield, Dake, Chafer, Walvoord, Watson, Ryrie, LaHaye/Jenkins, Darby, and Ironside, are unaware of how recently derived their ideas and beliefs are. For centuries upon centuries, there was no exegesis anywhere near those now imagined by these writers. Modern pop-prophecy lectures and conferences spew forth false interpretations that would make the saints of old roll over in their graves. Futuristic-focused charts, hanging like wall paper in churches, mislead congregations into thinking they present what Jesus and the Apostles foretold.

Their modern scenario goes something like this: Christ's offer of a Kingdom for the nationalistic Jews was rejected by them, so the 70th week of Daniel was postponed, leaving a gap, now, of over 2,000 years. In the future, the Antichrist (the Prince) will make a covenant with the Jews who have rebuilt their Temple and are again offering animal sacrifices. (The Antichrist will have arisen from a restored Roman Empire, perhaps the European Union!). At the end of 3½ years, the Antichrist will break the Covenant, and will initiate a Great Tribulation period (based on Matthew 24:21), which will only end with a return of Christ. Christ will then set up a literal throne in Jerusalem and reign for a literal thousand year period, after which there will be a Great Throne Judgment of all the nations.

Throw in a "secret rapture" of the Gentile Church, and an apocalyptic battle of biblical proportions at Armageddon, and a mark of the Beast, and you have the whole bucket load carried by these modern propheteers. The way we are supposed to know when these things will all come to pass is their list of *end-time signs,* or *signs of the times.* It should be noted that every generation since 1830 has these advocates claiming that their generation was the end-times generation because all of the "signs" were recognizable in their time! However, every one of those prophecy teachers have been wrong. 100% failure rate! 100% erroneous expectations!

They ignore the fact that Jesus' listing of calamities in Matthew 24 (verses 4–13) were not concerning an end, but were related, by Jesus, to a *beginning* (vs 8). And, as has already been noted, *great tribulation* (distress affliction, persecution; *thlipsos,* Gk.) is not to be translated "The Great Tribulation" as if it were a proper name of a period of time. They make this mistake. They treat, also *the Gospel being preached in all the earth* as future, when the Apostles declared that it was fulfilled within their life-time.

The *Prince* of Daniel's prophecy, who normally would refer to events at the destruction of the Second Temple, is removed off into the future as an Antichrist. Yet Daniel 9 speaks only of an *Anointed One*, not of any anti-anointed one. The words of Gabriel mention the rebuilding of (Ezra's Temple) and its destruction later in the time of the Messiah . . . and the angel never mentions the rebuilding of a Third Temple after that.

No covenant is "made or broken" in Daniel 9. One is only *made to prevail (or confirmed)* for the *many*, which *put an end to sacrifice and offering.* These are words that accurately describe the sacrificial death of Jesus on the cross, and the confirmation of the New Covenant. They, in no way, can be construed to refer to an Antichrist covenant with the Jews.

We concur with George Murray who pined, *"It is not without sorrow of heart, therefore, that we listen to men, whose sincerity we do not question, emphasizing . . . that an end is not made of sin, that everlasting righteousness is yet to be brought in and going so far as to attribute to a wicked Antichrist that which our glorious Lord has brought about by His sacrifice on the cross, the abolition of the oblation and sacrifice." (Millennial Studies, pp. 104–105)* (Read Hebrews 9:14–20; Matthew 26:28, covenant for the "many".)[8] And with this sentiment we add the insight of Philip Mauro:[9]

> *"According to the view we are now considering, the passage is taken to mean that there is a "prince" who is to "come" at some unknown time yet future, which prince will be of the same nationality as the people (the Roman armies) by whom the city and the Sanctuary were to be destroyed. It is further* **assumed**, *and taught with much confidence, that this "coming prince" will be in league with Antichrist, if indeed he be not Antichrist himself.*
>
> *"This is a very* **radical idea**, *one which changes the entire meaning of this basic prophecy, and affects the interpretation of all prophecy. It transfers the main incidents of the prophecy of the Seventy Weeks from Christ to Antichrist, and removes them bodily from the distant past to the uncertain future,*

---

8   Consider a word study on "many" and its use in the New Testament: Isaiah 53:11; Luke 1:16, 2:34; Matthew 20:28, etc.

9   Mr. Mauro, a brilliant patent attorney, gradually switched from Dispensationalism in his earlier writings, to a more sane interpretation of scripture. Much of his *Seventy Weeks* book is commendable; parts needed work.

thus separating them far from all connection with the period of seventy weeks to which God assigns them.

"This manner of dealing with Scripture is, so far as our experience goes, without parallel or precedent in the field of exegesis. Is it sound and sober interpretation of Scripture, or is it **playing pranks** *with prophecy?"* (Philip Mauro, *Seventy Weeks,* p. 75, emphasis mine)

Switching the meaning of "The Anointed One, the Prince" does the greatest possible violence to words which are not at all obscure or of uncertain meaning. It is a scheme fabricated upon speculation, contrived by a sect in Ireland of dubious credibility. And its modern proponents, with their end-time list of signs, are given to exploiting the fears, and curiosity of believers.

On the one hand, militating against this contrivance, are the records of Flavius Josephus describing the Jewish Zealot rebels, **people** of Judea that Jesus warned about. And on the other hand, there stands the Triumphal Arch of Titus in Rome, depicting the Menorah and other instruments of the Second Temple, which were carried in procession by this Roman **people**. With either fulfillment of the words of Daniel's prophecy, there remains no need for any future speculation about someone arriving over two thousand years beyond the destruction of the Temple in 70 A.D. No need for a future Prince to accomplish what has already been accomplished in the first century.

(D) JULIAN THE APOSTATE

In *A Dictionary of Early Christian Biography* (the abridged edition edited by Wace and Piercy, 1911), there is an interesting account of the attempt of Emperor Flavius Claudius Julianus (Julian the Apostate) to rebuild the Temple at Jerusalem (pp. 593–4). We include it here as a warning to those modern souls who might desire to rebuild this Temple as well. It reads:

"Julian had apparently wished to reconcile the Jewish people, and was quite ready to grant Jehovah a place amongst the other local deities. It seems probable, therefore, that his chief motive in wishing to restore the temple at Jerusalem was the desire to increase the number of divinities who were propitious to him, and to gain the favour of the Jewish God in the prosecution of his Persian campaign.

"This is substantially the account given by Socrates, who tells us that he summoned the Jews to him and asked why they did not offer sacrifice. They replied that it was not lawful for them to do so, except at Jerusalem; and he therefore determined to rebuild the temple of Solomon . . .

"There is, however, an air of great probability in the statement of Philostorgius that he wished to falsify the prediction of our Blessed Lord as to the utter destruction of the temple (vii. 9). Nor could the enmity of the Jews against the Christians be otherwise than very pleasing to him. Julian provided very large sums for the work, and entrusted its execution to the oversight of Alypius of Antioch, an officer who had been employed by him in Britain and who was his intimate personal friend.

"The Jews were exultant and eager to contribute their wealth and their labour. The rubbish was cleared away and the old foundations were laid bare.

"But a stronger power intervened. To quote the words of Ammianus: 'Whilst Alypius was strenuously forcing on the work, and the governor of the province was lending his assistance, fearful balls of flames, bursting out with frequent assaults near the foundations, and several times burning the workmen, rendered access to the spot impossible; and in this way the attempt came to a standstill through the determined obstinacy of the element.

"No doubt the Christians saw in this defeat of their oppressor not only a miracle of divine power, but a peculiarly striking fulfillment of the old prophecies in which fire is so often spoken of as the emblem and instrument of judgment (e.g. Deut. 32:22; Jer. 21:14, and particularly, perhaps, the historical description of Lam. 4:11, 'The Lord hath accomplished His fury; He hath poured out His fierce anger, and hath kindled a fire in Zion, and it hath devoured the foundations thereof'). They thought also, of course, of our Lord's own words, now more completely verified than ever.

"Julian retained his wide knowledge of the text of Scripture, as we see by his writings, and these prophecies doubtless irritated him by their literal exactness. The *'globi flammarum probe* **fundamenta** *erumpentes'* of the heathen historian are an undesigned coincidence with the words of Hebrew prophecy.

"From . . . heathen testimonies, and from the fathers and historians of the church, Dr. Newman has put together the following detailed account of the occurrence, in which he chiefly follows Warburton . . . 'They declare as follows: The work was interrupted by violent whirlwind, says Theodoret, which scattered about vast quantities of lime, sand and other loose materials collected for the building. A storm of thunder and lightning followed; fire fell, says Socrates, and the workmen's tools, the spades, the axes, and the saws were melted down.

" 'Then came an earthquake, which threw up the stones of the old foundation, says Socrates, filled up the excavation, says Theodoret, which had been made for the new foundations; and, as Rufinus adds, threw down the buildings in the neighborhood, and especially the porticoes in which were numbers of the Jews who had been aiding in the undertaking, and who were buried in the ruins.

" 'The workmen returned to their work; but from the recesses, laid open by the earthquake, balls of fire burst out, says Ammianus; and that again and again as often as they renewed the attempt. The fiery mass, says Rufinus, raged up and down the street for hours; and St. Gregory, that when some fled to a neighbouring church for safety the fire met them at the door and forced them back, with the loss either of life or their extremities.

" 'At length the commotion ceased; a calm succeeded; and, as St. Gregory adds, in the sky appeared a luminous cross surrounded by a circle! Nay, upon the garments and the bodies of the persons present crosses were impressed, says St. Gregory; which were luminous by night, says Rufinus; and at other times of a dark colours says Theodoret; and would not wash out, adds Socrates. In consequence the attempt was abandoned.' (Newman, Essay on Miracles in *Early Eccl. Hist.* p. clxxvii)

"All these incidents present a picture consistent with the extraordinary operations of the forces of nature. Even for the luminous crosses there are curious parallels in the history of storms of lightning and volcanic eruptions . . . The cross in the sky has its likeness in the effects of mock suns and parhelia. But even so, a Christian may still fairly assert his right to call the event a miraculous interposition of God's providence. It fulfilled all the purposes we can assign to the Scripture miracles. It gave 'an impression of the present agency and of the will of God.' It seemed to shew His severe disapproval of the attempt and fulfilled the prophecy of Christ. It came, like the vision of Constantine, at a critical epoch in the world's history. It was, as the heathen poet has it, a *'dignus vindice nodus.'* All who were present or heard of the event at the time thought it, we may be sure, a sign from God. As a miracle it ranges beside those Biblical miracles in which, at some critical moment, the forces of nature are seen to work strikingly for God's people or against their enemies."

* * * * *

ACT II
PERSONAL PERIPATOLOGY

NOW BROTHERS, ABOUT TIMES AND dates we do not need to write you, for you know very well that the Day of the Lord will *come like a thief* in the night. While people are saying, "Peace and safety," destruction will come on them suddenly, as labor pains on a pregnant woman, and they will not escape.

— *1 Thessalonians 5:1–4*

THE LORD IS NOT SLOW IN KEEPING HIS promise, as some understand slackness. He is patient with us, not desiring that anyone perish, but that everyone come to repentance.

But the day of the Lord will *come like a thief*. The heavens will disappear with a roar; the elements will be destroyed by fire, and the earth and everything in it will be burned up.

— *2 Peter 3:9–10*

CHAPTER 24

BUT OF THAT DAY and hour knoweth no man, no, not the angels of heaven, but My Father only. ³⁷ But as the days of Noe *were*, so shall also the coming of the Son of Man be. ³⁸ For as in the days that were before the flood they were eating and drinking, marrying and giving in marriage, until the day that Noe entered into the ark, ³⁹ And knew not until the flood came, and took them all away; so shall also the coming of the Son of Man be. ⁴⁰ Then shall two be in the field; the one shall be taken, and the other left. ⁴¹ Two *women shall be* grinding at the mill; the one shall be taken, and the other left.

⁴² ¶ Watch therefore: for ye know not what hour your Lord doth come. ⁴³ But know this, that if the goodman of the house had known in what watch the thief would come, he would have watched, and would not have suffered his house to be broken up. ⁴⁴ Therefore be ye also ready: for in such an hour as ye think not the Son of Man cometh. ⁴⁵ Who then is a faithful and wise servant, whom his lord hath made ruler over his household, to give them meat in due season? ⁴⁶ Blessed *is* that servant, whom his lord when he cometh shall find so doing. ⁴⁷ Verily I say unto you, That he shall make him ruler over all his goods. ⁴⁸ But and if that evil servant shall say in his heart, "My lord delayeth his coming;" ⁴⁹ And shall begin to smite *his* fellowservants, and to eat and drink with the drunken; ⁵⁰ The lord of that servant shall come in a day when he looketh not for *him*, and in an hour that he is not aware of, ⁵¹ And shall cut him asunder, and appoint *him* his portion with the hypocrites: there shall be weeping and gnashing of teeth.

CHAPTER 25

THE PARABLE OF THE TEN VIRGINS

THEN SHALL THE KINGDOM of heaven be likened unto ten virgins, which took their lamps, and went forth to meet the bridegroom. ² And five of them were wise, and five *were* foolish. ³ They that *were* foolish took their lamps, and took no oil with them: ⁴ But the wise took oil in their vessels with their lamps. ⁵ While the bridegroom tarried, they all slumbered and slept. ⁶ And at midnight there was a cry made, "Behold, the bridegroom cometh; go ye out to meet him." ⁷ Then all those virgins arose, and trimmed their lamps. ⁸ And the foolish said unto the wise, "Give us of your oil; for our lamps are gone out." ⁹ But the wise answered, saying, "*Not so;* lest there be not enough for us and you: but go ye rather to them that sell, and buy for yourselves." ¹⁰ And while they went to buy, the bridegroom came; and they that were ready went in with him to the marriage: and the door was shut. ¹¹ Afterward came also the other virgins, saying, "Lord, Lord, open to us." [12] But he answered and said, "Verily I say unto you, I know you not." [13] Watch therefore, for ye know neither the day nor the hour wherein the Son of Man cometh.

THE PARABLE OF THE TALENTS

FOR THE KINGDOM *of heaven is* as a man travelling into a far country, *who* called his own servants, and delivered unto them his goods. [15] And unto one he gave five talents, to another two, and to another one; to every man according to his several ability; and straightway took his journey. [16] Then he that had received the five talents went and traded with the same, and made *them* other five talents. [17] And likewise he that *had received* two, he also gained other two. [18] But he that had received one went and digged in the earth, and hid his lord's money. [19] After a long time the lord of those servants cometh, and reckoneth with them. [20] And so he that had received five talents came and brought other five talents, saying, "Lord, thou deliveredst unto me five talents: behold, I have gained beside them five talents more." [21] His lord said unto him, "Well done, *thou* good and faithful servant: thou hast been faithful over a few things, I will make thee ruler over many things: enter thou into the joy of thy lord." [22] He also that had received two talents came and said, "Lord, thou deliveredst unto me two talents: behold, I have gained two other talents beside them." [23] His lord said unto him, "Well done, good and faithful servant; thou hast been faithful over a few things, I will make thee ruler over many things: enter thou into the joy of thy lord." [24] Then he which had received the one talent came and said, "Lord, I knew thee that thou art an hard man, reaping where thou hast not sown, and gathering where thou hast not strawed: [25] And I was afraid, and went and hid thy talent in the earth: lo, *there* thou hast *that is* thine." [26] His lord answered and said unto him, "*Thou* wicked and slothful servant, thou knewest that I reap where I sowed not, and gather where I have not strawed: [27] Thou oughtest therefore to have put my money to the exchangers, and *then* at my coming I should have received mine own with usury. [28] Take therefore the talent from him, and give it unto him which hath ten talents. [29] For unto every one that hath shall be given, and he shall have abundance: but from him that hath not shall be taken away even that which he hath. [30] And cast ye the unprofitable servant into outer darkness: there shall be weeping and gnashing of teeth." ◄ KJV

ACT II
PERSONAL PERIPATOLOGY
MATTHEW 24:35 – 25:30

Heaven and earth will pass away, but My words will never pass away. No one knows about that day or hour, not even the angels in heaven, nor the Son, but only the Father.

— MATTHEW 24:35–36

ACT I CLOSED WITH THE OMINOUS CLOUD HANGING OVER THE INCENSE-FILLED JEW-ish Temple of the first century. Though mixed with the dust kicked up by hundreds of thousands of devout pilgrims coming to celebrate the Passover holiday, the air was a toxic smog of hypocritical ritual and empty spirituality. It stunk to high heaven, and was offensive to the Main Character for whom the Temple was built: the Son of Man who came from heaven.

Enough was enough! That physical Temple had to go. *"When?"* the Twelve disciples had asked. Within the life-time of their contemporaries . . . within that generation . . . by 70 A.D. And what about signs? For the Jews were always wanting proof and confirmation of a prophet's "word." They were told not to look for international affairs, nor internal church dynamics. What they ought to watch out for was the encroachment of the mighty lean machine, the Roman legions invading Judea.

The Romans weren't going to mess around, and neither was God: desolations were decreed . . . to the very end of the Temple . . . until the "times of the Gentiles" were accomplished . . . which Daniel enumerated with detailed accuracy . . . 3½ years of clashing swords and fiery arrows. Immediate flight was mandatory . . . across the hills, and through the river . . . to Pella in Perea . . . to a tenuous safety. Jerusalem was to have no Deliverer.

But . . . but inquisitive disciples . . . but don't mistake that annihilation for the *end of the world!* Don't misconstrue the end of the Second Temple Era with all its omens and precursory signs as the final Judgment Day. My words aren't to be taken lightly; *they won't pass away* like a tumbleweed blown by a Sirocco wind storm. So listen up!

Heaven and earth **will** *pass away: no one knows about that Day or Hour, not even the angels in heaven, nor the Son, but only the Father.* (24:36–36) The end of the world is going to be different than the end of the Second Temple Era in that no *end-time* signs will be given. *I, the Son, cannot provide any because even I don't know when it will occur!* The world will indeed pass away, but only the Father knows when . . . and He "ain't tellin' " He won't even give a hint . . . not even the *times or seasons (chronous ē kairous,* Gk. Acts 1: 7).

Notice! This emphatic statement by Jesus precludes any biblical or prophetic commentator from applying each and every "signs of the times" listed in the previous thirty-four (34) verses, to the end of the world, or to the final Judgment Day. This statement also gave God's approval on the metaphorical (spiritual) interpretation of the Coming of Christ in clouds of glory (24:30–31) . . . which was considered a *sign.*

> Hence it appears plain enough, that the foregoing verses are not to be understood of the Last Judgment, but, as we said, of the Desolation of Jerusalem. There were some among the disciples (particularly John), who lived to see these things come to pass. With Matthew 16:28, compare John 21:22. And there were some Rabbins alive at the time when Christ spoke these things that lived until the city was destroyed. (John Lightfoot "Commentary", 1658)

Those days of vengeance and divine retribution, announced by Jesus, no doubt were quite unnerving to the Twelve; but at least they were being warned and being given an escape plan.

THE GREAT DAY

The topic, first dealt with in the Olivet Discourse, was one that covered many days, many years . . . 40 years zeroing in on the last traumatic 3½ years. That was a lot of days for "standing firm" and not giving in to "anxiety." (24:6, 13)

But, then, *concerning* the next topic about *heaven and earth passing away,* the disciples were to consider the time frame to be just a *day,* or less, just an *hour.* This switch from the plural to the singular is indicative of the change of events Jesus wanted to deal with . . . and which the disciples had inquired of. "Are there signs of the **end times**?" "End of the **world**?"

The usage of a certain day in conjunction with teaching about the final Judgment had been a common practice throughout Jesus's ministry:

> *Many will say to me in that day,* etc. (Matthew 7:22)

> *But I say unto you, It shall be more tolerable for Tyre and Sidon at the* **Day of Judgment**, *than for you . . . But I say unto you, that it will be more tolerable for the land of Sodom in the* **day of Judgment** *than for thee.* (Matthew 11:22, 24)

> *Every idle word that men shall speak, they shall give account thereof in the day of Judgment.* (Matthew 12:36)

So, here, on this mountain, the disciples knew that Jesus had switched subjects and had spoken with reference to the end of all things as we know it. Nowhere in the New Testament is the Second Advent referred to with the "plural" of days.

The modern propensity for futurists to speak of "the last days" in reference to the Second Coming or Final Judgment does not coincide with the New Testament usage of that phrase. The plural, *last days,* always describes the whole New Covenant era (what some call, the Church Age), from the First Advent to the Second Advent. It is **not** "just a short period" just before the Second Advent. This phrase is **not** used in the Bible as a period of time designated by "Signs of the times" just before the Final Judgment. The Bible gives no justification for that usage that is common in modernists' books and lectures. It is a figment of propheteers' imagination melded with their misinterpretation of the first topic in the Olivet Discourse.

> *God, who at various times and in divers manners spake in time past unto the fathers, by the prophets, has in these last days spoken unto us by His Son . . .* (Hebrews 1:1)

> *This is that which was spoken by the prophet Joel: 'And it shall come to pass in the last days,' saith God, 'I will pour out My Spirit on all flesh.'* (Acts 2:16–17)

> *Christ, a lamb without blemish or defect. He was chosen before the creation of the world, but was revealed in these last times for your sake.* (1 Peter 1:19–20)

Plurality is used in the Bible only when the "whole" New Covenant age is in mind, and singularity is the form when the Second Advent and Judgment Day are referred to.

NOTHING OUT OF THE ORDINARY

> *As it was in the days of Noah, so it will be at the Coming of the Son of Man, for in the days before the flood, people were eating and drinking, marrying and being given in marriage up to the day Noah entered the ark, and they* **knew nothing** *about what would happen until the flood came and took them all away.*
> *That is how it will be at the coming of the Son of Man.* (Matt. 24:37–39)

> *It was the same in the days of Lot. People were eating and drinking, buying and selling, planting and building. But the day Lot left Sodom, fire and sulfur rained down from heaven and destroyed them all.*
> *It will be just like this on the day the Son of Man is revealed.* (Luke 17:28–30)

To drive home the difference between the announced events surrounding the Destruction of the Temple, on the one hand, and unheralded Advent, on the other, Jesus introduced three (3) illustrations, and then three (3) parables.

1. ANCIENT JUDGMENTS — The first illustration drew from *judgment day* on two groups of people that most scripture readers — and secular literary savvy scholars — are familiar with: the pre-alluvial inhabitants of the earth, and the residents of the plains of Jericho in Sodom and Gomorrah. Both of their stories are recorded in the book of Genesis, so Jesus is indirectly putting His imprimatur on that ancient document.

The point was: neither of them *knew* about what was going to happen to them until it occurred. The *day, the very day* Noah and his family entered the ark, the rain began to fall on the earth. The people were caught off guard, and all perished. So also with the residents of Sodom: they never *knew* what hit them, until it was too late.

Jesus listed a handful of societal activities the people were carrying out to show that "life was going on as usual." There were no signs of any kind . . . no catastrophes . . . no unusual disasters . . . no alarms to speak of.

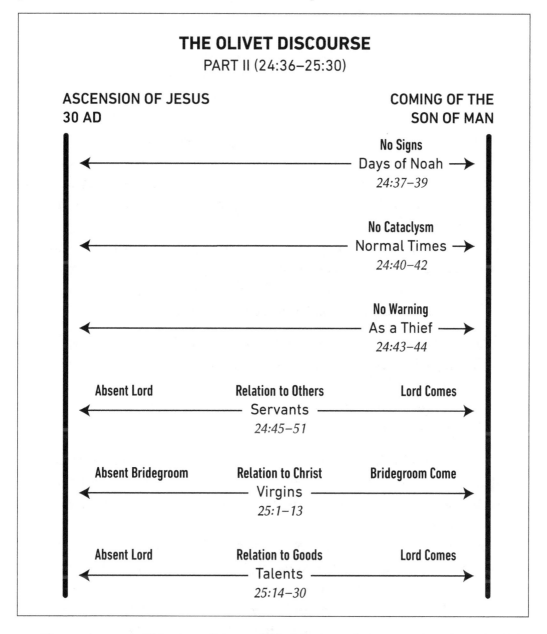

THE OLIVET DISCOURSE
PART II (24:36–25:30)

ASCENSION OF JESUS
30 AD

COMING OF THE
SON OF MAN

No Signs
Days of Noah →
24:37–39

No Cataclysm
Normal Times →
24:40–42

No Warning
As a Thief →
24:43–44

Absent Lord	Relation to Others	Lord Comes
	Servants	
	24:45–51	

Absent Bridegroom	Relation to Christ	Bridegroom Come
	Virgins	
	25:1–13	

Absent Lord	Relation to Goods	Lord Comes
	Talents	
	25:14–30	

That is how it will be (it will be just like that) *at the coming* (revelation) *of the Son of Man*, is how Jesus concluded His illustration of those ancient judgments: normal activities right up unto the end . . . right up unto the Second Advent. There could be nothing more clear.

And yet . . . and yet . . . mystery upon mysteries, modern biblical teachers who pride themselves of having studied prophecy for years, do not hesitate to rant and rave about how wicked and dark the end-time will be just before the Second Advent. The minute they hear the word, *Noah,* their mind conjures up all sorts of visions of evil societal conduct: divorce, debauchery, rapes, murders, covetousness . . . and the list goes on and on. They totally miss the point of Jesus's illustration.

To make sure He was *not* misunderstood, Jesus mentioned the type of activity He wanted the days of the Second Coming to be compared to: (a) eating and drinking . . . something that Jesus even partook of (*the Son of Man came eating and drinking,* Matthew 11:19), and in the blessed time of Solomon, they were eating and drinking; (b) marrying and given in marriage . . . activities instituted and sanctioned by God Himself (marrying is the holy ordinance that men do, and being "given" is what happens to women in Judea); (c) buying and selling . . . two actions that even Jesus commanded some of His disciples to do! ("sell your cloak and buy a sword", Luke 22:36; John 13:29, Matt. 19:21); (d) planting and building . . . hardly nefarius conduct committed by wicked men.

What Jesus should have mentioned was that prophecy teachers would, in the last days, teach just the opposite of the Bible, and they themselves become wicked in contradicting the words of the Son of Man!!! (We, for a moment, are entertaining the folly of there being a "last days" period just before the Coming of Christ.)

> *Two men will be in the field; one will be taken and the other left. Two women will be grinding with a handmill; one will be taken and the other left.*
>
> *Therefore keep watch, because you do not know on what day the Lord will come.* (vss. 40–42)

2. MORNING OR EVENING — Jesus gave the illustration of normal occupation activities. Men get up early and head out into the fields to plow, hoe, or harvest the grains. This is what men normally do to provide for their families, for if a man does not work, nobody eats.

In the evening, when the men come home with the harvested grain, the women set about grinding or milling it so that baking bread and cooking can be done. Quite normal for the agricultural household.

But the "cleavage" that will happen at the Second Advent will be so unexpected that both the believers and unbelievers will be "caught" doing the same work at the same time. The separation will occur instantaneously with no warning or precursory sign.

What did Jesus mean by the word *taken* (passive of *paralambanō*, Gk.)? It is a generic word that has several meanings depending upon the context of the passage of scripture, or the intent of the speaker. For instance, it is the same word used when Jesus "took" Peter, James, and John, up the mountain of transfiguration (Matthew 17:1; See also John 14:3)

It is the same word used when He "took" Peter and the two sons of Zebedee into the garden of Gethsemane. So the implication is that it means "to cause to be with one's self", that is as a companion or friend. In the Bible, it referred to a bridegroom "taking" his betrothed to his home (Matthew 1:20) . . . a very close friend, indeed.

On the other hand, it is also used of "taking" someone as a prisoner (John 19:16; Acts 23:18). So that we are left with some uncertainty as to what Jesus meant. On the one hand, the parables of Matthew 13 tell of the angels gathering the wicked *first*, at the end of the world. They take out the evil who are offensive to the Kingdom, then the righteous are the ones *left behind.*

On the other hand, we are told in other passages that the Second Advent will be like a bridegroom coming for his bride . . . Jesus coming for His Church . . . the Lover for His Beloved (Ephesians 5:25–27; Revelation 19:6–9). But whichever meaning was intended, the main point was that the "taking" would be sudden and without any signs. The normal economic fluctuations, natural catastrophes, international espionage, and meteorlogical disturbances were not to be taken as harbingers of the Second Advent. Although they often interrupt normal routines of life, the mundane affairs of humanity would continue unabated until Christ comes back . . . unannounced . . . daytime or night time. In fact, Mark added:

> . . . *You do not know when the owner of the house will come back* . . . *whether in the evening* (9 pm), *or midnight* (12 o'clock), *or when the rooster crows* (3 am), *or at dawn* (6 am). *If he comes suddenly, do not let him find you sleeping.* (Mark 13:35–36)

Nobody knows the time of day, or even the hour, when Jesus is going to return to end this age: Stock market crash, the oil shortage (or surplus), the hostage crisis, the subway bombings, Mideast conflicts, toilet paper shortage, ebola epidemics, power outages, movie box office busts . . . none of these abnormal normalities of a nation's history do, nor will, signal the Coming of the Son of Man.

> *Now listen up! If the owner of the house had known at what time of night the thief was coming, he would have kept watch and would not have let his house be broken into.*
>
> *So you also must be ready, because the Son of Man will come at an hour when you do not expect Him.* (24:43–44; also, Luke 12:39)

3. SNEAKY THIEF — The third illustration is drawn from that occasion most of us have been unfortunate to experience: the break-in of a *thief.* Jesus mentioned something we could relate to more than we ever want to: the intrusion of someone who thought he had more rights to our possessions than we did.

Even with all the modern electronic security devices invented to thwart off this pesky fellow, there is nothing that takes the place of someone standing guard with a shotgun, awake and alert, ready to respond at the slightest sound! And the key word here is *awake.* To *keep watch* a guard has to be awake. That is the only way a person could be considered *ready.*

This same warning is picked up on by saints. Peter and Paul. (1 Thessalonians 5:1–4, 2 Peter 3:9–10.) What is interesting is that immediately after the Coming of Christ as a thief in the night, *the heavens will disappear with a roar; the elements will be destroyed by fire, and the earth and everything in it will be burned up!* The Second Advent is closely tied in with the "end of the world". The unmistakable shutting down of human history. The closing of the curtain with thunderous angelic applause, accompanied by a fireworks display that would make any Fourth of July organizers green with envy.

And yet, modern prophetic sensationalists teach, write pamphlets, publish novels, and make movies, portraying the *Thief in the Night* episode as being followed by normal days and times — with missing Christians who have been 'raptured' causing some consternation — instead of the event described by the inspired biblical apostles! Just as with the first century Pharisees, these contrarians have blinders on so that they cannot *see with understanding the scriptures that are read every Sunday (Sabbath).* (Acts 13:27; 2 Corinthians 3:14–15)

A *secret Church rapture exists* only in the imaginations-gone-wild of seminary professors and illiterate revivalists alike, and **not** in the systematic theology of the Apostolic writings. The immanent return of the Son of Man (the Lord) is followed by a cosmic catastrophe that would even make Carl Sagan sit up and take notice! It is **not** followed up by reports on the 5 o'clock evening news about missing persons. This false teaching is preposterous, if not diabolical . . . it is a tradition of men that makes the Word of God of none effect.

PERIPATOLOGY PARABLES

Next, in Jesus's teaching about the Day of the Lord (or the Coming of the Son of Man), we are given three parables about how we are to live until it happens.

SERVANTS — Relation to Others (24:45–51)
VIRGINS — Relation to Christ (25:1–13)
TALENTS — Relation to Goods (25:14–30)

In each case there is a period of time when the Lord or Bridegroom is absent . . . and then returns unexpectedly, unannounced, without warning, without any end-time signs . . . and then rewards or punishes appropriately.

1. My master is staying away a long time (24:48)	The master will come on a day when he does not expect him. (24:50)	He will cut him to pieces and assign him a place with the hypocrites. (24:51)
2. The bridegroom was a long time in coming. (25:5)	While they were on the way to buy oil, the bridegroom came. (25:10)	"Open up!" But he answered, "I tell you the truth, I don't know you." (25:12)
3. It will be like a man going on a long journey. (25:14)	After a long time the master returned. (25:19)	"Throw that worthless servant outside." (25:30)

Peripatology is the studying about "how we should live," or "how we should walk and conduct ourselves as we travel down the bumpy, pot-holed, highway of life . . . that is fraught with highway men and bush-whackers . . . and scenic distractions . . . as well as rose gardens and refreshing inns . . . and traveling companions of a varying sort.

So it was quite appropriate that Jesus hand the disciples a travelogue or handbook for this pilgrimage. A guidebook that would not only warn of the dangers, but also prepare for the major relationships that a disciple incurs.

1. THEM FOLK

The first topic was their relationship with each other: *Servant to servant . . .* man to man . . . person to person. And Jesus reassured them that if they were good to each other . . . took care of one another . . . *gave them their food at the proper time . . .* they would be rewarded with a greater position, and undoubtedly, higher wages with all the perks that go along with it!

One can't help but read all the epistles to the congregations of the early church and come away with the Apostles' great concern that *brotherly Love* be manifest as a major characteristic of Christians, and that the *Royal Law of Love* would reign supreme in their midst. *Oh, how they love one another!* was the response they wanted the world to exclaim. (Ephesians 4:22 – 5:33; James 2:8)

"Favoritism" was not to be shown to the rich (James 2:5–13), nor act of prejudice against any nation (Gentile), gender, or social standing. (Romans 15:1–16; Colossians 3:11–17) Fraternity, equality, charity, in Christ.

On the other hand, Jesus forewarned about maltreatment of fellow human beings. Those who would devalue the sanctity of human life by beatings, starvings, abuses, rioting, drunken brawls, and the torture of the innocent (aborting by tearing limb from limb, or prolicide for the purpose of selling body parts) . . . would all face certain punishment! Dante's hell would be a starting point, *a place with the hypocrites where there will be wailing and gnashing of teeth.* And their ending? The Master knows.

The "gnashing of teeth" is a common phrase in Old Testament literature. (Psalm 112:10; Lamentations 2:16) And previously, Jesus used it to describe the condition of the wicked at *the end of the age.* (13:39, 49) It is correct, then, to interpret the second act (Act II) of the Olivet stage as one dealing with the final ending of the world.

2. WEDDING BANQUET

The second parable concerned their relationship to Christ, the Bridegroom. Although other scriptures using this metaphor picture the Church as the Bride of Christ, here the wedding attendants (*ten virgin lamp-bearers*) are used to show the need to be constantly prepared to meet the Groom. It is incumbent on everyone to be prepared for the Coming (*parousia*) of Jesus at the Second Advent.

The scene here is that of a Mideastern culture wedding. The engagement had taken place, and the betrothal ceremony a year earlier at the bride's home. Now the bridegroom was to leave his father's home and go fetch his bride, then in a large procession return for the grand wedding banquet.

Some commentators go to great lengths in search of the meaning of the "oil", literal or symbolic in relation to the Christian life; others venture to make conclusions about the percentage of prepared Christians and unprepared ones; and still others worry about which door is shut: The door of salvation, or the door of heaven, etc.

But it needs be observed that most parables deal with only one topic; they have only one "punch line", or one theme that the speaker wished to convey. To go beyond that intent is unwarranted, and can lead to all sorts of invalid conclusions. It is best to simply focus upon the most apparent — and usually stated — proverb.

The concluding admonition here, has the expressed purpose of drawing our attention to the need for preparation so when the Bridegroom arrives all will be ready to meet Him. *Personal* preparation is underscored by His mentioning that the foolish virgins could not rely upon any others to supplement their needs. Each person must look out for their own readiness.

An Eastern marriage feast

And it does not do any good to "just get by." Since no one knows — in this case the ten virgins — *what day or what hour* the Return will happen, there must be concern for on-going *watchfulness,* and adequate preparation for the short duration or the long haul. A once-in-a-while, or sporadic, assessment of readiness just might not be sufficient. As the old pilgrims used to say, *we must always be prayed up, so we can be caught up.* Whether the Lord comes sooner or later, the suddenness will not allow any deficiencies to be made up at the last moment. Especially if the arrival happens to be *after midnight!* No store would be open at that time for buying oil.

We are reminded of the crowds of people who accompanied Jesus at His *Triumphant Entry* into Jerusalem as King. (Matthew 21; Zechariah 9:9) The expectancy and exuberance they exhibited with their shouts of praise and waving of palm leaves is the kind of attention Christ should be receiving from us at His Second Advent. *Extinguished lighting* will hardly brighten His roadway, nor His radiance.

3. THE SMELL OF MONEY

As in the preceding parables, there was a delay or space of time before the main character returned, and both then proceed to deal with how the disciples ought to deal with their time: the first in personal relationships, and the second in personal piety.

In this story, the master *called his employees and entrusted his property to them.* Here, money, cold cash currency, is the type of property doled out. But for all intents and purposes, this parable told today, could include any type of economic holdings that may be entrusted to us. And if we considered divine Providence for a moment, we would realize that any possessions we "own" are really property belonging to the LORD that is only temporarily placed within our hands to be frugally and purposefully handled. Thus the directive to Israel:

> *The land must not be sold permanently, because the land is Mine and you are but aliens and My tenants. Throughout the country that you hold as a possession you must provide for the redemption of the land.* (Leviticus 25:23–24)

> *Every firstborn male in Israel, whether man or animal, is Mine.* (Numbers 8:17).

> . . . *Every animal of the forest is* **Mine**, *and the cattle on a thousand hills. I know every bird in the mountains, and the creatures of the field are* **Mine**. *If I were hungry I would not tell you, for the world is* **Mine**, *and all that is in it.* (Psalm 50:10–12)

*The silver is **Mine** and the gold is **Mine**, declares the LORD
Almighty.* (Haggai 2:8)

In this life, each person is given abilities, and resources for the productive func-
tioning of those abilities, and is expected to show some profit when he/she meets up
with his/her Master to give an account Although financial gain is the topic of this
parable, the accrued benefits one may enhance the Kingdom with may be nonphys-
ical as well: charity or a word of encouragement, Habitat for Humanity or consoling
the bereaved, offerings or mentoring a youth, providing jobs to the unemployed or
the ultimate sacrifice — martyrdom.

Those who share the resources God has entrusted them with — and enlarge the
influence of the Kingdom to the glory of God — will share in the Master's happiness!
Notice that the reward given to the servant who only had two (bars of gold) is the
same as that given to the faithful servant who invested five. So it is not the amount,
or skills level, or great acumen, that a person has, that is necessarily important . . . it
is *accomplishment flowing out of a 'good and faithful' character.*

The "worry free" life Jesus had enjoined in the Sermon on the Mount did not
mean that just because God would always provide, one did not have to work for a
living . . .The apostle Paul, later, would admonish:

> In the name of the Lord Jesus Christ, we command you, brothers, to keep
> away from every brother who is **idle** . . . For you yourselves know how you
> ought to follow our example, we were not idle when we were with you, nor
> did we eat anyone's food without paying for it . . . We gave you this rule:
> 'If a man will not work, he shall not eat.' (2 Thessalonians 3:6–10; see also
> Proverbs 13:4; 12:11)

The diligent, hard worker who abounds in every good work, will have enough
harvest or wages left over that he will be able to be generous in supplying the needs
of God's people. And *because of the service by which you have proved yourselves,
men will praise God for the obedience that accompanied your confession of the Gospel of Christ.* It is true that *whoever sows sparingly will also reap sparingly, and
whoever sows generously will also reap generously.* (2 Corinthians 9:6–15; 1 Peter
4:10–11)

The third servant (employee) was criticized for being "lazy" and therefore,
"wicked." His only excuse was "fear." This, is reminiscent of the man in Ecclesiastes
who watches the wind and will not plant, or looks at the clouds and will not reap.
(11:4; compare 11:6) Fear easily becomes an excuse for idleness . . . which an industrious company manager (boss) can not stomach. To him, *a worthless servant* belongs

outside in the darkness . . . where there will be deep regret (weeping and gnashing of teeth).

To underscore the seriousness of Jesus's parable we need only recall the Old Testament prophetic passages from which Jesus drew His phrases:

> *. . . Do not **fear what they fear**, and do not dread it. The LORD Almighty is the one you are to regard as holy, He is the one you are to fear, He is the one you are to dread, and He will be a sanctuary . . .*
>
> *If they do not speak according to this word, they have no light of dawn. Distressed and hungry, they will roam through the land: When they are famished, they will become enraged and, looking upward, will curse their king and their God.*
>
> *Then they will look toward the earth and see only distress and darkness and fearful gloom, and they will be **thrust into utter darkness**.* (Isaiah 8:12–13, 20–22)

Faithless inactivity, and lack of a practical use of the possession a man is entrusted with, while positioned in the time between the First Advent of Christ and the Second Coming, will cause one to miss out on the joy of the Lord, and on hearing those satisfying words, *Well, done, thou good and faithful servant!* We are to "occupy" until He comes. *(Do business until I come back,* Luke 19:13 NKJV.)

As an "aside", it is interesting that Einstein once quipped that "the greatest force in the universe was compound interest!" Money that is put into circulation increases exponentially.

On the other hand, money that *is buried* in an old sock and put under a mattress is "dead money." It not only does not work to produce interest, but it decays in value because it does not even keep up with the rate of inflation that often plagues a nation. It's buying power decreases with time.

A gentleman on the television reality show, *Shark Tank*, also warned that money that is spent on a possession (stereo, car, clothes, etc.) becomes dead money. Eventually stored in an attic (buried in basement), it is worthless.

[Caution must be taken concerning who is being charged "interest". Even though this is an Old Testament reference, there is New Testament application: Leviticus 25:35–38]

Thus Act II ended . . . in stark contrast to Act I. In very picturesque, and pointed, imagery, Jesus answered the remaining questions swirling around in the tornado of the Apostolic mind: These troublesome days, stand firm and stay the course;

in that Day, finish the course nobly (with *noblesse oblige*). The Day of the Lord in judgment, the end of the Jewish covenant, would take place within a lifetime (*this generation*), but the Day of the Lord, the end of the world and Final Judgment, would occur unannounced after an undetermined length of time.

But wait, there's more. There's another Act in the wings, ready to take center stage. Take a break, buy some popcorn . . . and after intermission, fasten your seat belt!

CONTRASTING EVENTS

There is a definite and clear contrast between the content (subject matter) and the emphatic warnings of the two Acts: Act I (Matthew 24:1–34) and Act II (Matthew 24:35 – 25:30). It can only be concluded that they describe two different events: the First Advent (with its Days of Vengeance), and the Second Advent (at the end of the world).

ACT I	ACT II
Specific signs are given	Absence of explicit signs
Christians are to flee	No time for fleeing
Judgment on earth for conduct	Judgment with heavenly rewards
Cataclysmic activity: wars, treason, disasters	Normal everyday living with common ups and downs
Events to happen within 'this generation' (soon)	Long delay for waiting for the Lord, Bridegroom, etc.
3½ years of Gentile army trampling across the land	Immediate appearance and coming at once of the Lord
Plural "days" and "times" (of the Gentiles)	Singular "day" and "hour"
End of the Second Temple era	End of the world as we know it
Local destruction in Judea	Heaven and earth pass away
Abomination of desolation; desolate house	Wedding feast; joy of the Lord; promotion
Specific warnings: "do this, don't do that"	General admonition: "Watch" "be ready" "do good"
Snakes, brood of vipers; hypocrites, blind guides: all beyond redemption	Faithful and wise servant; wise virgins; good and faithful servants (as well as worthless servants)

ADDENDA

*I marvel that you are turning away so soon from Him
who called you by the grace of Christ, and are turning to a
different Gospel — which really is no Gospel at all!
Some who are confusing you are trying
to pervert the Gospel of Christ.*

— GALATIANS 1:6–7

WHY NO SIGNS?

Christian congregations in every generation are bombarded with the television programs, prophecy conferences, published literature, and sermons of thousands of men who claim to be able to recognize *end-time signs* that they assure them, are *fulfillments* of biblical verses interpreted *literally*, according to their conjured "Golden Rule of Biblical Interpretation."

As a direct result, congregations are whipped into a frenzy of expectation with questionable consequences:

1. They are urged to buy all the latest books cranked out by non-stop publishing houses' printing presses. Millions of dollars are spent by them to try to satisfy their curiosity about who the Antichrist is, or if the European Union is really the "revived Roman Empire" that's going to take over the world, or if the latest skirmish in the Mideast is the harbinger of "the big one" (Armageddon).

    Money that could have gone to more worthy missions programs, charity, or pastoral outreaches (what used to be called evangelism), instead is spent on rows of books collecting dust on shelves loaded with other outdated publications. What's known as "dead money" could have been kept in circulation, pumping life, spiritual life, into a biblically illiterate culture.

2.   The lecturing on "end time signs" generation after generation after generation after generation, ad nausium, . . . *without there being an End* has been a major point of disillusionment to faithful church goers. This repeated nonsense has had a failure rate of 100% for the past two thousand years! Yet prophetic charlatans continue to raise the expectations of church members, only to let them down in time . . . for time is the enemy of these con-men . . . time proves them all wrong in their interpretations of scripture. The interest in serious Bible study that was piqued lays shattered on the floor like expensive lead crystal pushed off a table hitting hard marble stone. Their faith in the Word of God is diminished, not realizing that it's the Tradition of Men that should be shunned.

3.   Much of the sensationalizing about the alleged end-times has an adverse psychological affect as well. *Fear, anxiety, hand-wringing, helplessness, resignation, uncertainty,* and *restlessness* are all symptomatic of listening to telepastor after pastor orate about the coming Beast, Antichrist, War of Armageddon, and False Prophet.

The fear of being *left behind* in the event of a Secret Rapture for the truly faithful also sits in the back of believers' minds like a disruptive school boy known for shooting spitwads and causing other disturbances. The anxiety of thinking that a dear relative or close friend may not make it "up" with you also haunts them . . . to think that they might get the Mark of the Beast . . . dreadful thought!

Many believers are paralyzed into being ineffective in their Christian walk with such teachings of men. They are as zombies just placing one foot ahead of the other, going down the bumpy path of life, without the enthusiasm of a warm-hearted, Spirit-filled, born-again, devil-chasing, hopefulness.

4.   This incessant date-setting, timing of the End, and observance of signs, has had the deleterious effect of taking the eyes of the people off from Christ, and placing them on world events. Instead of focusing on Jesus and looking for the blessed hope of His returning, they focus on the appearance of the unholy trinity: Beast, False Prophet, and Antichrist. What a diabolical turn of events!

Old Screwtape himself could not have come up with a better plan to change the outlook of Believers. He must be dancing an Irish jig to think that evangelical preachers are accomplishing what he and his demons have been wanting to do all along. Like the stormy waves that caused Peter to take his eyes off Jesus walking on the water, the sweaty preaching and armwaving of the Judaizers and telepastors has effectively distracted sincere believers from feasting their eyes on the One who alone can bring peace of mind and soul satisfaction.

Christians are to be *Christ-centered*, and not sign-centered. As one dear expositor admonished, "We are not to be waiting for the Coming of the Lord so much as for the Lord who is coming." There is inherent wisdom in that.

5. Another extremely tragic consequence of raising up churches full of *sign seekers* is the "yanking of laborers off the field of the harvest." We we told by the Loving Savior who has a heart of compassion and sense of urgency, to *pray that the Lord of the Harvest would send out laborers into the field that was ripe for reaping.* On another occasion, Jesus called all His disciples to "trade until I come back" ("occupy" KJV). Keep busy. Invest your time, treasure, and talent while the Lord is away.

But the nasty, obscene, result of end-time hysteria has been the pulling out of society in crucial areas because of the defeatist mentality of the Rapture teaching. Instead of *getting involved* for the long haul, in political legislation (or running for office from the grass-roots upward), or becoming a lawyer with the intent of eventually becoming a righteous judge, or getting an education so the School Boards and the university professorships could be filled with god-fearing teachers . . . pseudo-prophets have instilled an *escapist* out-look and perspective on life and life's occupations.

Christians so influenced have abrogated Christ's directive to be a light on a hill, and salt in society, and turned the job of running their country over to the atheists, hedonists, and immoral. (And then they whine on Sunday because the world is getting darker and darker!) They have forgotten the proverb that informed us that "when the righteous rule, the people rejoice." How can the righteous rule, if they don't run for office? And why should they run, if they daily anticipate leaving this old world behind in an imminent Rapture out if it?

Looking at end-time signs that are precursors of the Rapture has caused America to suffer needless spiraling down in to depravity and debauchery.

6. "Signs" of contemporary political movements, especially in the Mideast, have also had a deleterious effect on foreign policy and international affairs. Prime Ministers and Presidents (with their Secretary of States) have been unduly influenced by propheteers misinterpreting scriptures that deal with

the State of Israel, and allegedly, countries like Russia, Iran, Egypt, Syria, and even the European Union. Through tweaking phonetics and appealing to ancient terminology, they come up with end-time signs that portend wars, conflicts, and the big one: Armageddon!

They do not hesitate to tickle the ears of politicians about the central part that Israel is supposed to play in last days intrigue, and try to drum up support for this anti-Christ nation (which will take tourists' money, but diligently persecutes Christians living there!). That land which the book of Revelation called "Sodom", these preachers designate as "Holy Land." And the Temple which Jesus decreed as *desolate*, they wish to rebuild. And the throne of David, which Jesus now occupies in heaven (Acts 2), they want to transfer to earth so He can reign in Jerusalem here instead of the heavenly Jerusalem that Abraham looked forward to. (Hebrews 11:16; 12:22)

Such contrariness boggles the Christian mind. But such are the nefarious effects of these end-time signs propheteers. The teaching that the world is teetering on the brink of an imminent world war has left the Gospel far behind and is proclaiming different messages than what Christ intended. (Galatians 1:6–9)

By not giving any end-time signs (signs of the times) Jesus hoped to avoid grandiose speculations, false prophet fabrications, foolish forecasting, anticipatory anxiety, private interpretations, senseless sensationalism, financial scams, chart calculations, deleterious date-setting, cultural irrelevance, fear fostering, duty diluting, focus shifting, and a fatalistic world view.

The unannounced, any-moment Coming of Christ with certain assessment of each person's conduct (accountability), was designed and implemented to promote action more than contemplation . . . character more than speculating . . . spirituality more than sensationalization. This was the Apostle's plea:

> Now we beseech you, brothers, by the coming of our Lord Jesus
> Christ, and by our gathering together unto Him, that you be **not**
> **soon shaken** in mind, or be **troubled**, neither by spirit, nor by
> word, nor by letter as if from us that the day of Christ is present.
> (2 Thessalonians 2:1–2)

Whether waiting for the Day of Judgment on Jerusalem, or anticipating the Day of Judgment on the whole world, the Christian believer is not to be dominated by a spirit of fear or anxiety because of some charlatan's fabricated speculations. Rather, as Jesus taught, the believer ought to be given to charity, character development, and ceaseless watchfulness.

Loraine Boettner, summarized the strategy of Jesus quite succinctly when he wrote in his scholarly book, *The Millennium,* that if . . .

> . . . men knew that the time of His coming was far off, they would tend to become careless, indifferent about moral and spiritual values. On the other hand, if they knew that the time was very near they would become frenzied and excited and neglect their assigned work.
>
> In either event, they would not live normal lives . . . [God] seeks from us that which is the true fruit of our natures, not that which is excited and motivated by the expectation of immediate reward or punishment. This life is for every person primarily a time of testing for character and achievement. (p. 329)

A Roman triumph.

ACT III
DENOUEMENT

GOD WILL "GIVE TO EACH PERSON according to what he has done." (Psalm 62:12) To those who by persistence in doing good seek glory, honor and immortality, He will give eternal life.

But for those who are self-seeking and who reject the truth and follow evil, there will be wrath and anger. There will be trouble and distress for every human being who does evil: first for the Jew, then for the Gentile. But glory, honor and peace for everyone who does good: first for the Jew, then for the Gentile, for God does not show favoritism.

— Romans 2:6–11

WHEN THE SON OF MAN shall come in His glory, and all the holy angels with Him, then shall He sit upon the throne of His glory: [32] And before Him shall be gathered all nations: and He shall separate them one from another, as a shepherd divideth *his* sheep from the goats: [33] And He shall set the sheep on His right hand, but the goats on the left. [34] Then shall the King say unto them on His right hand, "Come, ye blessed of My Father, inherit the kingdom prepared for you from the foundation of the world: [35] For I was an hungred, and ye gave Me meat: I was thirsty, and ye gave Me drink: I was a stranger, and ye took Me in: [36] Naked, and ye clothed Me: I was sick, and ye visited Me: I was in prison, and ye came unto Me." [37] Then shall the righteous answer Him, saying, "Lord, when saw we Thee an hungred, and fed Thee? or thirsty, and gave *Thee* drink? [38] When saw we Thee a stranger, and took *Thee* in? or naked, and clothed *Thee*? [39] Or when saw we thee sick, or in prison, and came unto Thee?" [40] And the King shall answer and say unto them, "Verily I say unto you, Inasmuch as ye have done it unto one of the least of these My brethren, ye have done it unto Me." [41] Then shall He say also unto them on the left hand, "Depart from Me, ye cursed, into everlasting fire, prepared for the devil and his angels: [42] For I was an hungred, and ye gave Me no meat: I was thirsty, and ye gave Me no drink: [43] I was a stranger, and ye took Me not in: naked, and ye clothed Me not: sick, and in prison, and ye visited Me not." [44] Then shall they also answer Him, saying, "Lord, when saw we Thee an hungred, or athirst, or a stranger, or naked, or sick, or in prison, and did not minister unto Thee?" [45] Then shall he answer them, saying, "Verily I say unto you, Inasmuch as ye did *it* not to one of the least of these, ye did *it* not to Me." [46] And these shall go away into everlasting punishment: but the righteous into life eternal. ◀ **KJV**

ACT III
DENOUEMENT
MATTHEW 25:31–46

When the Son of Man comes in His glory, and all the angels with Him, He will sit on His throne in heavenly glory. All the nations will be gathered before Him, and He will separate the people from each other like a shepherd separates the sheep from the goats. He will put the sheep on His right, but the goats on His left.

MATTHEW 25:31–33

ACT II CONTAINED THREE SCENES IN WHICH INDIVIDUALS WERE ALLOTED VARIOUS responsibilities. At the end of a protracted period of time, the one by whom they were employed returned unannounced and unexpectedly. The three arrivals (a Bridegroom and two Masters) prefigured the appearing of the Main Character in Act III: the Son of Man.

This arrival is the *climax*, not just of the melodrama played out on the stage of Judean history, but is the dramatic *parousia* (arrival of state)[1] of the *King of all the earth*. It is the coming of the Son of Man at a *day and hour* which was eagerly anticipated with faith and hope, but which was totally unknown. (24:37–39)

---

1   The Greek word, *parousia*, was used by the ancients for the "visitation of a dignitary or head of state, and also in reference to the manifestation of a divine figure. It is often used for the climactic "arrival" of Jesus royal and divine in essence. His "comings" are of a dignified category.

This was the Son of Man whom the Spirit of God had predicted would suffer, and then enter into glory: Be resurrected and coronated on a throne of all encompassing power and authority! (1 Peter1:10–12; Acts 2:22–36) This is He who has watched over His Kingdom from afar, but now has lifted His scepter toward the cosmos, and decreed: *The end!*

He is revealed by Matthew's Gospel as *sitting on His throne in* **Heavenly glory**. The phrase, "He will sit" does not mean the Son of Man hasn't been King already, during the Kingdom Age (Church age). And certainly, it does not mean that He won't be king until He sits on a material throne of David in a rebuilt Temple in a millennial Jerusalem.

Rather, He *sits on His throne in* **heavenly glory**. His Kingship and His Kingdom are eternal. Only spiritual realities are eternal; physical ones decay and pass away. (1 Corinthians 15:50–54; 2 Corinthians 4:16–18) He reigns from heaven's domain. Angels are His courtiers. The disembodied saints are His audience.

And that He *will sit on His throne* to judge, does not mean He isn't endued with judiciary abilities already, no more than a county judge "just becomes" a judge when he sits in on a case. He is judge before that time as well. The Son of Man is come to sit in on a case that would make the O. J. Simpson trial seem like a junior high debate practice. "All rise!" Now "All bow."

This *sitting* that Jesus mentioned in the Olivet Discourse really meant that He was switching from a period of gracious intercession to a time of judgment. (Hebrews 4:16 "throne of grace"; Matthew 25:31 "heavenly throne of separation") This was a climactic change, so much that Peter, who was listening in, later wrote:

> *The Day of the Lord will come like a thief. The heavens will disappear with a roar; the elements will be destroyed by fire. Both the earth and everything in it will be burned up* (laid bare, NIV).
>
> *Therefore, since all these things will be dissolved* (destroyed, NIV) *in this way, what kind of people ought you to be? You ought to live holy and godly lives* (holy conduct and godliness, NKJV) *as you look forward to the Day of God . . . That day will bring about the destruction of the heavens by fire, and the elements will melt with fervent heat.*
>
> *But in keeping with His promise we look forward to a new heaven and a new earth, in which righteousness dwells* (the home of righteousness, NIV).
>
> *So then, beloved, since you are looking forward to this, make every effort to be found spotless, blameless and at peace with Him.*
> (2 Peter 3:10–14)

This is not some "night court" in a suburban ghetto attended by a clerk and few witnesses. He will sit, and *all the angels* with Him, saying 'Oyez, oyez, oyez.'

We are astonished at the simple presentation of the "coming" (designated, *parousia*), and "sitting" of Christ at *that day and hour*. The Son of Man comes, and immediately follows the Day of Judgment . . . *that day and hour* when "heaven and earth shall pass away." (24:35–36) [We are later informed by Paul that after the gavelling of the court session, Christ will hand the Kingdom over to the Father. (1 Corinthians 15:24–26)]

And we notice that these concomitants are not preceeded, nor interrupted, by any of the end-time events nor even "signs of the times", that modernist propheteers opine. None! There is no mention of an alleged Secret Rapture of the Church, no One-world Government, no Revived Roman Empire, no Rebuilding of a Jewish Temple, no Millennium on earth, no Davidic Throne in Jerusalem, no Reinstitution of the sacrifices of red heifers . . . nada . . . zilch . . . not . . . zero!

In fact, if there were any of these (especially an alleged Seven-Year Tribulation period) they would be a flat contradiction of Jesus's clear statement that His Coming would have no harbingers nor hints nor omens. A seven-year period, according to sensationalists' charts, would mean that those living during that time would know

Christ is about to return, when the seven years was up. All the modern (since 1830) two-, or three-, or four-phase presentations of the Second Coming are silliness . . . foolish speculation . . . if not, heresy.

DANIEL'S IMAGERY

What the Spirit-inspired psalmist wrote concerning the Exaltation and Corona-tion of Christ, Daniel repeated, but in different imagery. (Psalm 110, confirmed by Peter, Acts 2:34–36)

> *In my vision at night I looked, and there before me was one like a*
> *Son of Man, coming with the clouds of heaven. He approached the*
> *Ancient of Days* (God), *and was led into His Presence.*
>
> *He was given authority, glory, and sovereign power; all people,*
> *nations, and men of every language worshiped Him. His dominion*
> *is an everlasting dominion that will not pass away, and His King-*
> *dom is one that will never be destroyed.* (Daniel 7:13–14)

In previous verses, there was mention of a "fourth beast" which most reliable scholars have identified as the vast Roman Empire. And it was indeed during the time of the Caesars that Christ's **First Advent** occurred. (Luke 2:1) It was then that the Son of Man was crucified, risen, and exalted to the position that Daniel described. Christ has ruled and reigned ever since then . . . on His throne of grace. (Hebrews 4:16)

It was then, quite appropriate that Jesus use the same imagery in this Olivet Dis-course to describe His **Second Advent**: *The Son of Man comes in His glory, and all the angels with Him.* (25:31, as well as 24:30–31; *"coming on the clouds"*, describing His first advent) "Heavenly glory" and "clouds of heaven" all speak of His divin-ity . . . something that the Pharisees who were looking for an earthly Conqueror to squelch the Roman oppression, could not grasp. They could not realize that David's Son was David's "Lord". (Matthew 22:41–46) Nor did they comprehend that He would be "Judge."

DENOUEMENT

At the end of a Perry Mason television program, the detective Drake and the sec-retary Della would sit in their office and wonder how on earth Perry Mason knew who the guilty person was. What hint or evidence did he discover that put him on the right track? What clue gave it away, and led him to the perpetrator?

Then Perry Mason would arrive, sit down, and proceed to explain the circumstances that led him to the right conclusion: "The shoes on the victim were muddy . . . and there was no rain." "The purple umbrella didn't match the green dress of . . ."

The same type of conversation would occur at the end of a Sherlock Holmes mystery. His detective companion, Dr. Watson, would inquire as to how he figured out who really did commit the crime. And the proverbial response was always: "Quite elementary, my dear Watson!" Then Mr. Holmes would reveal the clues that unravels the criminal's plot.

In literary circles this is called the *denouement*, the unraveling of all the knotty schemes that keeps the reader tied up in suspense. It is the time when "all" is revealed and explained. The motives, the methods, the manners. It's all laid out on the table, so to speak.

Such is the situation at the Great Judgment Day after the climactic arrival and sitting of the King (Judge). First there is a *separation of all the sheep from the goats.* Christ reveals to the whole universe, all those who really are evil. All the hypocrisy . . . the robes of religiosity . . . the whitewashed conduct . . . the sanctimonious "put on's" . . . all of it is whisked away. Everyone "stands naked and open" *before the eyes of Him to Whom we must give account.* (Hebrews 4:13) *Nothing in all creation* is hidden from God's sight. Denouement! Open revelation. Nothing held back. Wolves in sheep's clothing are exposed. False "ministers of light" are defrocked. False apostles are denuded. (Compare Ezekiel 34:17, "I judge between . . . rams and he-goats")

Just as the detectives and secretaries were surprised at some of the outcomes of their mysteries, so there will be a lot of surprises on Judgment Day. Those we thought were sheep will be found to be goats after all. And those we had dismissed as goats (thieves on a cross of their own doing) might just end up being revealed as lost sheep who found their way in the nick of time! Some in "a Muslim grave might really have a Christian resurrection." And some buried in a Christian church-yard cemetery just might not . . .

But the denouement will not stop there. The Word of God will judge *the thoughts and attitudes (intents) of the heart.* (Hebrews 4:12) Secret thoughts will be open scandal in heaven at that time of unraveling. Underlying motives will be brought to the surface like a fishing bobber released from its lead weight, popping up above the water.

All the closed-door meetings of politicians will become front page headline news on that Day. All the secret cabals, revolutionary conspiracies, and top-secret memos will be on the Living section for all the angels to read. Newspaper boys (angels) will be shouting out, "Judgment Daily, get your paper here. Read all about it!" "Conspiracy exposed! Perpitrator revealed. Hoax uncovered! Propheteers brought to justice!"

I, the LORD, search the heart, I try the reins, even to give every man according to his ways, and according to the fruit of his doings. (Jeremiah 17:10)

Can any hide himself in secret places so that I will not see him? saith the LORD. Do not I fill heaven and earth? (Jeremiah 23:24)

Death and destruction lie open before the LORD—how much more the hearts of men? (Proverbs 15:11)

O LORD Almighty, You who examine the righteous and probe the heart and mind, let me see Your vengeance upon them, for to You I have committed my cause. (Jeremiah 20:12)

And (Jesus) did not need for any one to testify of man for He knew what was in man. (John 2:25)

O LORD, You have searched me and You know me. You know when I sit and when I rise; You perceive my thoughts from afar. You discern my going out and my lying down: You are familiar with all my ways. Before a word is on my tongue You know it completely, O LORD. (Psalm 139:1–4)

A man's ways are in full view of the LORD; and He examines all his paths. (Proverbs 5:21)

More accurately than Perry, and more thorough than Sherlock, Jesus will explain to the whole universe what was behind the events of history, and what were the motivations of all the participants. And He will also reveal the awesome Providential intervention that God carried out to keep things from totally getting out of hand.

Those times when we saw only one set of footsteps in the sands of time were when He was carrying us . . . and we thought we were alone. All those accidents that were kept back by the Hand of God . . . that we were unaware of. All those blessings that came our way . . . and we had thought it was because of our greatness. All these will become broadcast on the airwaves of heaven. We will then realize that *by the grace of God we are what we are.* (1 Corinthians 15:10)

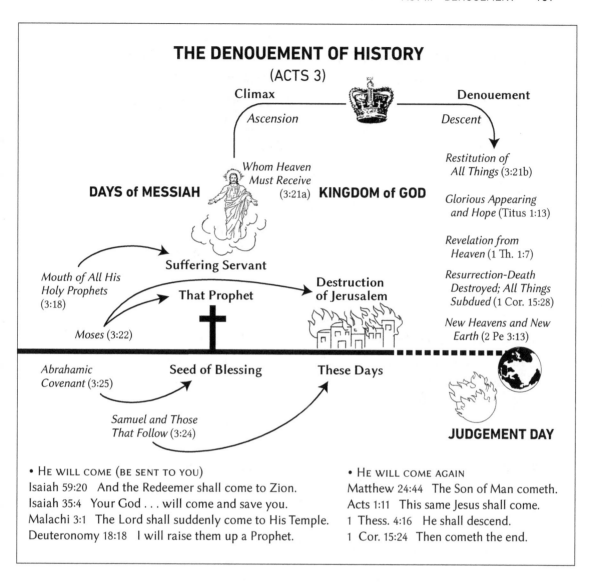

THE DENOUEMENT OF HISTORY
(ACTS 3)

Climax

Denouement

Ascension

Descent

Whom Heaven Must Receive (3:21a)

DAYS of MESSIAH

KINGDOM of GOD

Restitution of All Things (3:21b)

Glorious Appearing and Hope (Titus 1:13)

Revelation from Heaven (1 Th. 1:7)

Suffering Servant

Mouth of All His Holy Prophets (3:18)

That Prophet

Destruction of Jerusalem

Resurrection-Death Destroyed; All Things Subdued (1 Cor. 15:28)

Moses (3:22)

New Heavens and New Earth (2 Pe 3:13)

Abrahamic Covenant (3:25)

Seed of Blessing

These Days

Samuel and Those That Follow (3:24)

JUDGEMENT DAY

- HE WILL COME (BE SENT TO YOU)
Isaiah 59:20   And the Redeemer shall come to Zion.
Isaiah 35:4   Your God . . . will come and save you.
Malachi 3:1   The Lord shall suddenly come to His Temple.
Deuteronomy 18:18   I will raise them up a Prophet.

- HE WILL COME AGAIN
Matthew 24:44   The Son of Man cometh.
Acts 1:11   This same Jesus shall come.
1 Thess. 4:16   He shall descend.
1 Cor. 15:24   Then cometh the end.

In the light of this coming denouement at the Judgment Throne of the Son of Man, every man ought to be on his guard against *hypocrisy, for there is nothing concealed that will not be disclosed, or hidden that will not be made known. What you have said in the dark will be heard in daylight, and what you have whispered in the ear in the inner rooms will be proclaimed from the housetops!* (Luke 12:1b–3; see Romans 2:1–11)

After the shock of the thought of standing naked before the whole world, and having all our life . . . thoughts exposed, we regain our composure and return to the passage of scripture before us. We sit back in our cushy theater seats and listen to the King (Judge) give his verdict to us and them, the sheep and the goats.

THE TEN COMMANDMENTS	THE ROYAL LAW OF LOVE
FEAR OF PUNISHMENT	**COMMAND TO LOVE**
THOU SHALT NOT (DO & DIE!)	THOU SHALT (DO & LIVE!)
SINS OF COMISSION	SINS OF OMISSION
Blasphemy	Not feed the hungry
Idolatry	No water for thirsty
Murder	No hospitality
Theft	Not clothe the naked
Adultery	Not heal the sick
Lying	Not care for imprisoned
Covetousness	
FALLEN NATURE PROPENSITY	BORN AGAIN NATURE
Redeemed by blood of bulls	Redeemed by blood of Lamb
Covered over	Transformed heart
Personal restraint	Community activism
Civility struggle	Charity outreach
TEMPORAL, SOCIETAL,	ETERNAL, SPIRITUAL,
NATIONAL JUDGMENT!	INDIVIDUAL JUDGMENT!

NEW KING, NEW LAW

In this scene, the audience, is given a hint of things to come. A whole new way of doing business is at hand . . . a new regime is about to take over . . . a superior covenant will be confirmed . . . and with it, a new kind of judging.

One cannot but help see here, a surprising and different approach to what Judgment Day would be all about. Under the Mosaic Covenant, and the Rabbinical culture (that tweaked it a lot), judgment was based on sins of commission. If a person broke the "Thou shalt not . . ." of the basic Ten Commandments, punishment was in order. The Apostle Paul referred to this in his epistles; and he addressed the motivation for doing well: *fear!* (Galatians 3:10; 1 John 4:18; Deuteronomy 27:26)

Under the old Mosaic Covenant, external compliance with laws ruled the day. And those who sinned could bring sacrifice so blood could *cover over* their transgressions. The mercy seat blocked the view of God so He couldn't see the people's rap sheet within the Ark of the Covenant:

> *But it could never, by the same sacrifices repeated endlessly year*
> *after year, make perfect those who draw near to worship . . . They*
> *were an annual reminder of sins, because it is impossible for the*
> *blood of bulls and goats to take away sins.* (Hebrews 10:1–3)

As a result, the whole history of Israel was a struggle to maintain *civility*, a struggle it usually lost. Injustice, corruption, and economic tyranny won out repeatedly. And with that moral failure came swift and certain judgment:

> *Son of man, this is what the Sovereign LORD says to the land of*
> *Israel: the End!, The end has come upon the four corners of the land.*
> *The end is now upon you and I will unleash My anger against you. I*
> *will judge you according to your conduct and repay you for all your*
> *detestable practices. I will not look upon you with pity or spare you:*
> *I will surely repay you for your conduct . . .* (Ezekiel 7:2–4)

God came (in the clouds) and brought temporal, societal, national, judgment. In fact, the desolation of Judea in 67–70 A.D. was one of those times!

But this time, the Day of Wrath, through the instrument of the Roman Legions, was not just about the destruction of a building (Temple), it was the end of an era—the end of the Old Covenant Mosaic era—and importantly, the beginning of a New Covenant era . . . the manifestation of the Kingdom of God . . . the reign of the Son of Man in power and great glory (in the clouds).

And at the end of this new era (the age to come that the old rabbis anticipated), Jesus, the Son of Man, the *King* (25:34), will judge people according to *their sins of omission*. Why? Because the Royal Law of Love was the statute of the New Covenant. "Love your neighbor as thy self" had become the expressed fulfillment of all the Law and Prophets. (James 2:8; Matthew 7:12; 22:34–40; Galatians 5:14; Romans 13:8–10)

All people are to do acts of charity (THOU SHALT . . . instead of THOU SHALT NOT) with diligence and intention . . . not by compulsion . . . but out of hearts of love, willingly, and wanting to. But how is this possible with the same *propensities of fallen nature* that have plagued mankind for millennia? The answer lay within the method of entering into the Kingdom of God: By being born again! By being transformed in spirit.

> *Now that you have purified yourselves by obeying the truth so that*
> *you have sincere love for your brothers, love one another deeply,*
> *from the heart. For you have been born again, not of perishable*
> *seed, but of imperishable, through the living and enduring word of*
> *God.* (1 Peter 1:22–23)

We know and rely on the love God has for us. God is love. Whoever lives in love lives in God, and God in him. In this way, love is made complete among us so that we will have confidence on the Day of Judgment, because in this world we are like Him.

There is no fear in love. But perfect love drives out fear, because fear has to do with punishment. (1 John 4:16–18)

So, with this perspective, we can understand the way that the Son of Man, the King, will judge all mankind. It is the approach to justice that a most loving God would be expected to take. A God who cares about people.

ACTS OF KINDNESS

I was hungry and you gave me something to eat, I was thirsty and you gave me something to drink. I was a stranger and you showed me hospitality. I needed clothes and you clothed me. I was sick and you looked after me. I was in prison and you came to visit me. (25:35–36)

This list of "acts of kindness" and humanitarian aid is repeated four times in this Judgment scene for emphasis by Jesus. People's well-being is utmost on His mind. The sufferings of humanity are His greatest sorrow. Blessing His creation is His greatest joy. People matter; life is sacred.

Other ethnic (Gentile) cultures have intermittently come and recognized the virtue of compassion and have written down a similar list. This grouping of acts of kindness is found in rabbinical writings as well. When Jesus lifted these off the dusty shelves of the Sabbath school's libraries, He was, in effect, saying, "You all know better. There is no excuse for not living up to them. Here they are right in front of you!"

1. Feed the hungry.
2. Quench the thirsty.
3. Show hospitality.

4. Clothe the poor.
5. Tend to the sick.
6. Visit the prisoner.

The Jewish nation had for millennia, been the caretakers of the Word of God. They were privileged more than any other nation with divine revelation and inspired prophets. They even had heard and seen God . . . manifestation on Mount Sinai with all its pyrotechnical extravaganza and surround-sound blowing of the trumpet of God! They had received the Big Ten: a code of ethics acknowledged through history as the best social contract ever written down as a nation's guide to social felicity and personal safety.

But time has shown that "knowledge of the truth" alone does not insure moral conduct. Jews — as well as the rest of nations — have proved to be hypocrites. While recognizing the favor of God, they lived like the devil. Such that the major message of the prophets, B.C. and A.D., was a cry against social injustice. (Isaiah 58:1 – 59:16; Amos 5:7–13; Micah 6:9–12)

Taking food out of the mouths of the common folk, stealing the wine from the vineyards, despising the stranger, ignoring the poor beggars littering the streets, quarantining the diseased and sickly, and throwing people in prison without a fair trial . . . lack of justice in the land . . . innocent blood spilled in the courtyards . . . economic corruption . . . broken contracts . . . unfair wages (withheld benefits) . . . political lies . . . turning from one's own flesh and blood.

This conduct incurred the wrath of God in the Old Testament history of Israel. Warlike nations would march across their territory, sent by God in hopes of getting their attention and changing their ways . . . in hopes of repentance and restitution . . . in hopes of restoring civility and humanitarian acts of kindness.

Alas, the social condition during the First Advent of Christ saw the same aberration. As we saw in Matthew 23, hypocrisy was lord of the hearts of the people . . . and as we discovered in Matthew 24, another army was to come.

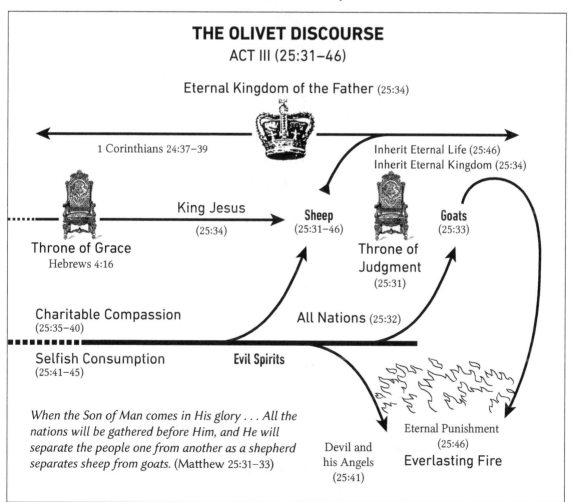

THE OLIVET DISCOURSE
ACT III (25:31–46)

Eternal Kingdom of the Father (25:34)

1 Corinthians 24:37–39

Inherit Eternal Life (25:46)
Inherit Eternal Kingdom (25:34)

King Jesus (25:34)

Sheep (25:31–46)

Goats (25:33)

Throne of Grace
Hebrews 4:16

Throne of Judgment (25:31)

Charitable Compassion (25:35–40)

All Nations (25:32)

Selfish Consumption (25:41–45)

Evil Spirits

When the Son of Man comes in His glory . . . All the nations will be gathered before Him, and He will separate the people one from another as a shepherd separates sheep from goats. (Matthew 25:31–33)

Devil and his Angels (25:41)

Eternal Punishment (25:46)
Everlasting Fire

And as we see here in chapter 26, there is another Day of Judgment, the final one, in which these humanitarian acts of kindness will be the ruler by which all men are measured. The word, *nations*, is not to be taken collectively, but as "people individually brought together." The *them* (KJV) in the this verse is masculine plural, meaning single individuals. If nations were intended as a whole, the "neuter" form would have been used. *All the nations with the people comprising them, will be gathered together before Him, and He will separate* **the people one from another** . . . (Matthew 25:32; see NIV)

THE FATHER'S KINGDOM

> *Come, the blessed by My Father; take your inheritance: the Kingdom prepared for you since the creation of the world.* (Matthew 25:34)

This awesome reward for humanitarian deeds—as an outworking of salvation, not a merit for salvation—is the ushering into the royal and divine Kingdom of the Father . . . for eternity! Eternal life (vs. 46)! Everything that the Pharaohs of ancient Egypt hoped for when they inscribed the *ankh* on the walls of the deep passageways of their pyramids . . . will instead be the inheritance of the righteous sheep, the kind Christians . . . the *blessed of the Father.*

It is important to point out: This statement of Jesus did not mean that the Kingdom of God was not yet in existence. Jesus repeatedly taught on the spiritual nature of His Kingdom—the one given to the Son of Man (Daniel 7)—and spoke parables illustrating the *present existence* of it in the hearts of believers. (John 18:36, "now"; Matthew 4:17; 9:35; 11:12; 12:28; 16:28) And Jesus had spoken many parables showing the long time progression of the Kingdom, spreading throughout the whole earth. (Matthew 13 especially; and Matthew 25:1, 14)

What He is emphasizing here at the Day of Judgment is the eventual transfer of His Kingdom up to the Father, at the end of the world, and when death is finally conquered. (1 Corinthians 15:23–28) This is why He had taught: *The righteous will shine like the sun in the* **Kingdom of their Father**. (Matthew 13:43) And combining the thought of the Kingdom with the reward of helping the poor, Jesus had previously taught:

> . . . *do not worry . . . for the pagans run after all such things, and your Father knows that you have need of them. But seek His kingdom and all these things will be given unto you.*
>
> *Do not be afraid, little flock, for your Father has been pleased to give you the Kingdom. Sell your possessions and give to the poor. Provide purses for yourselves that will not wear out, a treasure in*

*heaven that will not be exhausted, where no thief comes near and
no moth eats.* (Luke 12:29–33)

What an honor and tremendous reward to be part of the Kingdom of the Son of
Man and to reign with Him now. (Colossians 3:1) And we ought to join in with the
Colossian church *joyfully giving thanks to the Father who has qualified us to share in
the* **inheritance of the saints** *in the Kingdom of Light.* (Colossians 1:12) This Kingdom of the Son of Man . . . and the Kingdom of the Father. This age, and the age to
come! What an inheritance . . . reward.

It is, then, folly to focus on a physical, material kingdom of sorts here on earth,
as a fulfillment of the teachings of Jesus. There is not the slightest hint, in Jesus's
picture of the End, that an earthly Millennial kingdom is to be ruling with a Davidic
throne set up on some real estate in the Mideast, when Jesus comes at the Second
Advent. Such a concept is a step down from the awesome glory of the *parousia* of
the Son of Man.

Such carnal thinking is nixed by the apostle Paul: *Since then, you have been
raised with Christ, set your hearts on things* **above**, *where Christ is seated at the
right hand of God. Set your mind on things above,* **not** *on things of earth. For you
died, and your life is now hidden with Christ in God. When Christ, who is your life,
appears, then you also will appear with Him in glory.* (Colossians 3:1–4)

After the sheep are judged and rewarded, Christ emphatically declared that *the
righteous go away to eternal life.* (Matthew 25:46) They do not board a plane for
a trip to Israel! They do not indulge themselves in the grapes and pomegranates
of Judea for a thousand years. Their joy is an expectation of "eternity" with the
Father . . . a restoration of the communion Adam once had before the Fall . . . *and
fellowship with His Son.* (John 14:1–3)

If there were to be a material, earthly millennium as alleged by the modern
Dispensationalists, this would have been an excellent opportunity for Christ to mention it. But He seemed to be oblivious to any such earthly utopia . . . and we should
follow suit.

Instead, as the whole tenor of the Olivet Discourse proclaimed, we ought to
give the earnest heed to occupy until He comes . . . be diligent to maintain personal
integrity . . . and assiduously perform acts of kindness. To be found doing these
when He arrives (*the great Parousia*) will reap for us the greatest joy and fulfillment
of our human existence! (Mark 8:35–9:1; Luke 9:25–27; Matthew 24:46) The believers who are resolute in the service of the Kingdom, and *stand firm to the end* will
be aptly rewarded with abundant life here in this age, and with *eternal life* in the
age to come. (Matthew 24:13; Hebrews 3:12–14; Colossians 1:23; 1 Corinthians 15:58;
2 Corinthians 4:16)

HELL FIRE

> *Then He will say to those on His left, "Depart from Me, you who are cursed, into the eternal fire prepared for the devil and his angels" . . . They will go away to eternal punishment.* (25:41, 46)

To some, "virtue is its own reward." To others, compassion out of a pure heart spurs them on to good deeds. And to still others, it takes the motivation of a desire to escape the *eternal fires of hell* to shake them out of their lethargy and self-centeredness.

There is much debate on the aspect of hell, hell-fire, eternal punishment, and annihilation of the wicked. Whether the exegete is to take these as literal (physical, Celsius or Fahrenheit) or symbolic has inspired many commentators to write volumes of books by manufacturing paper from many trees — a forest full of trees — and fill them with ink from a source the size of Niagara Falls. Although these are replenishable natural resources, *time* is not, so we do not wish to spend a lot of it arguing the case, either way. But we do observe with utmost sobriety that *fire* is a constant theme associated with punishment . . . and it doesn't sound good, at all!

> *I* (Daniel) *kept looking until the beast was slain and its body destroyed and thrown into the blazing fire.* (Daniel 7:11)
>
> *If we deliberately keep on sinning after we have received the knowledge of the truth, no sacrifice for sins is left, but only a fearful expectation of judgment and of raging fire that will consume the enemies of God.* (Hebrews 10:26–27)
>
> *The ax is ready at the root of the trees, and every tree that does not produce good fruit will be cut down and thrown into the fire.* (Matthew 3:10) (Notice the cool, refreshing remedy: *"I baptize you with water for repentance."* vs. 11; That will put out any fire! Compare Matthew 7:15–20)
>
> *His* (Christ's) *winnowing fork is in His hand, and He will clear His threshing floor, gathering His wheat into the barn and burning up the chaff with unquenchable fire.* (Matthew 3:12)
>
> *Anyone who says to his brother, 'Raca'* (an Aramaic term of contempt) *is answerable to the Sanhedrin. But anyone who says, 'You fool!' will be in danger of the fire of hell.* (Matthew 5:22)

As the weeds are pulled up and burned in the fire, so it will be at the end of the age. The Son of Man will send out His angels, and they will weed out of His Kingdom everything that causes sin and all who do evil.

They will throw them into the fiery furnace, where there will be weeping and gnashing of teeth. (13:40–42)

Then they (the fishermen) sat down and collected the good fish in baskets, but threw the bad away. This is how it will be at the end of the age. The angels will come and separate the wicked from the righteous, and throw them into the fiery furnace, where there will be weeping and gnashing of teeth. (13:48–50)

It is better for you to enter life maimed or crippled than to have two hands or two feet and be thrown into eternal fire. It is better to enter life with one eye than to have two eyes and be thrown into the fire of hell. (18:8–9)

It is better to show kindness, and to treat Jesus humanely. Jesus? What does it mean to "Show kindness to Jesus"?

MY BROTHERS

Then the righteous will ask, "Lord, when did we see You hungry and feed You" . . . The King will reply, "I tell you the truth, whatever you did for one of the least of these My brothers, you did for Me." (Matthew 25:37, 40)

Showing kindness to normal, everyday people is just like doing deeds of kindness unto Christ! Interesting. Even though Jesus is ascended, we are not "let off the hook" with an excuse for not being kind to Him.

We're to serve the needs of the *brothers of Jesus* from the greatest unto *the least of them.* (25:40) But Jesus didn't mention "the greatest" superlative, just the diminutive, *the least* (a derivative of *mikros*, Gk.). He already knew that human nature gravitates toward the "rich and famous." The next time someone famous or well-known walks into the office, just see if heads don't turn, including yours. See if their presence causes your conversation with "a commoner" to be interrupted, or even halted. You have gravitated.

In this politico, socio-economic, hero-worshiping culture, socialites and some pastors give the advice: "Friend up." Associate with those better than you. It is not common to hear, "Marry up," as well. Now, there is nothing wrong with this advice if one wants to enhance the occupational skills or technological abilities that will help him be more industrious in life.

But Jesus knew that "looking up" usually seeps over onto motives of self aggrandizement and stains character. He deliberately mentioned *the least of . . .* Previously, in light of Judgment Day, no doubt, Jesus admonished Christian believers who were inclined to *give a luncheon or dinner (banquet)* to not invite their friends, their brothers or relatives, or rich neighbors. If they did so, they might get invited back by them, and so receive back "payment" for their invite. But

> *. . . when you give a banquet, invite the poor, the crippled, the lame, the blind, and you will be blessed. Although they cannot repay you, you will be repaid at the resurrection of the righteous.*
> (Luke 14:12–13)

In the estimate of social climbers, and those wishing to gain a reputation or higher station in life, that strategy would seem offensive, or as the hippies would say, "obscene." But they fail to keep in mind that there is "life" *and* there is "life to come . . ."

Just who did Jesus mean to refer to by the use of the word, *brothers (adelphon,* Gk.)? The answer may intentionally be vague so that the believer will show acts of kindness to all he meets in life.

It was common for citizens in Israel to call each other brothers. (Acts 22:1, 5) Just as common, or more so because of their relationship in the Family of God, the Christians called each other brothers. (Acts 21:7, 17, 20; Hebrews 2:11–12; Matthew 18:15)

Some commentators note the similarity of Jesus's rebuke to His disciples on a previous occasion when they want to know who would be the "greatest" in the Kingdom of Heaven:

> *Therefore, whoever humbles himself like this child is the greater in the Kingdom of Heaven. And whoever* **welcomes a little child** *like this in My Name* **welcomes Me.**
>
> *But if anyone causes one of these* **little ones** *(mikron, Gk.) who believe in Me to sin, it would be better for him to have a large millstone hung around his neck and to he drowned in the depths of the sea.* (Matthew 18:4–6)

Conduct directed toward, not only the "least" but also the "little", is a reflection on Jesus. It is tantamount to messin' with God, and is punishable.

Some expositors have deduced that Jesus was referring to "the brotherhood of man". Jesus, in a sense, came to earth and shared in the suffering of all men. He was hungry, He thirst, He became poor (2 Cor. 8:9), He was rejected by men, He was afflicted, He was ostracized, He was scorned . . . Jesus became just as us — yet without sin — in the grand fraternity of human existence. (However, consider Matthew 12:49–50, those who do the will of God)

But whatever the meaning of "brother" it wouldn't hurt to touch all bases: Do works of charity to those within and without the Kingdom of God, to those whom society turns its back on . . . and to those who even demonstrate a hatred toward you. (Luke 6:35–36, God is kind to the wicked.)[2]

> *You have heard it said, "Love your neighbor, and hate your enemy" but I say, "Love your enemies and pray for those who persecute you, so you may be sons of your Father in heaven . . .*
>
> *If you love those who love you, what* **reward** *will you get? Do not even the tax collectors (those beasts among men!) do that? And if you greet only your brothers, what are you doing more than others? Do not even pagans do that?*
>
> *Be perfect, therefore, as your heavenly Father is perfect.* (Matt. 5:43–48)

There is one more warning that Jesus gave about acts of kindness in relation to Judgment Day that is found in the sixth chapter of Matthew:

> *Be careful not to do your 'acts of righteousness' before men to be seen by them. If you do, you will have* **no reward** *from your Father in heaven.*
>
> *So when you give to the needy, do not announce it with trumpets, like the hypocrites do in the synagogues and on the streets, so they can be honored by men.*
>
> *I tell you the truth, they have received their* **reward** *in full! But when you give to the needy, do not let your left hand know what your right hand is doing, so that your giving may be done in secret. Then your Father, Who sees what is done in secret, will* **reward** *you.* (Matthew 6:1–4)

In the parable of the Good Samaritan, Jesus highlighted the necessity of reaching out to those He called *neighbors*, not necessarily *brothers*. *Love your neighbor as*

---

2   That the "surrogate principle" does not simply apply to children (Little ones), Jesus mentioned "those whom He sends" (ministers, prophets, etc.) in this respect, as well. (John 13:20) These men are indeed, *brothers.*

yourself. (Leviticus 19:18; Luke 10:25–37) The whole story of the kind Samaritan was given in response to the evasive question, "And just who is my neighbor?"

The man who had mercy on him is the true neighbor, according to Jesus. "Go and do likewise," remains today a command by which the sheep and the goats will be eventually judged. It will differentiate between the cursed and the *blessed . . . between eternal punishment and eternal life. (25:46)*

ADDENDA

END TIME EVENTS

It can be seen that Jesus was concerned about the disciples knowing the truth about the Jewish people, about the on-going conduct of Christian believers, and about the end of the world. He prophesied the End of the Second Temple Era . . . with no one coming to the rescue; it was over, finished . . . ended. God's focus was to be on "all nations."

Jesus then admonished through several parables, all believers to live with integrity, charity, and transparency. There would be an indefinite period of time before the Second Coming, and it required that they conduct themselves with circumspect at all times because Christ will judge each individual accordingly.

And concerning the End of the world, when that great Judgment will be held, Jesus informed the disciples that there would be absolutely no signs of its approach. There were to be no "signs of the times" nor "last days" events to look for to reveal its nearness.

MASS MEDIA MADNESS

And yet, horror of all horrors . . . modernist evangelical preachers do not hesitate to teach contrary to the clear words of Jesus! . . . think nothing of televising program after program of stories about alleged end-time events (happening "right now in our generation!") . . . continue to contradict the scriptures by listing "signs of the times" . . . and endlessly fabricate events that are figments of their imagination.

Brothers and sisters in Christ around the world are being exploited, mentally manipulated, and fleeced by these wolves in sheep's clothing. Like lemmings led astray by Pied Pipers, the children of God are misled with abandon by pulpit pastors engrossed in futurism. How are they misled?

Novels and fictitious movies have taken the place of "sola scriptura" as the main source of truth and understanding about the End of the world. Serious exegesis by congregations is trumped by sensationalistic exposé regarding the latest news item out of the Mideast and its all-edged relationship to end-time prophecies! It takes less energy for a believer to sit back and watch a movie while eating buttery popcorn, than it is to go and dust off reference books, and the Bible, and do personal research.

It is also easier for pastors to "dip from each other's cup" (spread pulpit gossip, in effect) than to do deep word studies and in-depth research into matters of eschatology from Jesus's point of view. (Jeremiah 24:30) Lazy leadership results in egregious error, and perpetuation of false doctrine.

Both pastor and congregant alike tend to interpret prophecies about the end of the world *according to what's happening in their own nation (America)*. If economic disaster strikes, if meteorological catastrophe happens, if terrorism erupts . . . they consider these as "signs" of the end of the world . . . when in effect, these are only (perhaps) signs of the end of a nation. After all, nations come and go . . . but it isn't the end of the world. Signs of national decay are just that, signs of a nation.

It may be shocking news, but one's own nation is not the North Star of prophetic understanding. There's a lot more to history, and the future, than the destiny of one nation.

A lack of historical knowledge, especially ancient history leaves most Christian believers without the foundation necessary to see if prophecies have already been fulfilled. Since prophecy deals with historical events, a true understanding can only come from knowing ancient, middle-age, and, as well, present events. Most believers don't get past reading the news in their daily newspaper (and their horoscope, sports, and comics sections). Their limitation of time is marked by how far back they can remember who won last year's Super Bowl. An occasional documentary on public television might give them a small glimpse through the window of history, but that's about it.

A lack of knowledge about and an underestimate of the seriousness of the Fall of Jerusalem in 70 A.D. also hampers a believer's grasp of prophetic insight. The Jews— without a Temple, without a daily sacrifice, without a sanctuary for Messiah to come to—know the tremendous effect the Roman invasion had on Judaism. Christians don't generally comprehend such tragedy. The writings of Flavius Josephus once graced the book shelves of Church libraries *(History of the Jewish Wars)*, but emerging churches are oblivious to this tome and its importance. As a result many of the events Jesus outlined in the Olivet Discourse, referring to this catastrophe, are wrenched out from their context and placed at the End-of-the-world scenarios.

Without knowledge of *Church history*, modern Christians have left themselves open to theological manipulation, as well. They are gullible and susceptible to the rantings of "futurism" because they are unaware that it was the clandestine efforts of false sects that introduced it into churches. They don't realize that Jesuit spies dressed up as Protestant ministers infiltrated England with a futurism doctrine that was designed to let Catholicism off the hook of accusations of being Antichrist! And it worked. The librarian for the Archbishop of Canterbury, Edward Irving, John Darby, as well as others, grabbed this torch and ran with it. It eventually was the main theme of the *Scofield Reference Bible* and the Plymouth Brethren who inundated England and America with this heresy-laced literature. Modern believers just don't realize that for millennia, the Church theologians never, ever taught this perspective of prophecy. They mistakenly think it is normal, and orthodox.

Modernist evangelical telepastors also misled congregations by their habit of *leap-frogging over the New Testament*. Instead of letting the New Testament apostles (and Jesus) interpret the Old Testament prophecies, the propheteers take the predictions about the Jewish Nation (and its alleged restoration) and jump over into modern history. They maintain that the major theme of the Bible, and of God's purposes in the earth, are the Jewish people and their national prominence among nations. They underscore the Pharisees' nationalistic spirit, with a prejudice against the Gentiles. (Modernists get rid of the Gentiles by "rapturing them up in a secret Church event", and thereby avoid the stance of being prejudiced.)

By doing this leap-frogging, modern expositors think they can avoid any "spiritualizing" or "allegorizing" of Jewish prophecies which the apostles tended to do. Literalism is the linchpin of propheteers.

"Literalism" is sacrosanct with telepastors. It has become the new *shibboleth* (password) of fellowship. Just mention the spiritualizing of Jesus and the Apostles, then watch their jugular veins bulge, and their face burn red with ire. Literalism has become their "Golden Rule of Interpretation" — yet they themselves, are not consistent with it, it ought to be noted. It trumps all other principles of hermeneutics. It will take symbolism and contort it into literal nonsense, and come up with an End-time prophetic event!

Why all this massive tsunami of "signs of the times" propaganda? One reason cannot be overlooked: Fear sells! There are big bucks in sensationalism (Dispensensationalism). Movies manufacture ticket sales. Books about the latest end-time sign generate revenue for the telepastors; it cannot be denied.

Are there end-time events like a Secret Rapture of the Church, or a future Antichrist, or some Covenant of the Devil with the Jewish nation, or the reguilding of a Temple, or a humongous Tribulation of seven-years duration . . . ad nauseum?

The plain truth, and the simple answer is *"No!"* We have Jesus's word on it.

Are there "signs of the times" noticeable that we should be concerned with? Are there signs that this is the last generation before the coming of Christ? Are we near the End for certain?

The plain truth, and the simple answer is *"No!"* We have Jesus's word on it.

Should believers be aroused by the latest announcement of propheteers, and buy their books, watch their television programs, or go to their movie presentations? Will they accurately inform us, or equip us as believers?

The plain truth, and the simple answer is *"No!"* We have Jesus's word on it.

> *Heaven and earth will pass away, but My words will never pass away.* **No one knows** *about that Day or Hour, not even the angels in heaven, nor the Son, but only the Father . . .*
>
> *You must be ready, because the Son of Man will come at an hour when you* **do not expect** *Him . . .*
>
> *Keep watch because you* **do not know** *the day or the hour.*
> (Matthew 24:35, 36, 44; 25:13)

Anyone who claims to know, is a liar, and the truth is not in him. Keep your money in your pocket. (Or give it to charity.) Rather, be circumspect, and *watch* (keep your eyes on the prize). Work diligently for the Kingdom of God where you are, and may you (we) be so doing when He does return!

COUP DE THEATRE

DAUGHTERS OF JERUSALEM, DO NOT weep for Me; weep for yourselves and for your children. For the time will come when you will say, "Blessed are the barren women, the wombs that never bore and the breasts that never nursed!"

Then "they will say to the mountains, Fall on us!" and to the hills, "Cover us!" (Hosea 10:8) For if men do these things when the tree is green, what will happen when it is dry?

Two other men, both criminals, were also led out with Him to be put to death. When they came to the place called Calvary (the Skull), they crucified Him . . .

—Luke 23:28–33

AND IT came to pass, when Jesus had finished all these sayings, He said unto His disciples, [2] "Ye know that after two days is *the feast of* the Passover, and the Son of Man is betrayed to be crucified." [3] Then assembled together the chief priests, and the scribes, and the elders of the people, unto the palace of the high priest, who was called Caiaphas, [4] And consulted that they might take Jesus by subtilty, and kill *Him.* [5] But they said, "Not on the feast *day,* lest there be an uproar among the people."

[6] ¶ Now when Jesus was in Bethany, in the house of Simon the leper, [7] There came unto Him a woman having an alabaster box of very precious ointment, and poured it on His head, as He sat *at meat.* [8] But when His disciples saw *it,* they had indignation, saying, "To what purpose *is* this waste? [9] For this ointment might have been sold for much, and given to the poor." [10] When Jesus understood *it,* He said unto them, "Why trouble ye the woman? for she hath wrought a good work upon Me. [11] For ye have the poor always with you; but Me ye have not always. [12] For in that she hath poured this ointment on My body, she did *it* for My burial. [13] Verily I say unto you, Wheresoever this gospel shall be preached in the whole world, *there* shall also this, that this woman hath done, be told for a memorial of her."

[14] ¶ Then one of the twelve, called Judas Iscariot, went unto the chief priests, [15] And said *unto them,* "What will ye give me, and I will deliver Him unto you?" And they covenanted with him for thirty pieces of silver. [16] And from that time he sought opportunity to betray Him.

AFTER TWO days was the feast of the Passover, and of Unleavened Bread: and the chief priests and the scribes sought how they might take Him by craft, and put Him to death. [2] But they said, Not on the feast *day,* lest there be an uproar of the people.

[3] ¶ And being in Bethany in the house of Simon the leper, as He sat at meat, there came a woman having an alabaster box of ointment of spikenard very precious; and she brake the box, and poured *it* on His head. [4] And there were some that had indignation within themselves, and said, "Why was this waste of the ointment made? [5] For it might have been sold for more than three hundred pence, and have been given to the poor." And they murmured against her. [6] And Jesus said, "Let her alone; why trouble ye her? she hath wrought a good work on Me. [7] For ye have the poor with you always, and whensoever ye will ye may do them good: but me ye have not always. [8] She hath done what she could: she is come aforehand to anoint My body to the burying. [9] Verily I say unto you, Wheresoever *this* gospel shall be preached throughout the whole world, this also that she hath done shall be spoken of for a memorial of her.

[10] ¶ And Judas Iscariot, one of the twelve, went unto the chief priests, to betray Him unto them. [11] And when they heard *it,* they were glad, and promised to give him money. And he sought how he might conveniently betray Him. ◄

NOW THE feast of unleavened bread drew nigh, which is called the Passover. [2] And the chief priests and scribes sought how they might kill Him; for they feared the people.

[3] ¶ Then entered Satan into Judas surnamed Iscariot, being of the number of the twelve. [4] And he went his way, and communed with the chief priests and captains, how he might betray Him unto them. [5] And they were glad, and covenanted to give him money. [6] And he promised, and sought opportunity to betray Him unto them in the absence of the multitude. ◄

Coup de Theatre
MATTHEW 26:1–16

When Jesus had finished the Discourse, He said to His disciples, "As you know, the Passover Feast is two days away . . . and the Son of Man will be handed over to be crucified!"

Then the chief priests and the elders of the people assembled in the palace of the high priest, whose name was Caiaphas. They plotted to arrest Jesus in some covert way and kill Him. "But not during the Feast," they said, "or there may be a riot among the people.". . .

Then one of the twelve, the one called Judas Iscariot, went to the chief priests and asked, "What are you willing to give me if I hand Him over to you?" So they counted out for him thirty silver coins. (arguria, Gk.) From then on, Judas watched for an opportunity to hand Him over.

— MATTHEW 26:1–5, 14–16

A SURPRISING, STARTLING, OR TRAUMATIC 'TURN OF EVENTS' IN A THEATRICAL drama is called a *coup de theatre* (Fr.). An audience often is lulled to sleep by the usual outcome of "Man against man," "Man against nature," or "Man against unrelenting fate." The actors seem to trudge across the stage with the usually spoken lines that lead to the inevitable conclusion, with a few quips here and a few lines of emoting there.

But in a well-scripted play, a *coup de theatre* pops up out of nowhere . . . although, the learned listener alertly suspects something is afoot . . . and the audience sits upright, with mouth agape and heart a'pounding. *"It's not suppose to end that way!" "What a revolting state of affairs!" "I never saw that coming, did you Martha?" "Well, blow me down, sport."*

The drama takes on a new, deeper, perhaps existential, meaning. The mundane becomes *nouveau*. The ordinary becomes spectacular. And more importantly, the mind becomes engaged.

Such is the case of the drama unfolding before us in the Evangel of Saint Matthew. Jesus had just informed the Twelve that He, the Son of Man, would be seen coming in the clouds of great glory. He would triumphantly bring judgment on the corrupt hypocrites of Judean politics and synagogue. Drawing from the prophecy (and imagery) of Daniel, He declared that He would reign over the Kingdom of God for a protracted period of time . . . even if as an absentee land-Lord . . . interacting with His citizenry through *messengers (aggelos;* prophets and pastors). And He would return as King and Judge of all mankind, *in glory with all the angels with Him.*

But then, He dropped a bomb-shell: There was soon to be a *coup d'etat!* The chief priests and elders were to rise up in rebellion, and seize the Son of God, and *hand Him over to the Romans to be crucified!* (26:1–2) The King of the Jews was to be "cut off" and end up with nothing. (Daniel 9:26–7)

The throne-room scenery was to be changed by the stage-hands. A two-faced actor was to take center stage. There was to be a mood swing of biblical proportions. There was to be a transition of power, but not in the usual way. As an aside, the stunned (some say dense) disciples were to wait for three days, whatever that meant.

ROAD SIGNS

The prophetic signs posted along the avenue of the Old Testament prophets are phenomenal! They were more than sufficient to lead the Magi from Persia to the little town of Bethlehem. No other religious figure in planetary history has had such an amazing introduction.

The supernatural signs that confirmed the Messianic character of Jesus are also mind-boggling. Those that describe His earthly ministry of miracle-working, and of His Divine character demonstrated miraculously, are unlike any other dignitary in human history. They were sufficient enough to bring peace of mind to John the Baptizer at his moment of martyrdom. Those signs were pointed enough to stop the thinking man in his tracks, and confront him with the greatest decision of his life: Bow before the Son of Man and accept His lordship.

The terrifying signs confirming the pending doom of Jerusalem and the destruction of the Temple were outstanding, as well. The *signs of the times* were as plain as the nose on an anteater . . . if only the rulers were not so blinded that they could not see them! (Luke 12:54–56) To those whose eyes were treated by the eye-salve of grace and mercy, those signs were able to warn them to flee to safety in times of most horrible conflagration and suffering.

TRANSITION SIGNS

Right after finishing the Olivet Discourse, Jesus repeatedly laid out 'the plans—and confirming sign—that would signal the *transition* from the Old Testament Mosaic Covenant to the New Testament Kingdom Covenant. He had previously given the "sign of Jonah" to describe this on-coming event, but few understood what He meant. (Luke 11:29–32; Matthew 12:38–42) Jesus had referred to this before. (Matthew 16:21; 17:22–23) Now He plainly declares:

> *As you know, the Passover is two days away, and the Son of Man*
> *will be handed over to be crucified.* (26:1–2)

Just outside of Jerusalem, in the suburb of Bethany, a woman came and anointed Jesus with very expensive perfume . . . to the chagrin of the self-interested disciples and the snooty Pharisees. But Jesus stopped eating His dinner, and announced in a sober tone, *When she poured the perfume on My body, she did it to prepare Me for burial.* (26:12) The Holy Spirit had given the humble lady more insight than all the religious men gathered around the Rabbi from Nazareth.

Amazingly, this event was foretold, by the inspiration of the Holy Spirit upon David, in the 23rd Psalm! This song-ode expressed the thoughts of Jesus just before the fateful Passover crucifixion:

> *The LORD is my Shepherd, I shall not want . . . He leads me . . . He*
> *guides me . . . even though I walk through the valley of the shadow of*
> *death, I will fear no evil for You are with me . . ..*
>
> *Thou preparest a table before me in the presence of my enemies.*
> *You anointest my head with oil; my cup overflows. Surely goodness*
> *and mercy (love) will follow me all the days of my life, and I will*
> *dwell in the House of the LORD forever.* (Psalm 23)

Just before His crucifixions Jesus was anointed at the dinner table in the presence of His antagonizers! Truth had been revealed unto "babes" and hidden from the "wise and learned" . . . Matthew 11:25) This woman's act is remembered "everywhere the Gospel is preached throughout the world"!

The death of Jesus, then, was the pivotal act — not just because it was foremost on the mind of Jesus — but it would be the fulcrum on which rested the transition from the worship at the Second Temple to worship in the new Kingdom of Heaven. The crucifixion would rip down the curtain of the Holy of Holies, and free the Presence of God to go dwell in the hearts of believers . . . in the inner sanctum of the souls of saints . . . in the minds of the multitudes who seek after holiness. (Matthew 27:51; John 14:23)

This act of ultimate rejection of Jesus by the Jewish establishment was the final straw that broke the camel's back on which had ridden all the ceremonial righteousness of the Israelis. *Fill up, then, the measure of sin of your forefathers. You snakes, you brood of vipers! How can you escape being condemned to hell?* (23:32–33) The destruction of the magnificently built Second Temple was sealed . . . it was only a matter of time . . . time which Jesus designated as *within the generation* (40 years, or 70 A.D.). The crucifixion was the point of no-return.

It now only had to be worked out, and for that, the Pharisees needed a mole, a spy, a Judas goat (26:14–16). The bribery would only cost 30 pieces of silver (27:1–10).

We are told that later, with pangs of conscience, Judas tried to return the money, but the Rabbis had a limit to their greed: no blood money! Notice the irony. These are men who had no qualms about ripping off widows, withholding money from orphans, setting up selling booths in the holy Temple mount with exorbitant exchange rates . . . but they didn't want to accept "blood money". That was beneath their dignity!

THE PROPHET DANIEL

This transition point is underscored by the amazing prophecy of Daniel in the ninth chapter of his book. With precise accuracy he foretold of the crucifixion . . . and the pivotal consequences associated with it: The end of the Second Temple with total desolation *and* the establishment of a New Covenant with no more need for daily sacrifices.

> *After sixty-two sevens* (years) *the Anointed One will be cut off, and there shall not be to Him* (a people) *. . . He will confirm a Covenant with the many for one "seven"* (years). *In the middle of the seven* (year period) *He will put an end to sacrifice and offering.* (Daniel 9:26–27)

After 3½ years of ministry, Jesus was indeed "cut off" (killed) by a people who had rejected Him from the get-go. This once-for-all death of Christ, as the Passover Lamb, forever put an end to animal sacrifice as atonement for mankind's sins. (Hebrews 10:1–12; see also 1 Peter 1:18–19)

This rejection of Christ by His own people was heart-breaking. He was a marked man from birth (by Herod) . . . He was mocked by rulers of the synagogue . . . He was hunted down by assassins of the Pharisees . . . He was unjustly arrested and beaten by corrupt police . . . and innocently convicted as a felonious criminal for blasphemy. He had no "people" on His side, nor anyone to "watch His back."

> *He came to His own (people), and His own receive Him not.* (John 1:11) *As He approached Jerusalem . . . He wept.* (Luke 19:41)

Jesus was a "cornerstone" rejected by the movers and shakers of Israel. He was forever bidding people come "to supper", but none showed up. He was faithfully working in His Father's vineyard, but the husbandmen decided to kill Him. (Matthew 21:42; Luke 14:23–24; Luke 20:13–19) He was "cut off" and with "no people to call His own," like Daniel prophesied.

But . . . good news! In the midst of all this sad commentary on human nature, there is the working out of the Providence of the Almighty: A New Covenant is "confirmed." And with it, the ending of all the animal sacrifices. More about this later.

Right now, we need to recognize the dire consequences of the evil act of rejecting the Messiah by killing Him. Daniel also mentioned these events in chapter nine . . . and he ties them in with the "cutting off."

> *The people of the Prince who will come will destroy the city, the Sanctuary. The end will come like a flood; war will continue until the end, and desolations have been decreed . . . on the wing of the Temple he will set up an abomination that causes desolation . . .* (Daniel 9:26–27)

As we have seen, this has been the topic of Jesus from the scathing review of the Pharisees in Matthew chapter 23, through the description of this desolation in chapter 24. Jesus even referred to the prophet, Daniel, and warned the people to take note of this foreboding doom he spoke about. (24:15) The destruction of Jerusalem and the Temple were to be totally devastating . . . wiped clean out . . . finished with.

And, in the fantastic Providence and Sovereign plan of God, it was for good reason: That something better may take place. It is hard to remodel an old, rickety house with a crumbling foundation, as every construction company foreman knows. It is better to bull-doze all the rotten wood, and cracked walls, and shattered windows, and leaking roof tiles . . . and haul them away . . . and build on a better foundation, if need be, from scratch. It may take a little more effort and sweat and time, but the end product is much better in the long run. It's a pivotal decision.

In the sacrifice of the Lamb of God, in the crucifixion of Christ, in the giving of His own Son, in this pivotal deed, God was about to open up the free gift of salvation to the whole world . . . to all peoples . . . Jew or Greek, rich or poor, ugly or handsome, prostitute or professional! The *wrath of man* was going *to bring praise to God* in a unique way. (Psalm 76:10) It would precipitate the ending of the Old Covenant, but it would usher in with fullness, the Kingdom of God!

NOW, NOT YET

It should be noted that several biblical commentators refer to the Kingdom as "Now, Not yet". To them it seems that some of the statements of Jesus claim the Kingdom is *present*, that is, it has come. But they have problems with other verses which seem to imply that the Kingdom is yet *future*. They have come up with the compromising phrase, "Now, and not yet." They look for some future inauguration, or such.

This confusion can easily be resolved, like noon-day sun-rays clearing away the morning fog, when scholars realize that just like any other "switching of the guard", there is a *period of transition*. There is always a short time period when one entity exits and the other begins in an overlapping fashion.

Such is the case with the Kingdom of God (Heaven). When Jesus was making His pronouncements about this exciting spiritual Establishment, the old Mosaic system was still in place in Israel. The great Temple, redecorated by Herod, was still standing. Animal sacrifices were still being slaughtered, and offered on altars. There was still a Levitical high priest walking around the halls.

Indeed, the Kingdom that Jesus taught was "at hand." But the sweeping away of the physical obstacles still needed to be done . . . and this was accomplished in 70 A.D. when the Old Covenant Temple was totally destroyed . . . desolate . . . demolished . . . thrown into the historical dust-bin of discarded cultures. The Davidical kingdom concept was swept aside by the broom of John the Baptizer, so that Jesus, *the King of the Jews* (and everybody else) could take the throne! But it took the Roman legions, later, to finish the job of clearing away the debris . . . what military men call a "mopping up action."

The Kingdom of God could accurately be called "at hand" by Jesus, but clear evidence of it would only finally be when the Temple was destroyed a little later. The transition period, then, would be from 30 A.D. to 70 A.D.

There is nothing in the teaching of King Jesus that would necessitate thinking there is to be some future aspect of the Kingdom that has not already been realized. *The king is dead, long live the King!* is most appropriate now. Jesus reigns in majesty! Jack Hayford's chorus "Majesty" tells it all! *His anthem we raise!* Jesus, now, is King of Kings, and Lord of lords.

This does not mean all is rosy. There are many traitors, invaders, in the realm. Not all the citizens get along peaceably. Some elders are not "public servants" but "lord it over" the people. But all these will be dealt with eventually, when the Day of Judgment comes, and a pure, noble kingdom will be handed over to the Father by Jesus. (1 Corinthians 15:24)

The rest of the citizens enjoy the benefits of a most gracious and benevolent King. They revel in the Presence of His glory and power. They rejoice, along with the angels, in the splendor of His holiness. And they hope in a most glorious consummation of His reign!

TIMES THEY ARE 'A CHANGING

From that time on Jesus began to preach, "Repent, for the Kingdom of Heaven is at hand." (Mtt. 4:17) The Law and the Prophets were until John; since that time the Gospel of the Kingdom of God is being preached. (Luke 16:16)

The Law was put in charge to Lead us to Christ . . . now that faith has come, we are no Longer under the supervision of the Law. (Gal. 3:24–25)

O Jerusalem, Jerusalem, you who kill the prophets and stone those sent to you . . . Look, your House is Left to you desolate. (Luke 13:34)

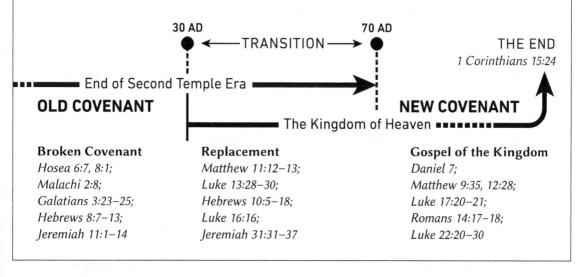

Broken Covenant
Hosea 6:7, 8:1;
Malachi 2:8;
Galatians 3:23–25;
Hebrews 8:7–13;
Jeremiah 11:1–14

Replacement
Matthew 11:12–13;
Luke 13:28–30;
Hebrews 10:5–18;
Luke 16:16;
Jeremiah 31:31–37

Gospel of the Kingdom
Daniel 7;
Matthew 9:35, 12:28;
Luke 17:20–21;
Romans 14:17–18;
Luke 22:20–30

The end of the Second Temple era occured in 70 AD, and the Third Temple, *the spiritual* or *heavenly Temple not made with hands* was to be the focus of the Church. And for centuries Jesus and His Church were given due attention, but in modern times these have been replaced with "the nation of Israel"! Instead of recognizing the initiation of a *New Covenant* with the Kingdom of Heaven, modern prophecy televangelists have promoted Judaizers' perspectives just like the Pharisees who replaced Jesus's teaching with a nationalistic hope.

True "replacement", however, acknowledges the Good News of Jesus's reign in grace and mercy, instead of the Law of Moses which could never make anyone perfect, as the Holy Bible teaches.

MODERN COUP D'ETAT

Many Judaizers have infiltrated the modern evangelical arena and battled against those who seem to advocate a *Replacement Theology*. With gladiator ferocity they mock such an idea, and maintain that the nation of Israel is, and will always be, the center of the "plan of the ages" They accuse those who advocate the centrality of "Christ and the Church" of replacing the Jews with Gentiles . . . of switching the Israeli nation with the Christian congregations . . . of changing a Jewish nationalistic hope with a spiritual emphasis.

But a survey of history will show just the opposite! From the first century of Gospel presentation until the middle of the 1800s, the majority of believers taught the centrality of Christ as savior for all people groups. Believers preached that the Old Testament prophecies were fulfilled in the establishment of a New Covenant wherein the Church played the prominent role. It has been the new sects like Darbyism and Messianic congregationalism that *replaced the Church* with a Jewish nationalistic focus! Those guilty of "replacement theology" are relatively modern prophecy teachers and televangelists who have fallen prey to another Gospel. (Galatians 1:6–9)

WHAT JESUS TAUGHT

Why did the Early Church and the believers for centuries thereafter have Christ and the Church as the focus of their catechisms? It was because Jesus introduced the idea and drove it home to His disciples and Apostles. The Luke epistle recorded the beginning of the Gospel (good news) by writing that the Christmas angels declared: *I bring you good news of great joy that will be for **all** people. Today . . . a Savior has been born.* (Luke 2:10–11)

To be sure, for all people to have a Savior, Jesus had to walk down a bumpy road with a lot of obstacles put in His way . . . by Rabbis . . . by religious seminarians of all people . . . by demons, even. *He came unto His own (people) but they received Him not. But to all who received Him, to those who believed in His name, He gave the right to become Sons of God.* (John 1:11–12) The Messianic message Jesus presented, the Gospel of the Kingdom at hand, eventually led to His being crucified, "cut off", and buried.

But during all of this contention and controversy, Jesus saw glimmers of hope sparkling in the eyes of common folk . . . Roman soldiers . . . Phoenician foreigners . . . and prostitutes, tax-collectors, and the like! He recognized perked up ears, and lifted heads, eager to hear more about the Kingdom of Heaven. He saw fertile soil in the open hearts of burdened pilgrims, ready for the planting of the seeds of the *evangelion*. If the establishment would not receive Him, these people certainly would. The riotous rabbis would be replaced by the meek and lowly in spirit. Rejected by the synagogue, Jesus would build a Church, and the gates of hades would not prevail over it!

> *Jesus saith unto them, "Did you never read in the Scriptures, 'The Stone which the builders rejected, the same is become the Head of the corner; this is the Lord's doing, and it is marvelous in our eyes'? Therefore I say unto you, the Kingdom of God shall be taken from you, and given to a nation bringing forth the fruits thereof."* (Matthew 21:42–43)

> *Go out into the highways and hedges, and compel them to come in, that My house may be filled. For I say unto you, that none of these men which were bidden shall taste of My supper.* (Luke 14:23–24)

> *I will send My beloved Son; it may be they will reverence Him when they see Him. But when the husbandmen saw Him, they reasoned among themselves) saying, "This is the heir; come, let us kill Him, that the inheritance may be ours." . . . What therefore shall the Lord of the vineyard do unto them? He shall come and destroy these husbandmen and shall give the vineyard to others . . . And the chief priests and the scribes . . . perceived that He had spoken this parable against them.* (Luke 20:13–19)

> *Jesus said to (the chief priests and elders), "I tell you the truth, the tax collectors and the prostitutes are entering the Kingdom of God ahead of you."* (Matthew 21 :31)

> *I say to you that many will come from the east and the west, and will take their places at the feast with Abraham, Isaac, and Jacob in the Kingdom of Heaven. But the citizens of the Kingdom will be*

> *thrown outside, into the darkness, where there will be weeping and*
> *gnashing of teeth.* (Matthew 8:11–12)

In a very real sense, Jesus Himself was an advocate of *replacement theology!* He did not hesitate to fill the Kingdom pews with a church full of people from all nations (Gentiles; Gk. *ethnos*) . . . and eject the brazen bullies who hogged the "chief seats." He instituted a Church that was spiritual in nature, replacing the nationalistic interpretation of the scribes and elders. Jesus put a premium on holiness of heart, ousting those who were heady and high-minded. In a way, those who walk in the footsteps of Jesus can wear this label as a badge of honor! With the fulfilling of prophecy, Jesus replaced Moses.

Those who wish to revert back to the nationalistic propensities of the Pharisees and Sadducees, and who want to place undo emphasis upon a physical nation of Israel, are the ones who should be embarrassed by the label of "replacement theologians." They are replacing the teaching of Jesus with non-biblical ideology. They are *reverting back* to an old and obsolete covenant of curses. (Galatians 3:1–14)

SPIRITUAL KINGDOM

There is nothing more clear in the Gospels than the fact that Jesus came to establish a *spiritual kingdom*, and not rule over Israel like a human king does. (John 6:15) He presented Himself to Israel *as gentle, riding on a donkey, on a colt, the foal of a donkey, with children shouting praise.* (Zechariah 9:9; Matthew 21:1–17) At first, He was given a crown of thorns . . . placed on a wooden throne . . . hailed by pagan soldiers . . . coronated by a Roman governor . . . and anointed with spit. (Matthew 27:27–32) This was hardly the beginning of an Israeli kingship of a nationalistic nature.

Instead, Jesus heralded the transition from the idea of a kingdom headquartered on some real estate in the Mideast, to the reality of a spiritual kingdom where the King's domain was centered in the hearts of meek and lowly citizenry . . . where the King's power would be manifest over spiritual powers (demons, evil spirits, and human nature) . . . where justice and righteousness reigned supreme. (1 Corinthians 3:16)

This replacement was actually the fulfillment of Old Testament prophecies . . . of all that the Mosaic system symbolized . . . of all that the holy men of old looked forward to. It was the desire of the ages! (Malachi 3:1; Matthew 13:17)

> *From the days of John the Baptizer until now, the Kingdom of*
> *Heaven has been suffering violence, and the violent take it by force.*
> *For all the Law and Prophets prophesied* **until** *John.* (Mtt. 11: 12–13)

The Law and the Prophets were proclaimed **until** *John. Since that time, the Gospel of the Kingdom of God is being preached . . .* (Luke 16:16)

And of His fullness we have received blessing after blessing. For the Law was given through Moses; grace and truth came through Jesus Christ. (John 1:6–17)

If I cast out demons by the Spirit of God, then the Kingdom **has come** *upon you!* (Matthew 12:28)

Once, having been asked by the Pharisees when the Kingdom of God would come, Jesus answered, "The Kingdom of God does not come with your careful observation, nor will people say, 'Here it is,' or 'There it is,' because the Kingdom of God is within you. (Luke 17:20–21)

Let the little children come unto Me and do not hinder them, for the Kingdom of God belongs to such as these. I tell you the truth, anyone who does not receive the Kingdom of God like a little child will never enter it. (Luke 18:16–17)

The nationalistic Pharisees of the first century did not respond very favorably to Jesus's announcement of the Kingdom and of its spiritual nature . . . nor do twenty-first century evangelical prophecy teachers like this idea of a transition from thinking of a physical kingdom to a spiritual kingdom. But they have no say in the matter! It is the word of the King that is the law of the realm. He is the Master Teacher at whose feet true disciples must sit. His teaching takes precedent over evangelical novels and movies and conference lectures. (Matthew 23:8–10) There can be no more clearer statements: God's kingdom is a spiritual realm with citizenship open to **all** peoples who believe. And the Church remains the major proclaimer of this message until Christ returns in glory. *Local churches* are embassies in all nations for the Kingdom of God!

DAVID'S THRONE

The angel Gabriel announced to Mary the birth of Jesus with a fantastic prophecy that underscored the institution of a *spiritual kingdom* ruled over by Christ:

Behold, you will conceive in your womb, and bring forth a Son, and shall call His name 'Jesus'. He will be great, and will be called the Son of the Most High. The LORD God will give Him the throne of His

> *father David, and He will reign over the House of Jacob forever. His*
> *Kingdom will never end!* (Luke 1:31–33)

A topical study of the words "king" and "kingdom" in the Gospels does confirm that Jesus announced to the Jews that *"the kingdom was at hand"*, and that a person had to repent, humble himself, and be born again—that is, be born of the Spirit (John 3:5–8)—in order to become a citizen of it. He prophesied that people in the first century would see it manifest in power. (Mark 9:1; Luke 9:27)

But, in spite of Jesus's teaching, there are Judaizers (wolves in sheep's clothing) who insist that Gabriel's words have not been fulfilled. They look forward to a day when Jesus will rule on a literal, physical throne in the Mideast city of Jerusalem, with a rebuilt Mosaic/Davidic Temple with animal sacrifices. They insist upon a "physical" interpretation of all the angel's words.

Since, they argue, the first three aspects of this announcement were "physical" (literal), then the last two, concerning the rule, and reign, must also be physical in nature. Jesus has to sit on a real stone throne (or gilded wood), and govern a nation of Israelites in the capitol city of Jerusalem, situated in the piece of real estate known today as the Mideast.

FLAWED HERMENEUTIC

This type of reasoning is flawed on several points, and it ignores the teaching of Jesus about His own Kingdom. Any teaching like this dogma, which is contrary to the Gospel, can only have serious consequences which must be warned about.

First, notice that the *ruler* of the Kingdom of God was not just a physical man grown from a physical baby of normal birth. Jesus was not a common human being. He was conceived by the *Holy Spirit*. His Father was God! And it must not be forgotten that God is a *spirit*. (John 4:24) So Jesus was a "spirit-man", that is, God incarnated. Jesus was divine spirit Who had a human body prepared for Him to temporarily occupy. (Hebrews 10:5; Psalm 40:6 LXX)

Therefore, it is more reasonable to conclude that Jesus would be more interested in establishing a spiritual type of kingdom, than an earthly, temporal type. Deity, a divine Spirit, would hardly be satisfied with ruling over something that grows old and passes away. *For what is seen is temporary, but what is unseen is eternal.* (2 Corinthians 4:18). Paul realized that the spiritual nature of Jesus, not the physical, must be kept foremost in our thoughts (2 Corinthians 5:16)—a point prophecy lecturers ignore.

Secondly, it is important to understand what is meant by interpreting the scriptures (or any piece of ancient literature). "Hermeneutics" is the science of exegesis, or drawing out from the text what is originally meant by the author to convey. The principles of this science prevent the reader from "reading into" the text ideas that aren't really there.

Note that the opposite of *literal* is not "spiritual", it is *figurative*, or symbolic. Beside the literal meaning of a passage, there are many "figures of speech" often employed in writing: hyperbole, simile, litotes, synecdoche, metaphor, metonymy, oxymoron, et al. Also note that the antonym of spiritual is not "literal", but "physical."

For our discussion, we must also acknowledge that the Holy Bible uses the method of *typology* to show fulfillment, or higher sense of fulfillment, of Old Testament persons, events, *and* prophecies (prophetic promises). (E.g. 1 Peter 3:20–22, where Noah's flood is a type of baptism.) Paul used *allegory* to demonstrate the casting out of the Old Covenant by referring to Hagar, Abraham's concubine. (Galatians 4:21–31) So literal, historical events can take on a *spiritual* meaning in New Testament theology.

Modern prophecy teachers (a.k.a., Judaizers), however, take the position of a dual hermeneutic. Instead of letting the New Testament be the basis for interpreting the Old Testament, they let men's interpretation of the Old Testament be the dominant factor in understanding the Bible. And they believe, as C. I. Scofield led them, "Historical Scriptures have an allegorical or spiritual significance . . . [But in prophetic scriptures] we reach the ground of absolute literalness." *(Scofield Bible Correspondence Course, Chicago: Moody Bible Institute)*

This means that they can find many *christological-ecclessiological* fulfillments in the historical parts of the O.T., but they will only allow *national Israeli* fulfillments in the prophetic parts. They admit allegory in the first, but only a strict literalism in the second! They resign the New Testament to the sphere of the Church (with Gentile emphasis), but they refuse to let the Old Testament be anything but the prophetic playground of the State of Israel.

Consequentially, all the aspects of Gabriel's announcement—which they would consider part of the Old Testament era (before the preaching of John)—must have a literal fulfillment that is to be applied only to the State of Israel, they argue. Jesus hasn't fulfilled these prophetic statements because He isn't sitting on a literal throne in Jerusalem, and He isn't reigning over the Israeli nation yet, they allege.

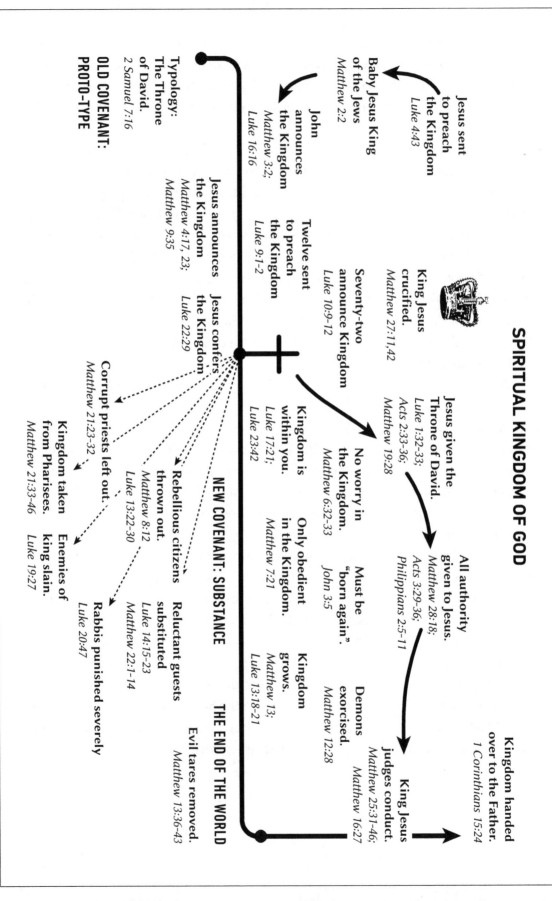

SPIRITUAL KINGDOM OF GOD

OLD COVENANT: PROTO-TYPE

Typology:
The Throne
of David.
2 Samuel 7:16

Jesus sent
to preach
the Kingdom
Luke 4:43

Baby Jesus King
of the Jews
Matthew 2:2

John
announces
the Kingdom
Matthew 3:2;
Luke 16:16

Jesus announces
the Kingdom
Matthew 4:17, 23;
Matthew 9:35

Twelve sent
to preach
the Kingdom
Luke 9:1-2

Seventy-two
announce Kingdom
Luke 10:9-12

King Jesus
crucified.
Matthew 27:11,42

Jesus confers
the Kingdom
Luke 22:29

NEW COVENANT: SUBSTANCE

Corrupt priests left out.
Matthew 21:23-32

Rebellious citizens
thrown out.
Matthew 8:12
Luke 13:22-30

Reluctant guests
substituted
Luke 14:15-23
Matthew 22:1-14

Kingdom taken
from Pharisees.
Matthew 21:33-46

Rabbis punished severely
Luke 20:47

Kingdom is
within you.
Luke 17:21;
Luke 23:42

Only obedient
in the Kingdom.
Matthew 7:21
John 3:5

No worry in
the Kingdom.
Matthew 6:32-33

Must be
"born again".
Matthew 7:21

Kingdom
grows.
Matthew 13;
Luke 13:18-21

Demons
exorcised.
Matthew 12:28

Jesus given the
Throne of David.
Luke 1:32-33;
Acts 2:33-36;
Matthew 19:28

All authority
given to Jesus.
Matthew 28:18;
Acts 3:29-36;
Philippians 2:5-11

King Jesus
judges conduct.
Matthew 25:31-46;
Matthew 16:27

THE END OF THE WORLD

Enemies of
king slain.
Luke 19:27

Evil tares removed.
Matthew 13:36-43

Kingdom handed
over to the Father.
1 Corinthians 15:24

This unyielding literalism has been strenuously advocated by Tim LaHaye, who wrote, "The best guide to Bible study is 'The Golden Rule of Biblical Interpretation . . . When the plain sense of Scripture makes common sense, seek no other sense, but take every word at its primary, literal meaning unless the facts of the immediate context clearly indicate otherwise." *(No Fear of the Storm,* 1992, p. 240)

However, a casual reading of LaHaye . . . and his fellow Judaizer's books reveals that they are not consistent with their own hermeneutic methodology. Such literalness leads to absurd interpretations. Consider the following:

— Is Jesus really going to "sit on David's throne"? Does David's throne still exist somewhere? Was it not demolished by the invading armies of Egypt or Babylon, long ago? Is the literal idea of a physical throne what we are to take away from this prophecy of Gabriel? Probably not!

— Is David the "father" of Jesus? Really? Are we to take this literally? Or could this be a figurative statement referring to a distant relative of Jesus (on His mother's side)?

  It is interesting that Jesus, just before His Olivet Discourse (Matthew 23–25), approached the Jewish scholars with this conundrum when He quoted Psalm 110:1 *(The LORD said to my Lord, 'Sit at my right hand until I put your enemies under your feet.),* "If then David calls him 'Lord', how can he be his son?"

  Obviously, parts of Gabriel's prophecy must be taken in a sense other than literal.

They also show the unfeasible nature of their methodology by interpreting Ezekiel's prophecies about warfare using "bows and arrows, war clubs and spears" as descriptions of jets, missiles, and atomic bombs! Not a violation of "The Golden Rule", but an adherence *to* it, leads to all forms of confusion and sometimes even heresy.

Although teleprophets on "Christian" media defy the authority of New Testament authors, and Jesus Himself, to interpret the Old Testament prophecies, still, *the best interpreter of Scripture is Scripture.* And this applies to the verses of our study here in Luke.

On the Day of Pentecost, Peter preached a rousing sermon that has echoed around the marbled halls of Judaism, and resounded in the cathedrals of nations across the blue planet. In it, he addressed this issue of Christ's reign upon the throne of David: Past, present, or way off in the future?

> *Men and brothers, let me speak freely to you of the patriarch David,*
> *that he is both dead and buried, and his tomb is with us to this day.*
> *Therefore, being a prophet, and knowing that God had sworn an oath*
> *to him that of the fruit of his body, according 'to the flesh, He would*
> *raise up the Christ* **to sit on his throne** *— he foreseeing this —* **spoke**
> **concerning the resurrection of the Christ,** *that His soul was not*
> *left in Hades, nor did His flesh see corruption.*
>
> *This Jesus God has raised up, of which we are all witnesses. There-*
> *fore, being* **exalted to the right hand of God,** *and having received*
> *from the Father the promise of the Holy Spirit, He poured out this*
> *which you now see and hear.*
>
> *For David did not ascend into the heavens, but he says himself:*
> *'The* LORD *said to my Lord, Sit at My right hand till I make Your ene-*
> *mies Your footstool.*
>
> *Therefore, let all the* **House of Israel** *[house of Jacob] know*
> *assuredly that God has made this Jesus, whom you crucified, both*
> *Lord and Christ.* (Acts 2:29–36)

When we leave behind the opinions of novelists and movie directors and turn from the speculations of prophetic conference lecturers . . . and rely upon the *inspired writings* of the Early Church . . . and stick to the pronouncements of Jesus Himself . . . we can clearly see that Jesus has been raised to sit on the Throne of David, and that He has been given all authority in heaven and in earth!

The Apostle Peter has made it clear that the burden of the Old Testament proph-ets — as well as the historical typology — was *concerning this salvation, the grace that was to come . . . predicting the sufferings of Christ, and the glories that would follow . . . They spoke of the things that have now been told you by those who have preached 'the Gospel' . . .* (1 Peter 1:10–12). The prophets foretold of the Gospel, not of Zionism.

As far as "the House of Jacob" is to be interpreted, Peter is not silent, either: . . .

> *You also, like living stones, are being built into a* **spiritual House** *to*
> *be a holy priesthood, offering spiritual sacrifices acceptable to God*
> *through Jesus Christ. For the Scripture says:*
>
> *See, I lay in Zion a stone, a chosen and precious cornerstone; and*
> *the one who trusts in Him will never be put to shame.* (See Isa. 28:16)
>
> *Now, to you who believe, this stone is precious. But to those who*
> *do not believe: "The stone the builders rejected has become the cap-*
> *stone"* (see Psalm 118:22)*, and, "a stone that causes men to stumble*
> *and a rock that makes them fall"* (see Isaiah 8:14).

> *They stumble because they disobey the message . . . but you are*
> *a chosen people, a royal priesthood, a holy nation, a people belong-*
> *ing to God, that you may declare the praises of Him who has called*
> *you out of darkness into His marvelous light. Once you were not a*
> *people, but now you are the people of God . . . (1 Peter 2:5–10)*

The "House of Jacob" that King Jesus reigns over is, according to the inspired Apostle, a *spiritual House*, comprised of believing Jews and of Gentiles, who offer up *spiritual sacrifices*, not physical animals in a rebuilt temple. This is the *holy Nation* that the Old Testament prophets foresaw in the Spirit . . . not a State in the Mideast.

If modern propheteers wish to throw accusations of "spiritualizing, allegorizing, and promoting typology", then it must be directed at the inspired holy men of the New Testament! Or . . . modernists could stop using the hermeneutic of the first century Pharisees who also looked for a nationalistic Messiah, but crucified Jesus when He spoke of a spiritual kingdom instead . . . and a spiritual King instead . . . and a "born again" citizenry instead of corrupt teachers of the Law. They could heed Peter's warning:

> *Above all, you must understand that no prophecy of Scripture came*
> *about by the prophet's own interpretation. For prophecy never had*
> *its origin in the will of man, but men spoke from God as they were*
> *inspired by the Holy Spirit.*
> *But there were also false prophets among the people, just as*
> *there will be* **false teachers** *among you. They will secretly introduce*
> *destructive heresies . . . (2 Peter 1:20–2:1)*

Just as there are "judases" today in the 21st century, there was the Judas in the 1st century. Having come from Judea, instead of Galilee like the other Eleven, he was indoctrinated in the nationalistic hopes of the scribes and Pharisees. Jesus's concept of a *spiritual kingdom* was a major let-down to him. For economic prosperity there must be a financial capitol.

The mole cooperated with the antagonists; the anti-hero tried to find some skinny on Jesus that he could take back to his sponsors; the betrayer looked for an occasion to trip Him up. Something, anything, to accuse Him of to Caesar or to Moses. He really had to earn his 30 pieces of silver.

He eventually returned to his conspirators, and they asked him what he had gathered for them. What information they could use in court. Judas could only reply: *I know where He prays.*

What?! You know where He prays?! No sin, no treason, no iniquity found in His mouth? The chief priests were irate. *I told you so,* an Aramithean said.

I know where He prays. That's all Judas could say.

Really, Judas! You expect us to . . . wait a minute . . . come here, Judas, I've got an idea. Everyone grab a torch.

And thus the *coup de theatre* burst forth on the night scene . . . under a full moon of hypocrisy . . . with a background of bleating lambs ready to be slain, and a praying Passover Lamb ready to be . . .

ADDENDA

CRISIS OF DECISION

In the tumultuous history of mankind there have been strategic moments when there was a crisis of decision. When Caesar reached the Rubicon . . . when Travis drew the line in the sands of the Alamo . . . when Eisenhower stepped across the English Channel . . .

The history of the Israeli people is no different. There were momentous challenges in their prophetic pageantry when "choice" was crucial. There were major occasions when a man of God confronted that nation with a "yes" or a "no" . . . progress, or the same old, same old . . . destiny or disaster.

FOUR PERIODS

There are four epochs in Jewish history that each extend over a period of approximately 400 years. The author of Galatians recorded a time of 430 years from Abraham to Moses (the Law) . . . The chronicler of the Kings gave a span of 480 years from Moses (the exodus) to Solomon (building of the Temple) . . . The prophets declared Israel would go into captivity "one year for each of her Sabbath years she desecrated" (70 × 7 = 490) during the times of the kings (Rehoboam to Josiah) . . . And there were 490 years from the return of the exiles unto Christ, the Messiah.

What is interesting is not just the similar length of time that each epoch occurred, but that each epoch ended in *disaster* . . . national punishment. The *first* one ended with the whole nation of people who had experienced the wonders of the Egyptian plagues and the crossing of the Red Sea, being slain in the wilderness of wandering . . . The *second* epoch ended with the traumatic ripping asunder of the grand Israeli nation that Solomon had made the envy of the world. Ten tribes split from the reign of David's Throne, inaugurating a whole history of oppression and tyranny . . . The *third* passage of time was marked by the invasion of Judah by the Babylonians with the destruction of the First Temple and the city of Jerusalem. While many of the *hoi polloi* were forced to maintain the crops and herds in the land, the cultural elite were all exiled to foreign lands and to strangers of foreign gods . . . The *fourth* and final era ended with the total destruction of the Second Temple, and a ransacking of all the land of Judea by the Roman Legions (which is the main thrust of our present study in Matthew).

CRISIS OF DECISION

At the end of every epoch, notice that the people were given a destiny-determining moment to decide their fate. The Israelis came to a point of opting which would determine whether they would be blessed in years to come, or not . . . whether they would have years of blessing and promised happy living out their days . . . or whether they would all die accursed and in sorrow. At each crucial time, God confronted them with a choice, a matter of faith or of doubt. The word "if" stands out unmistakably. It is such a small word, but it is a fulcrum upon which destiny is balanced. History teeters and totters on it.

On this little word the future of the Jewish peoples was placed time and again:

1. Would they have faith in God's ability to take them into the Promised Land in spite of the giants? *If* they believed, they were assured they could.
2. Would Solomon and his descendants remain upon the throne of David immemorably? *If* they followed the Lord whole-heartedly, without resorting to idolatry, they could.
3. Would Josiah's reforms be sufficient to change the hearts of the people away from cultural depravity, and ensure their future as a nation? *If* they were able to, they could.
4. Would Jesus's own people accept His messiahship, and message of the Gospel of the Kingdom? *If* they humbled themselves as a little child, they could. They could have.

PASSOVER

Notice that these important times of decision were highlighted by the Feast of Passover. By the offering of this sacrifice — and by the gracious acceptance of its shed blood in Heaven — all past sins were atoned for. At this moment, God was willing to "let bygones be bygones" so to speak. Jehovah God was not going to hold past failures as a hindrance to the people's destiny. History did not trump destiny. Sins were washed from the rap sheet of Jacob. The Lamb's blood atoned for all transgressions.

There were, therefore, no spiritual obstacles . . . no unresolved guilt . . . no demonic forces . . . that would have been able to prevent the Israelis from moving forward with God's blessing. By this sacrificial substitute, they would have received good from the hand of the LORD.

This Passover lamb was symbolic in the first three instances of crisis decision making, we must note. But all that the Passover pointed forward to in essence was fulfilled in Jesus and His crucifixion. (John 1:29, 1 Peter 1:18–19) Jesus was the Lamb of God, and it was through His blood that provision was made for the Jews to enter into the Kingdom of God and be blessed immemorial. (Along with all believing Gentiles)

(Solomon's sacrifice is not specifically mentioned as a Passover. He presented many animals to be sacrificed at his royal inauguration, though, which included, no doubt, sin offerings to atone for past iniquities and transgressions.)

40 YEARS

The charting of these epochs in Israeli history reveals, amazingly, that there was a time period of forty years between the moment of decision and the ultimate judgment when doubt trumped faith in God. This not only underscores the seriousness of decision-making, but the repetition of this exact number underlines the reality of *Providence in history.* There is no way that a person can say God's warning of judgment is carried out just by chance or coincidence. It puts to silence the voice of scoffers who say "nations come and go at will" . . . "everything goes on like it always has."

God speaks . . . things happen . . . His word does not return to Him voided by a serendipity of events. He speaks, and angels carry out His will without failure . . . right on time.

The Jewish rabbis should have realized that, based upon their past historical decisions, and God's stern response to them, that the words of Jesus should have been taken seriously. When He warned that all the threats of destruction would take place within *that generation,* they ought to have known they only had 40 years left. The pattern was too real to ignore. It is no wonder Jesus was so perplexed because they *could not discern the signs of the times,* nor the signs of past historical judgments. (Luke 11:50–51; 12:54–56; 13:34–35; 19:41–44)

CRISIS OF DECISION

	430 YEARS	Passover "If"	40 YEARS
Abraham	Gal. 3:17	Joshua (Moses)	Generation
Genesis 22:15–18		Exodus 12;	Destroyed
		Numbers 14	Deut. 2:14–15;
			Joshua 5:6

	440 YEARS	Passover "If"	40 YEARS
Exodus	1 Kings 6:1	Jedidiah (Solomon)	Empire
(Moses)		1 Kings 11;	Destroyed
Exodus 12		2 Chronicles 1:6	1 Kings 11:29–40

	450 YEARS (490–40)	Passover "If"	40 YEARS
		18 13 11 11 14	
Rehoboam	*70 Sabbaticals*	Josiah	Jerusalem
1 Kings 12:1–24	*Unobserverd*	2 Kings 23:21	Destroyed
	2 Chronicles 36:21		Jer. 25:1–11; 52:30;
			2 Chron. 36:15–17

	440 YEARS (490–50)	Passover "If"	40 YEARS
Ezra	Daniel 9:24–25	Jesus	Temple Destroyed
Malachi		(John)	70 A.D.
2 Chronicles		John 13:1	Matthew 23–24

The forty years for pending judgment also seem to emphasize for us, the fact that it only takes "one generation" of hard-hearted wickedness to bring about irreconcilable judgment. When a nation decides by judicial activism, or by secular education, or by cultural idolatry, or by political corruption, or by media immorality . . . to go their own way, and become *sons of Belial*, the die is cast. The next generation, indoctrinated and steeped in wickedness, has no hope of recovery. When the light of righteousness is snuffed out, people walking around in darkness tend to stumble. When a decision to forsake God is made, disaster is certain . . . justice comes knocking at the city gate.

SOVEREIGN PLAN

One more necessary commentary: We here notice the persistent and persevering character of Jehovah God in sticking with a nation to fulfill His plan for humanity's salvation, even though the vehicle through which He had chosen to accomplish it repeatedly and continually was bent on corrupting itself. God continued on through not one, not two, not three, but four epoch cycles of historical degradation, to bring all mankind to the revelation of the Messiah, the Savior of the world. God never gave up. Nothing was going to hinder the manifestation of *His love* for people in saving them from sin . . . from themselves . . . from a trivial life. (John 3:16)

Regardless of who He had to work with, God was able to see to it that there was a caretaker of the prophetic Word that would guide the wise in thought to Bethlehem. He put up with an obstinate aristocracy until it proved out to be a *schoolmaster* to lead mankind into a mature relationship with the Father God.

And lest we be wise in our own conceit, we hasten to admit that God puts up with us, vessels of clay, to continue to work out planetary history for good, and for His glory. (2 Corinthians 4:7; Romans 11:11–24) He has been merciful, as well, in saving a *remnant of Jewish people* in every generation . . . men like Simeon who've awaited for the Consolation of Israel, righteous, devout, and led by the Holy Spirit . . . women like Anna, who worship, fast, and pray, and give thanks to God for the Child, and speak to all who are looking forward to the redemption of Jerusalem (Luke 2:25–38)

CURTAIN
SPEECH

SPEAK TO ME, YOU WHO WANT TO BE under the Law, are you not aware of what the Law says? For it is written that Abraham had two sons: one by the slave woman and the other by the free woman . . . These may be taken figuratively, for these women represent **two covenants**. . . . Hagar stands for Mount Sinai, and gives birth to slaves—this Hagar is in Arabia, and corresponds to Jerusalem which now is, and who is in slavery with her children.

But the Jerusalem that is above (heavenly and spiritual) is free, and is the mother of us all. . . .

What does the scripture say? "Cast out the slave woman and her son." . . . Brothers, we, therefore, are not children of the slave woman, but of the free woman.

— *Galatians 4:21–31*

CURTAIN SPEECH
MATTHEW 26:17–30

JESUS INTRODUCED HIMSELF AS "THE SON OF MAN", THE MAIN CHARACTER IN THE Daniel-inspired drama who was to affect the history of Israel like no other ever could. He also effectively described the actors and stand-ins who were mainly antagonists and falling stars.

With the use of Hebraic idioms and figures of speech, as well as direct sanguinary predictions of dark and dire suspense, the plot of desolation never before experienced by a civilization of biblical magnitude, was revealed with all the pathos and sorrow a divinity could muster. What lay ahead for the land of Judea could only be described as a sinister toxic brew mixed with sorrow, tears, wailing, and gnashing of teeth, seething up to a Roman's boiling point of disgust and vengeance. It was to be preceded by omens that even the dense disciples could recognize.

As bad as this description of the end of the Second Temple era was, though, it was not to be construed as "the end of the world" nor the Second Advent. Even though the desolation was to happen within "a generation", the return of Christ was to be after a long period of time . . . and *unannounced* . . . no end-time signs of any sort . . . not!

And oh yes, the Second Coming would not only reunite Christ with His church, it would hail the arrival of the Judge of all the earth. The Great Judgment was to transpire . . . with rewards and punishments . . . with blessings and cursings . . . eternal life and hell fire.

But then the unexpected: a *coup de theatre!* Just when it looked like the hero, the righteous Son of Man, was victor over the corrupt antagonists . . . when it seemed like His conquest *with the clouds of heaven* was in hand . . . the worst scenario hit the news-stand. The Son of Man was to be kidnapped, incarcerated, and crucified.

Just like the death of Superman in the carnal comic book convention, the death of a real life hero usually signals *the end* of the story line. The tragedy is played out. All that is left is the *Curtain Speech.*

This speech can summarize the drama just enacted. It can scan the highlights like a pebble on the proverbial pond of thought. It can tie up some loose ends. It can announce "coming attractions." It can give appreciation and gratitude for the attentive audience, or list credits: all those involved in the gargantuan production with its multitude of tasks.

Jesus decided to be the Speaker. Some say He gave a curtain speech; others would describe it as an after-dinner speech given to the cast members. Which ever, He still had a lot to say. And He said it.

It was important that He not leave us in despair and without hope. Out of the old was to come the new. Out of the ashes was to arise beauty. Out of the grave, even, was to come . . .

For that you have to see the sequel: The Passion of the Christ.

New Meaning, New Challenge

MATTHEW 26

NOW THE first day of the *feast of* Unleavened Bread the disciples came to Jesus, saying unto Him, "Where wilt Thou that we prepare for Thee to eat the passover?" [18] And He said, "Go into the city to such a man, and say unto him, 'The Master saith, "My time is at hand; I will keep the passover at thy house with My disciples."'" [19] And the disciples did as Jesus had appointed them; and they made ready the Passover. [20] Now when the even was come, He sat down with the twelve. [21] And as they did eat, He said, "Verily I say unto you, that one of you shall betray Me." [22] And they were exceeding sorrowful, and began every one of them to say unto Him, "Lord, is it I?" [23] And He answered and said, "He that dippeth his hand with Me in the dish, the same shall betray Me. [24] The Son of Man goeth as it is written of Him: but woe unto that man by whom the Son of Man is betrayed! it had been good for that man if he had not been born." [25] Then Judas, which betrayed him, answered and said, "Master, is it I?" He said unto him, "Thou hast said." ◄

MARK 14

AND THE first day of Unleavened Bread, when they killed the Passover, His disciples said unto him, "Where wilt Thou that we go and prepare that Thou mayest eat the Passover?" [13] And He sendeth forth two of His disciples, and saith unto them, "Go ye into the city, and there shall meet you a man bearing a pitcher of water: follow him. [14] And wheresoever he shall go in, say ye to the goodman of the house, 'The Master saith, Where is the guestchamber, where I shall eat the passover with My disciples?' [15] And he will shew you a large upper room furnished and prepared: there make ready for us." [16] And His disciples went forth, and came into the city, and found as He had said unto them: and they made ready the Passover. [17] And in the evening He cometh with the twelve. [18] And as they sat and did eat, Jesus said, "Verily I say unto you, One of you which eateth with Me shall betray Me." [19] And they began to be sorrowful, and to say unto Him one by one, "Is it I?" and another *said*, "Is it I?" [20] And He answered and said unto them, "It is one of the twelve, that dippeth with Me in the dish. [21] The Son of Man indeed goeth, as it is written of Him: but woe to that man by whom the Son of Man is betrayed! good were it for that man if he had never been born." ◄

LUKE 22

THEN CAME the day of Unleavened Bread, when the Passover must be killed. [8] And He sent Peter and John, saying, "Go and prepare us the passover, that we may eat." [9] And they said unto him, "Where wilt thou that we prepare?" [10] And He said unto them, "Behold, when ye are entered into the city, there shall a man meet you, bearing a pitcher of water; follow him into the house where he entereth in. [11] And ye shall say unto the goodman of the house, 'The Master saith unto thee, "Where is the guestchamber, where I shall eat the passover with My disciples?"' [12] And he shall shew you a large upper room furnished: there make ready." [13] And they went, and found as He had said unto them: and they made ready the Passover. [14] And when the hour was come, He sat down, and the twelve apostles with Him. [15] And He said unto them, "With desire I have desired to eat this Passover with you before I suffer: [16] For I say unto you, I will not any more eat thereof, until it be fulfilled in the kingdom of God. . . .

[21] ¶ "But, behold, the hand of him that betrayeth Me is with Me on the table. [22] And truly the Son of Man goeth, as it was determined: but woe unto that man by whom He is betrayed!" [23] And they began to enquire among themselves, which of them it was that should do this thing. ◄ **KJV**

1. NEW MEANING

> *On the first day of the Feast of Unleavened Bread, the disciples came to Jesus and asked, "Where do you want us to make preparation for you to eat the Passover?"*
>
> *He replied, "Go into the city to a certain man and tell him, 'The Teacher (Master, KJV) says, "My appointed time is near (at hand). I am going to celebrate the Passover with My disciples at your house."'"* (Matthew 26:17–18)

> *Then came the day of Unleavened Bread on which the Passover lamb had to be sacrificed (killed, KJV). Jesus sent Peter and John, saying, "Go and make preparations for us to eat the Passover."* . . .
>
> *And when the hour was come, Jesus and His apostles reclined at the table (triclinium?). And He said to them, "I have eagerly desired to eat this Passover with you before I suffer."* (Luke 22: 7–8, 14–15)

With the passing of the old Second Temple Era there could have been unfathomable depression and unspeakable sorrow had there not been something new and meaningful to take its place. After the curtain dropped, *when Jesus had finished saying all those things* (26:1), there was a lot of apprehension, if not comprehension. What would take the place of *the* Temple? What's up?

To respond to that query, Jesus gave **seven (7)** *new* **directions** that the future would unfold. These new aspects of true spirituality would provide a theological template within which a fresh community of believers could live and accomplish all that God had planned for salvation of the nations.

First of all, Jesus gave the ancient holiday Feast of Unleavened Bread a *new meaning*. In the past, this Feast (also called Passover, *pascha*, Gk.) represented the sacrifice of a spotless lamb, whose blood splattered on the door-posts would keep a Death Angel from killing the first born of every Jewish family. The Egyptian families, without this sign on their houses, would not be so lucky.

This "plague" was so revolting, that Pharaoh finally decided to let the Israelite slaves leave Egypt and head for their Promised Land. Passover was therefore, to be observed in commemoration of this freedom by an act of God's intervention. (Exodus 12) It was also to represent the beginning of their calendar year from then on.

My time is at hand. I will keep the Passover . . . Not only was this new year at hand, Jesus indicated that "His time" was at hand. And Luke recorded Him as saying that instead of a usual observance, He *eagerly desired to* eat the Passover meal! (*"with desire I have desired . . . "* KJV, Gk.) This was emphatic! He coveted the opportunity with a great longing.

All these words imply that the purpose for which He was born (incarnated) and toward which He worked was about to come to pass. And He was excited about it . . . sort of . . . because He had added, *before I suffer.* Could it have been like the feeling of reluctantly going in for surgery to be cured? Exciting, but . . . painful . . . and wanting it to be over fast.

We in the twenty-first century have the advantage of chronology: We can look back at "history past" . . . or rather, at history already made. And when we focus on the first century Passover in Jerusalem we see the deep significance that Jesus was anticipating: He was to become *the* Passover Lamb, whose blood would redeem "the many" from every nation, freeing them from the penalty and power of sin. They would no longer be slaves to sin, but live righteous lives "in Christ." (Romans 5, 6)

> *We all like sheep have gone astray, each of us has turned to his own way; but the* Lord *has laid* **on Him** *the iniquity of us all. He was oppressed and afflicted, yet He did not open His mouth; He was led like a lamb to the slaughter, and as a sheep before her shearers was silent . . . He was cut off from the land of the living; for the sins of My people He was stricken.* (Isaiah 53:6–7, 8)

At this particular Feast, Jesus knew His time had come. The prophet Daniel had prophesied that at the end of *3½ years of ministry,* half of seven years, the Anointed One *(Messiah,* Heb., *Christ,* Gk.) would be "cut off", and that through His death the "end of sacrifice" would be accomplished. From Jesus's introduction by John the Baptist unto this night, it was that same length of time.[1] (Daniel 9:26–27) As eager as Jesus was to get this very personal Passover over with, it was the only way countless generations of people could ever recite with gratitude:

> *For God so loved the world that He gave His only begotten Son, so that whosoever believeth in Him, should not perish, but have ever-lasting life!* (John 3:16)

Jesus gave the Feast of Unleavened Bread a richer and deeper *new meaning,* for although physical slavery is brutal and dehumanizing, it is temporal. Slavery to one's inordinate lusts and covetousness, murderous thoughts, envious desires, dark attitudes . . . for all eternity, is infinitely worse; and freedom from the consequences, and from the fallen nature itself, conversely, is the greatest blessing a soul could have! Jesus's suffering provided mankind with that freedom.

---

1   Jesus's whole life was "on the clock." See Galatians 4:4; Romans 5:6; Matthew 16:21; Mark 1:9, 15; Luke 5:35; 9:51; John 2:4; 7:6, 13:1; 17:1. His life was programmed from before the Creation of the world: 1 Peter 1:19–20.

> *The next day John saw Jesus coming toward him, and said: "Behold, the Lamb of God, who takes away the sin of the world!"* (John 1:29)

2. NEW CHALLENGE

> *While they were sitting down to eat, Jesus revealed, "I tell you the truth, one of you will betray Me."*
>
> *The disciples were very saddened and began to deny to Him one by one, "Surely, not I, Lord?"*
>
> *Jesus replied, "The one who has dipped his hand into the bowl with Me will betray me. The Son of Man will go just as it is written about Him. But woe to that man who betrays the Son of Man! It would be better for Him if he had not been born."*
>
> *Then Judas* (Iscariot), *the one who would betray Him, said, "Surely not I, Rabbi?"*
>
> *Jesus answered, "Thou has said." ("You've answered your own question, Judas.")* (Matthew 26:21–25)

The famed Texan pastor, T. D. Jakes, once preached, *With new levels, comes new devils!* He underscored the reality that with new dimensions of life, there are new challenges. This is exemplified by the winning of the American lotteries: those who suddenly get the millions of dollars have a lot of new trouble to deal with . . . relatives, friends, parasites, vultures, revenuers, stock market brokers, venture capitalists, charities . . . all come flocking to their front lawn in a mad rush, like the 49ers seeking gold at Fort Sutter. It takes wisdom, discretion, and a massive amount of will power to keep from making rash decisions, or keep from "getting took" and losing all the riches. *Winner beware!*

When a person is promoted, by hard work or by fate, he faces new challenges that were non-existent in his lower job. How he learns to handle them will determine whether he succeeds or fails in his brand new position.

In fact, anyone who wants to progress to new levels as he lives out his life, must be skillful in meeting "the new devils" head-on. And some of these "devils" are not strangers. Not everyone will be happy with your success. Some whom you thought were your friends, faithful co-workers, or loving acquaintances, will turn on you! Some "bad press" you just ignore; some attacks you must deal with. One must be careful not to *pull out the weeds* at the expense of uprooting the wheat as well.

And . . . some opposition will in fact help your cause. It can be for your benefit, or for the improvement of your cause. Ironically, it may steel you for greater challenges down the road; it may prepare you for greater promotions ahead. That which seems to hurt you, can work out for your good. (Remember mom saying that when she gave you bitter medicine, sent you to the dentist, or spanked you?)

This is the situation that Jesus faced that Passover night. Jesus was excited about the promises from the Father about the *joy set before Him*, the glories that should follow, *the authority and power the Son of Man would receive*, and the coronation in a new Kingdom. With eager anticipation, He looked forward to the fulfillment of those grandiose prophecies. (Hebrews 12:2; Daniel 7:13–14, 1 Peter 1:11)

PRELIMINARIES

But He also knew that those glories were to be preceded by "sufferings" . . . that joy was to follow "discipline" . . . the reigning with His saints was only to happen after He dealt with a Judas.

Jesus was prepared for this opposition to His Kingship. He had read about it in the Scriptures. *The Son of Man will go (to the cross) just as it is written about Him.* (Matthew 26:24) In the parallel account given by John the Evangelist, Jesus even quoted one of the verses from the Old Testament:

> *Even my close friend, whom I trusted, he who shared my bread, has*
> *lifted up his heel against Me. But you, O LORD, have mercy on me;*
> *raise me up . . . (Psalm 41:9; John 13:18)*

There is an occasion during the Passover Feast when bread is dipped in a cup, and then eaten. Jesus took this opportunity to point out the one who was to betray Him . . . the devil He had to confront before He could see the accomplishment of the challenge of becoming King Jesus, Savior of the World, manifest Son of Man.

> *I tell you the truth, one of you is going to betray Me, . . . It is the one to*
> *whom I will give this piece of bread when I have dipped it in the bowl.*
> *Then, dipping the piece of bread, He gave it to Judas Iscariot, son*
> *of Simon. As soon as Judas took the bread, Satan entered into him.*
> *"What you are about to do, do quickly," Jesus told him, but*
> *no one at the meal understood why Jesus said this to him . . . As*
> *soon as Judas had taken the bread, he went out. And it was night.*
> (John 13:21–30)

And it was night. The reason John included this phrase in His script seemed redundant. The Passover Meal was **always** eaten in the evening. But it was "night" in more ways than one. A Shakespearean scene with witches brewing their toxic soup in the middle of the night would not even come close to depicting the darkness and dire foreboding of this "night" on the eve of Passover! It was a night of all nights.

The full moon of Passover was simply a cover-up, a luminary veil hiding the sinister and most diabolical event in human history. The Prince of Life was to be betrayed and killed in a most inhumane and cruel manner, disowned by His own people. (Acts 3:13–15) The darkened hearts of foe . . . and friend . . . defined the "night."

It is not the purpose of our study to go into depth in researching the biography of Judas . . . his motives . . . his pilfering the treasury . . . his affinity with demons . . . his punishment in eternity. Suffice it to say that in accepting the challenge of becoming the Savior of the world, and ultimately the reigning Son of Man, Jesus did not sidestep the opposition and adversity thrown at Him: He chose Judas to be one of the Twelve. (Matthew 10:4; John 6:70–71) He endured betrayal, but Jesus never took His eyes off the prize! He left us an example and bids us all to do the same. The challenge is worth it. If we rise to the occasion, God will raise us up in a most supernatural way. (In the meanwhile, focus and feast your eyes on Psalm 2!)

New Example, New Kingdom

LUKE 22

AND THERE was also a strife among them, which of them should be accounted the greatest. ²⁵ And He said unto them, "The kings of the Gentiles exercise lordship over them; and they that exercise authority upon them are called benefactors. ²⁶ But ye *shall* not *be* so: but he that is greatest among you, let him be as the younger; and he that is chief, as he that doth serve. ²⁷ For whether *is* greater, he that sitteth at meat, or he that serveth? *is* not he that sitteth at meat? but I am among you as he that serveth. ²⁸ Ye are they which have continued with Me in My temptations. ²⁹ And I appoint unto you a kingdom, as My Father hath appointed unto Me; ³⁰ That ye may eat and drink at My table in My kingdom, and sit on thrones judging the twelve tribes of Israel."

JOHN 13

NOW BEFORE the Feast of the Passover, when Jesus knew that His hour was come that He should depart out of this world unto the Father, having loved His own which were in the world, He loved them unto the end. ³ Jesus knowing that the Father had given all things into His hands, and that He was come from God, and went to God; ⁴ He riseth from supper, and laid aside His garments; and took a towel, and girded Himself. ⁵ After that He poureth water into a bason, and began to wash the disciples' feet, and to wipe *them* with the towel wherewith He was girded. ⁶ Then cometh He to Simon Peter: and Peter saith unto Him, "Lord, dost thou wash my feet?" ⁷ Jesus answered and said unto him, "What I do thou knowest not now; but thou shalt know hereafter." ⁸ Peter saith unto Him, "Thou shalt never wash my feet." Jesus answered him, "If I wash thee not, thou hast no part with Me." ⁹ Simon Peter saith unto Him, "Lord, not my feet only, but also *my* hands and *my* head." ¹⁰ Jesus saith to him, "He that is washed needeth not save to wash *his* feet, but is clean every whit: and ye are clean, but not all." ¹¹ For He knew who should betray Him; therefore said He, Ye are not all clean. ¹² So after He had washed their feet, and had taken His garments, and was set down again, He said unto them, "Know ye what I have done to you? ¹³ Ye call Me Master and Lord: and ye say well; for so I am. ¹⁴ If I then, *your* Lord and Master, have washed your feet; ye also ought to wash one another's feet. ¹⁵ For I have given you an example, that ye should do as I have done to you. ¹⁶ Verily, verily, I say unto you, The servant is not greater than his lord; neither he that is sent greater than he that sent him. ¹⁷ If ye know these things, happy are ye if ye do them."   ◄ KJV

* * * * *

3. NEW EXAMPLE

> *Also, a dispute arose among them as to which of them was considered to be greatest.* ("strife" *KJV*, Gk.)
>
> *Jesus said to them, "The kings of the nations lord it over them; and those who exercise authority over them call themselves 'Benefactors.' But you are not to be like that. Instead, the greatest among you*

> *should be like the youngest, and the one who rules like the one who serves.*
>
> *"For who is greater, the one who is at the table or the one who serves? Is it not the one who is at the table? But I am among you as one who serves."* (Luke 22:24–27)

> *It was just before the Passover Feast. Jesus knew the time had come for Him to leave this world and go to the Father . . . The evening meal was being served . . . so He got up from the meal, took off His outer cloak, and wrapped a towel around His waist.*
>
> *After that, He poured water in to a basin, and began to wash His disciples feet, drying them with the towel that was wrapped around Him . . .*
>
> *You call me 'Teacher' and 'Lord', and rightly so, for that is what I am. Now that I, your Lord and Teacher, have washed your feet, you also should wash one another's feet. I have set you an example that you should do as I have done for you . . . "* (John 13:1, 2, 4–5, 13–15)

Have you ever gotten together with relatives for an annual holiday party (feast), and a spat broke out? Or even an all out brawl? Hard feeling, miffed pride, unkind words . . . you get the picture.

Or how about recalling a national holiday event where thousands showed up . . . got drunk . . . became restless . . . and a mass riot erupted? Not a pretty sight. In come the security police . . . and things really get out of control.

At this Passover meal, the disciples weren't in fist a' cuffs, but pretty close to it. They were striven with anger over *who was the greatest among them*. They had just sat down and were ready to dig in when the conversation got over-heated. It wasn't just "boys will be boys." They were seriously in disputations, and it ruined the atmosphere of the meal. The ambiance of a deeply spiritual event was dissipated like morning dew driven off by the oppressive heat of a summer, dog-day's sun.

Perhaps the argument over being the greatest involved the seating arrangement. We have had insight into this custom from a previous teaching by Jesus (Luke 14:7–11). He *noticed how the guests picked the places of honor at the table.* Each person desired the table setting closest to the host or important person of honor. He noticed that some were embarrassed when they were asked move down to a lower seat, and that some were honored in front of all the others when they were allowed to sit up closer.

In our preceding study we saw how the hypocritical Pharisees *loved the place of honor at banquets and the most important seats in the synagogues.* (Matthew 23:6) They were known to bully their way into position.

BULLIES

If there is anything that history has taught us, it is the fact that nations are plagued with "bullies." They go by various names, but their conduct is recognizable: dictators, mafiosos, strong-arm thugs, generals, gangsters, county commissioners, corrupt judges, tycoons, fat cats, bad apple cops, ecoterrorists, popes, bishops, senior pastors, and school-yard bullies. They all want *to lord it over* other people, and those who *exercise authority* like to consider themselves as hot-shots, "Patrons looking out for the people." Like drug lords who are *benefactors,* giving money and food to poor villagers, they see nothing wrong with "how" they got their riches. This is what *the kings of the Gentiles do.*

Those who bully ingratiate and try to cover over their hypocrisy with not only euphemistic titles, but they deceive the people with empty rhetoric and vain philosophies that supposedly justify their actions. An example is the claim of the Russian Communist Party that it is the path to a utopian society, but its Ruling Party members have historically displayed selfish conduct in providing themselves with "steak and potatoes" while their countrymen starve to death. Even die-hard atheists have rethought their allegiance to the atheistic philosophy (and become theists) upon seeing the outworking of atheistic Communism with its oppression, tyranny, and self-aggrandizement of Party members. The common people are forced to steal, bribe, or work inordinate hours, just to survive.[2]

ELEEMOSYNARY EVANGELICALS

Disciples of Christ are not to be known as "bullies" nor use any pastoral authority in a "strong arm" manner. What Jesus announced here, the apostle Paul had to remind the Corinthian church. (2 Corinthians 1:24, "not that we lord it over your faith, but we work for your joy"; 13:9–10) Instead, Christians are to be noted for their *servant attitude and conduct.*

Luke quoted Jesus as saying, *I am among you as one who serves.* But it's only when we turn the pages to the book of John that we see what really went on that evening at the Feast. Instead of flaunting His "sonship" (Son of Man, Son of God), He, *though being in very nature God, did not consider equality with God something to be*

---

2   For a classic example of the abuse of the people by the elitists of the Communist Party in Russia, study the siege of St. Petersburg by the Germans in World War II. At a time of dire starvation, the Party lived "high on the hog."

grasped (white-knuckle tenacity), but made Himself nothing, taking the very form of a servant . . . He humbled Himself . . . and washed feet, the dirty feet of His arguing disciples. (See Philippians 2:1–11; John 13:1–17) Instead of following the example of rulers dotting the landscape, Jesus set *a new example* of relating to people.

It may have taken the disciples a while for this teaching to sink in, but Jesus never forgot it. Even after His amazing resurrection, having conquered death, demons, and every spiritual principality, having been proclaimed "the Champion," "Lord of lords," etc. . . . Jesus is seen on the shore of Galilee cooking breakfast for tired, frustrated fishermen who had worked all night! "Another biscuit, anyone? Some more tarter sauce for your fish and chips, Peter? Here's a napkin, Philip. Want seconds, John?" What a scene! What a Savior! What a Servant! (John 21:1–14)

4. NEW KINGDOM

> *I appoint unto you a Kingdom, as My Father has appointed unto Me, so that you may eat and drink at My table in My kingdom, and sit on thrones judging the twelve tribes of Israel.* (Luke 22:29–30)

Hidden in the narrative of Luke is a statement made during the Meal after Jesus gave the example of service (foot-washing). He mentioned an *appointing (a conferring,* NIV; *bestowing,* NKJV) *of His Kingdom.*

Recall the first century history of Judea. Herod the Great's extensive kingdom had been divided among his sons. And later Agrippa's descendants would lose more and more territory until the Roman procurators gained control of the government. Judean sovereignty was dissipating.

The meeting place of the Jewish governing body, the Sanhedrin, was to be totally demolished, according to the Olivet Discourse prophecy. No temple, no city, no Davidic kingdom remnant. This was occasion for Christ's disciples to be forlorn. Their government, such as it was, and their culture was to be trampled upon beyond recognition, and the future looked bleak . . . unless, however . . .

Not to worry, *I bestow upon* **you** *a Kingdom!* Jesus announced with an air of certainty. And guess what? **You** *will sit on thrones judging Israel!* You all, advancing to the colloquialism of John the Revelator, *will be freed from your sins . . . and made to be kings and priests to serve the (Lamb's) God and Father.* (Revelation 1:6; 5:10)

This is why the Apostle Paul could write: *God raised us up with Christ and seated us with Him in the heavenly realms in Christ Jesus . . .* (Ephesians 1:6) Because we have been *delivered from the authority of darkness and been translated into the Kingdom of the beloved Son, in Whom we have redemption (through His blood), the forgiveness of sins. (Colossians 1:13–14)*

Jesus, as He was accustomed to doing, drew the prophecy from Daniel 7 all the way across the bridge of time and laid it at the feet of the disciples. Joseph H. Thayer summarized this feat:

> Relying principally on the prophecies of Daniel, the Jews, realizing he had declared it to be the purpose of God that, after four vast and mighty kingdoms had succeeded one another and the last of them shown itself hostile to the people of God, at length its despotism should be broken, and the empire of the world pass over forever to the holy people of God, were expecting a kingdom of the greatest felicity, which *God through the Messiah* would set up, raising the dead to life again and renovating earth and heaven; and that in this kingdom they would bear sway forever over all the nations of the world. (Daniel 7:14, 18, 27; see 2:44)

But their self-centered, nationalistic interpretation was not to be thus fulfilled. Their self-righteous hopes and dreams of international supremacy were to lay in smoke and ashes at the bottom of the Kidron Valley. Instead of a strictly Jewish worldview,

> *Jesus employed the phrase Kingdom of God or of heaven to indicate that perfect order of things which He was about to establish, in which all those of every nation who should believe in Him were to be gathered together into one society, dedicated and intimately united to God, and made partakers of eternal salvation.* This kingdom is spoken of as now begun and actually present, in as much as its foundations have already been laid by Christ and its benefits realized among men that believe in Him. (Matthew 11:12; 12:28; 13:41; Luke 17:21; 1 Corinthians 4:20; *Greek-English Lexicon*, p. 97)

The *Son of Man* of Daniel 7 was to receive a kingdom, to be sure . . . but it was further revealed that *the greatness of the kingdoms under the whole heaven will be handed over to the saints, the people of the Most High! (7:27)* Or as Jesus phrased it for the surprised disciples to hear: *I convey, confer, bestow unto you a Kingdom!*

SAINTS PRESIDING

And one of the new jobs of the saints would be to administer justice in a fair and righteous government: They would be judges over the twelve tribes of Israel. We ought not to think this strange because ancient Israeli history recorded the appointment of *judges*, raised up by the LORD. (Judges 2:16) They not only approached the wayward about their conduct, but they also led them out and delivered them from the hands of their raiders and oppressors.

We also ought not to think Jesus's appointment applies to a future era (a carnal Jewish millennium) because in other verses Matthew spoke of Jesus giving *the keys of the Kingdom (symbols of authority)* to the disciples, and *whatever they bind on earth will be bound in heaven; whatever they loose on earth will be loosed in heaven.* (Matthew 16:18–19; 18:18–20)

The rest of the New Testament recounting the days of the Early Church, are filled with references to the use of ecclesiastical authority and local church government. (Acts 15; 5:1–11, 2 Corinthians 13:1–4, etc.) [3] There would come a time when the Pastor would be leaving (ascending), and the associate pastors would have to take over in the mundane matters of church life. This statement here in Luke would insure stability and progress in that fledgling organization. And that assurance continues to the present. Holy men of God, filled with the Holy Spirit, are given to the Church (Apostles, Prophets, Evangelists, Pastors, Administrators, Worker of miracles, Hosts, etc.) *to prepare God's people for work of service, so that the Body of Christ may be edified until we all reach the unity of the faith . . . and become mature . . .* (Ephesians 4:9–13)

Matthew recorded a similar pronouncement that resonates with Luke's verses: *I tell you the truth, at the Renewal of all things, when the Son of Man sits on His glorious throne, you who have followed Me will also sit on twelve thrones, judging the twelve tribes of Israel.* (Matthew 19:28).

The phrase, *at the Renewal of all things*, was the first century rabbinical way of describing the "age of the Messiah's reign". While they were rejoicing in the hope of blessings under the Messiah, their expectations were quite outlandish: National supremacy of Israel, subservience of all Gentiles, a kingdom that established peace and ended hostility from the enemies of Israel, etc. Throughout Jesus's ministry He was in conflict with the Pharisees over this materialistic interpretation, and had to continually correct them . . . and then run to keep from being stoned.

Just a few weeks after Jesus mentioned this amazing statement about the disciples becoming the judges of Israel — instead of the Sanhedrin — Jesus did sit on His glorious throne. After the resurrection, He ascended and was coronated with all that that entailed — authority, power, glory. (Matthew 28:18; Acts 2:29–36; Isaiah 9:7)

And with that event, the disciples were "seated *with Christ* in heavenly places . . . And the Kingdom of God was taken from the Pharisees and chief priests, and *given*

---

3   The phrase, "loosing and binding" was a very common rabbinical statement dealing with the authority of the scribes and legal scholars to determine creed and conduct. For example, a famous idiom was "Hillel binds, and Shammai looses", referring to the degree of strictness of dogma.

to the disciples who had produced the 'fruit of righteousness'. (Matthew 21:43) The disciples had become the new judges.

The image of the disciples *sitting on twelve thrones* was reminiscent of the ancient Persian suzerain (king) with many satraps (subservient kings) appointed underneath him (120 during Daniel's era!), such that the ruler was called "the king of kings", a title that John the Revelator gave to Jesus. (Revelation 17:14; 19:16; compare Zechariah 3:8 "associates")

The Revelator also gave us a picture of the judgeships of the disciples in his rendition of believers' authority over Satan: *I saw thrones on which were seated those who* had been given *authority to judge. And I saw the souls of those who had been beheaded because of their testimony for Jesus and because of the word of God . . .* (20:4) These were not some millennial saints according to modern interpretations, but were people who reigned before "the 1000 years, died, and *then came to life* and reigned some more with Christ (20:4)

We must keep in mind that Jesus did not set up a hierarchy of bishops, archbishops, cardinals, and popes (universal bishops). He forbade that nonsense (Matthew 20:20–28). He is merely installing *overseers* of local churches whose job it is to be *public servants.* (20:27–28) Ministers are deputized by Jesus, and He backs them up with His authority; they go forth *in the Name of the ~~Law~~ Lord!*

NEW COMMANDMENT

JOHN 13

THEREFORE, WHEN He was gone out, Jesus said, "Now is the Son of Man glorified, and God is glorified in Him. [32] If God be glorified in Him, God shall also glorify Him in Himself, and shall straightway glorify Him. [33] Little children, yet a little while I am with you. Ye shall seek Me: and as I said unto the Jews, Whither I go, ye cannot come; so now I say to you. [34] A new commandment I give unto you, That ye love one another; as I have loved you, that ye also love one another. [35] By this shall all *men* know that ye are My disciples, if ye have love one to another." ◄ **KJV**

* * * * *

5. NEW COMMANDMENT

> *A new commandment I give unto you to the intent you love one another as I have loved you, to the end that you also love one another.*
>
> *By this all men will know that you are My disciples: if you have love among one another.* (John 13:34–35)

The emphasis is clear in the original Greek: A new commandment is in the offing. Not "new" (*neos,* Gk.) in the sense of time, recent, but new (*kainos,* Gk.) denoting a reference to quality, freshness, not worn out. This love that is commanded does not merely have a foundation in mutual admiration . . . even the pagans do that . . . but it is to reflect the same, higher, divine compassion that Jesus Himself has, and will soon demonstrate even further, toward His brothers, His disciples.

Several times, in the Gospels, it was recorded that when Jesus looked across the landscape of Israel's hills, and saw the people milling about like sheep without a shepherd, that *He was moved with compassion.* When He espied a hurting or desperate person, His heart was crushed. With empathy He approached the outcasts of society.

And after His ascension the Apostle couldn't help but note that *when we were still helpless, Christ died for the ungodly. Very rarely will anyone die for a righteous man, though for a good man someone might possibly dare to die. But God demonstrates His own love for us to this extent: while we were still sinners, Christ died for us!* (Romans 5:6–8)

The Pharisees were accustomed to loving friends and hating enemies, showing love to Israelis and despising Gentiles, welcoming Jews and shunning Samaritans. Christ's own disciples were wanting to call fire down on the villagers who mocked them. These motivations were pagan, and of a fallen nature . . . of a different spirit . . . unchristian.

Christ had to make sure His disciples understood that. They needed a "new commandment" that would change their inner motivation. They needed to be reminded of the conduct that He had exemplified for the past 3½ years. *"I have loved you"* is in the aorist tense; the teaching had been done, class was over, school was out. But Jesus wanted to make sure the Apostles began *and continued* to love (the present tense).

LAW SCHOOL GRADUATES

Lawyers who are expert at asking questions occasionally tried to trip up Jesus with their queries. Once an expert at the Law (Levitical/rabbinical mixture) asked Him: *Teacher, which is the greatest commandment in the Law?* (Matthew 22:34–40) [Note, there were 613 Mosaic laws, and many more rabbinical statutes and sub-statutes, and sub-sub-statutes!]

Without batting an eye, He replied by giving the two that dealt with love: *Love God, love people* (Deuteronomy 6:5; Leviticus 19:18). *"All the Law and the Prophets hang on these two commandments."*

Checkmate! The scholar was stymied. He couldn't argue with that answer, nor embarrass Jesus by his legal prowess. Even the learned rabbi, Hillel, had taught it: *Love God, Love people; all the rest is commentary.*

On another occasion, a legal expert asked: *Teacher, what must I do to inherit eternal life?* (Luke 10:25–37) And Jesus answered a question with a question: *What is written in the Law; how do you read it?*

The lawyer's response was given in anticipation of Jesus's known belief about love: *Love God, and love your neighbor as yourself.* To this response, Jesus agreed. But the lawyer made the mistake of asking a second query: *And just who is my neighbor?* He tried to justify his self-righteousness.

What followed was the parable of "The Good Samaritan," which has become a well-known, oft-repeated story. The true neighbor, Jesus emphasized, is the one who demonstrates *love* to the needy . . . without considering ethnicity, social status, or denominational preference.

LOVE HAS NO BOUNDARIES. One can't be selective in determining who one's neighbor is. Love can't be packaged in social standing . . . it can't be dressed in political suits . . . it can't be wrapped in religious robes . . . it can't be decked out in tribal gear.

LOVE HAS NO LOOPHOLES. There is no justification for inaction . . . there is no excuse for a cold heart . . . there's no alibi for hating another person by simply walking away from a need. (1 John 2:4–11).

LOVE HAS NO LIMITS. It will break out of the bondage of selfishness . . . it will find a way . . . it will go the extra mile . . . it will soften the hardest mind . . . it will share the last cookie . . . it will sacrifice till it hurts!

LOVE HAS NO EQUAL. Of faith, hope and charity, the greatest is love . . . it can bring a man to his knees better than coercion . . . it can heal a marriage faster than apple pie . . . it can restore peace more securely than treaties. (See 1 Corinthians 13)

Jesus knew that you can't be a big person with a small heart . . . you can not find meaning when self is enthroned and love is in the lobby . . . and you cannot harvest in abundance unless you lift up your eyes unto the harvest field (and away from the smart-phone and television) with compassion.

UNIVERSAL GIVEAWAY

The most notable evidence that a community of believers, a local church, is certainly Christian, is love. *All men will know that you are My disciples by this: if you have love among one another.* (John 13:35) The ancient theologian and scholar, Quintus Florens Tertullianus (Tertullian, 160–230?), noticed what secular society used to say about the Christians: *See how they love one another; how they are ready even to die for one another. (Apology 39)*

Before the Church can be any relevance to its surrounding culture, it must first have "its own act together." This is why New Testament writers repeatedly admonished the congregations to manifest love within its walls as a foundation for outreach and charity in society. *Finally, all of you, live in harmony with one another; be sympathetic, love as brothers, be compassionate and humble.* (1 Peter 3 :8)

> **Love** *must be sincere. Hate what is evil; cling to what is good. Be devoted to one another in* **brotherly love** *. . . Honor one another above yourselves. Never be lacking in zeal, but keep your spiritual fervor, serving the Lord.*
>
> *Be joyful in hope, patient in affliction, faithful in prayer. Share with God's people who are in need. Practice hospitality. Bless those who persecute you; bless and curse not. Rejoice with those who rejoice; mourn with those who mourn.*
>
> **Live in harmony** *with one another. Do not be proud, but be willing to associate with people of low position (or, be willing to do menial work). Do not be conceited . . . If it is possible, as far as you*

are concerned, **live at peace** *with everyone.* (Romans 12:9–18; see 1 Corinthians 16:13; Galatians 5:6, 13–14; Ephesians 4:2–6, 15, 32)

James (Jacob, the brother of Jesus) also wrote about the "Royal Law" as a basis for, and incentive of, doing acts of kindness, without which a person's faith is unsubstantiated. (James 2:8) The Christian community must demonstrate to the world equality and fraternity, and live out its creed of unending charity. (1:27)

Love: an old commandment that has retained its newness, freshness, and vitality, and is as relevant now as it was the first day it was spoken by the Lawgiver. Such that Jesus may say, *a new commandment I give unto you. Love one another . . .*

Watch Me. I'll show you how.

New Covenant

MATTHEW 26	**MARK 14**	**LUKE 22**
AND AS they were eating, Jesus took bread, and blessed it, and brake it, and gave *it* to the disciples, and said, "Take, eat; this is My body." [27] And He took the cup, and gave thanks, and gave *it* to them, saying, "Drink ye all of it; [28] For this is My blood of the new Testament, which is shed for many for the remission of sins. [29] But I say unto you, I will not drink henceforth of this fruit of the vine, until that day when I drink it new with you in My Father's kingdom." [30] And when they had sung an hymn, they went out into the mount of Olives.	**AND AS** they did eat, Jesus took bread, and blessed, and brake *it*, and gave to them, and said, "Take, eat: this is My body." [23] And He took the cup, and when He had given thanks, He gave *it* to them: and they all drank of it. [24] And He said unto them, "This is My blood of the new Testament, which is shed for many. [25] Verily I say unto you, I will drink no more of the fruit of the vine, until that day that I drink it new in the kingdom of God." [26] ℙ And when they had sung an hymn, they went out into the mount of Olives.	**AND HE** took the cup, and gave thanks, and said, "Take this, and divide it among yourselves: [18] For I say unto you, I will not drink of the fruit of the vine, until the kingdom of God shall come." [19] ℙ And He took bread, and gave thanks, and brake *it*, and gave unto them, saying, "This is My body which is given for you: this do in remembrance of Me." [20] Likewise also the cup after supper, saying, "This cup is the new Testament in My blood, which is shed for you. . . . " [30] ℙ And He came out, and went, as He was wont, to the mount of Olives; and His disciples also followed Him.

◄ KJV

* * * * *

6. NEW COVENANT

There is no vacuum in the history of men. The very minute one dictator leaves the chair of government, another iron man comes and quickly sits down. When one king departs, a prince arrives on the scene to wear the crown. When one tyrant slips, another opportunist soon stomps on him to keep him down. Uprisings follow uprisings. Forms of government ebb and flow like the incessant ocean tide along the Atlantic seaboard.

Similarly, the sovereign plans of a providential God leave no gaps for chance or coincidence to fill in. With Jehovah God there is no happenstance. History happens and stands with firm "end" in view. "Purpose" is a major counselor in the war room of God.

The crucifixion of Christ was pivotal in the history of the Jewish nation, as well as was the consequence of such a tragedy: The destruction of the Second — and final — earthly Temple. But like the axis of a planet's rotation, ending one day and bringing in a new sunrise, these events saw the dawning of a *New Covenant era*, even though it seemed like the end of the world to the Jews . . . night-time for Phariseeism . . . twilight for Levitical sacrifice and ritual.

> *On the first day of the Feast of Unleavened Bread . . . the Master (teacher) said, "My appointed time is near . . . the Son of Man will depart just as it is written about Him."*
>
> *While they were eating, Jesus took bread, gave thanks and broke it, and gave it to His disciples, saying, "Take and eat; this is My body."*
>
> *Then He took the cup:, gave thanks and offered it to them, saying, "Drink from it, all of you, This is My* **blood of the new Covenant**, *which is poured out for many for the forgiveness of sins."*
> (Matthew 26:17, 18, 24, 26–28)

A new Covenant was to be established and confirmed by a "blood sacrifice." This procedure was traditional. It acknowledged the seriousness of the act. A covenant document stained with blood was not to be taken lightly. (Exodus 12:13) (See also Hebrews 10:29)

NEW COVENANT

It should have come as no surprise to the disciples of Jesus. The Old Testament prophets had foretold of one to be made that would replace the Mosaic Covenant. The revered prophet from Anathoth, in the territory of Benjamin, boldly declared under the inspiration of the Holy Spirit:

> *The time is coming, declares the* LORD, *when I will make a* **new covenant** *with the house of Israel and with the house of Judah. It will not be like the covenant I made with their forefathers when I took them by the hand to lead them out of Egypt, because they broke My covenant, though I was a Master (husband) to them.*
>
> *This is the covenant I will make with the house of Israel afterwards, declares the* LORD. *I will put My Law in their minds and write it on their hearts. I will be their God . . .* (Jeremiah 31:31–33)

The Israeli nation had a two thousand year history of "breaking covenant" with the LORD. The Sinai Covenant was repudiated by the sinful pilgrims who had left Egypt. The new covenant made at the entering in of the Jews into the Promised Land was annulled by adopting the life-style of the Canaanites. The covenant with the royal kings of Israel was abrogated by unfaithfulness. Etc.

With the breaking of covenant, of course, came the application of all the curses that were written out in advance. Some Jews died while wandering in the Wilderness. Some were taken captive by the Assyrians and Babylonians. And later, in history, the Romans put an end to the Temple worship by desolating Jerusalem. (See Hosea 6:7; 8:1; Malachi 2:8; Jeremiah 11:1–14) It was obvious that a covenant dealing with *external ritual and of a physical nature in observance* was not able to liberate men from the curse of fallen human nature. (Galatians 3:10–14; Romans 3:9–20)

What was needed was what the priest Ezekiel recognized, and forecast with hope: that God *would give a new heart and a new spirit inside; and remove the heart of stone, and replace it with a heart of flesh.* But more than just a new attitude (spirit), it was necessary that God would *place His (Holy) Spirit inside that would inspire man to follow God's decrees and be careful to keep His laws.* (Ezekiel 36:26–27) This was echoed by the prophet Joel: God's *Holy Spirit needed to be poured out on* **all** *people.* (Joel 2:28–29)

So Jesus Christ introduced the New Covenant, a covenant fortified by the infilling (indwelling) of the Holy Spirit! He actually did what John the Baptizer had told the throngs of common folk who came to listen to his seminars on the shore. He established the New Covenant, but not without instructing the disciples about being infilled with the Spirit. (John 14, 15, 16; these chapters are synoptic to our Matthew 23–26 study)

> *I baptize you with water for repentance. But after me will come One who is more powerful than I, whose sandals I am not worthy to untie. He will baptize you with the Holy Spirit and fire.*
>
> *His winnowing fork is in His hand, and He will clear His threshing floor, and gather His wheat into the barn, and burn up the chaff with unquenchable fire.* (Matthew 3:11–12)

Notice that the instituting of the New Covenant, which is based upon the regenerating power of the Holy Spirit on human nature, was accompanied by the removal of the Old Covenant in a dramatic and devastating way. "The chaff was burned up!" This thought reverberated in the hallways of the mind of the author of the book of Hebrews:

> *The ministry Jesus has received is as superior to theirs (the high priests of the old Mosaic Covenant), just as the Covenant of which He is mediator is superior to the old one, and it is founded upon better promises.*

> *If there had been nothing wrong with the First Covenant, no place would have been sought for another. But God found fault with the people . . .*
>
> *By calling this* **covenant** *'new', He has made the first one obsolete; and what is obsolete and aging will soon disappear.* (Hebrews 8:6–8, 13)

Remember that Hebrews was written before the Destruction of Jerusalem, so "will soon disappear" is in line with the prophecies of doom by Jesus in Matthew 23 and 24.

SPIRITUAL COVENANT

We have already seen that the New Testament presented Jesus as having instituted a *spiritual kingdom*, not a physical one with stone palaces, nor domains of planetary real estate, nor armies of trained soldiers to secure her borders. (See also John 18:36–37)

So also it is with the New Covenant. It is a *covenant of the Spirit*, a covenant not only spiritual in nature, but one dependent upon the Holy Spirit of Jehovah God. As the Apostle Paul would later write: "The Kingdom of God is righteousness, peace, and joy *in the Holy Spirit.* (Romans 14:17) The whole New Testament is the story of the Church under the New Covenant being instigated, infilled, and inspired by the Holy Spirit. The "birth of the Church" is by most theologians considered to be the Day of Pentecost when the core of first Christians gathered and were *filled with the Holy Spirit.* (Acts 2:4) And believers from then on are to live *by the Spirit* because the *fruit of the Spirit* is love, joy, peace, patience, etc. (Galatians 5:16, 22ff) And *since we live by the Spirit, let us keep in step with the Spirit!* (v. 25)

This radically new spiritual covenant was a consternation to many of the Rabbis and Jewish theologians of the first century. It involved a new way of approaching religion with all its observances and rituals, as well as creeds and dogmas. And in modern times, many Messianic congregations have a hard time letting go of Judaic traditions, many of which (by the way) are not Mosaic, but Massoretic. Habits of ritual and ceremonial customs are as addictive as chocolate candy . . . or even cocaine.

We recall that the person to whom Jesus spoke concerning the *new birth*, or *being born again (from above,* Aramaic) was not a filthy sinner, but a righteous Jewish elder! He was being instructed to enter a whole new kind of life . . . a new way of thinking . . . a new way of living . . . a new way of approaching God. (John 3:1–21) A believer must not just be religious, he *must he born of the Spirit.* That's what the New Covenant is all about.

TERMS OF THE COVENANT

The New Testament laid out several examples of what it means to live under the terms of the Covenant. We examine a few of them here:

- CIRCUMCISION — This ancient sign of relationship with God is no longer to be required of believers for membership in the Church (Kingdom of God). What is most important, rather, is a "circumcision of the heart" . . . this practice is to be spiritual in nature, not physical, so that all peoples (Jew and Gentile) may have fellowship in the family of God. (Romans 2:25–9; Galatians 5:2–6; 6:12–15; see also Galatians 2:3–6)

- BAPTISM — Ritualistic baptisms and cleansing by washing were a large part of ancient Judaism. But as John the Baptizer pointed out, not just "baptism of repentance" is necessary, but being "baptized in the Holy Ghost" by Christ must be done. (Matthew 3:11; Acts 1:4–5)

- GENEALOGY — Lineage through Abraham, Isaac, and Jacob, is no longer a token of special privilege. John warned those he baptized, *"Do not begin to say to yourselves, 'We have Abraham for our father.' For I tell you that from these stones God is able to raise up children for Abraham."* (Luke 3:8) What was, and is, important is the "producing of fruit worthy of repentance," not focusing on "endless genealogies". (1 Timothy 1:4; Titus 3:9) Jesus emphasized this by noting that even a Jew may be of "their father the devil" in spite of lineage through Abraham!

- EQUALITY — Related to the topic of special privilege because of lineage, is the concept of "equality" of races (ethnic groups, nations, clans) in the spiritual covenant of the Church. Instead of repeating the Rabbinical prayer, "I thank thee, O God, that thou hast not made me a dog, Gentile, or woman," a whole new acceptance and love for all people must be adopted. "God does not show favoritism." (Romans 2:11) *You are all sons of God through faith in Christ Jesus, for all of you who were baptized into Christ have clothed yourselves with Christ. There is neither Jew nor Greek, slave or free, male nor female, for you are all one in Jesus Christ. If you belong to Christ, then you are Abraham's seed* (figuratively speaking), *and heirs according to the promise.* (Galatians 3:26–29; see also, Luke 24:47; Romans 10:11–13; Colossians 3:11)

- PRIESTHOOD — The new, spiritual Covenant also has a new priesthood. It is not based upon *regulations as to ancestry, but on the basis of the power of an indestructible life.* (Psalm 110:4; Hebrews 7:16–19) Instead of a Levitical priesthood, it is of Melchizedek, who symbolically was without father or mother, *without genealogy, without beginning of days or end of life, like the Son of God He remains a priest forever.* (Hebrews 7:3)

This new priesthood was established by an oath from God, and because of this *Jesus has become the guarantee of a better covenant.* (Hebrews 7:22) It is better because *He is able to save completely those who come to God through Him, because He always lives to intercede for them.* (7:25) Jesus is the kind of High Priest Who is able to meet all our needs since He is *holy, blameless, pure, set apart from sinners, and exalted above the heavens. Unlike other high priests, He does not need to offer sacrifices day after day, first for His own sins, then for the sins of the people. He sacrificed for* **their** *sins once for all when He offered Himself.* (Hebrews 7:26–27; compare John 1:29)

Since the priesthood of Jesus is "permanent" this rules out any alleged reinstitution of the Levitical priesthood in a supposed rebuilt Temple in the future! Any attempt to do so would be an insult against God and His oath; and to teach so would be not only blasphemy, but heresy.

- SACRIFICES — Since Jesus offered Himself up as the "Lamb of God" for the redemption of all mankind, there is no need, ever, for sacrificing animals (or humans) for sins. Such rituals are forever finished. Sins are forgiven, *and where these have been forgiven, there is no longer any sacrifice for sin.* (Hebrews 10:18; see LXX, Psalm 40:6–8; Hebrews 10)

  Again, the reinstitution of animal sacrifice in an alleged future, rebuilt Temple would be an act of treason against the Kingdom of God, and a violation of the New Covenant. The attempt at breeding a new "red heifer" is a mockery of the crucified Christ and His redeeming blood. (Heb. 9:11–28)

  It should come as a relief to us all that we no longer have to bring animals to church to have the pastors slaughter them for us, in order to redeem us from our sins! Just as it was with a sigh of relief that the American Indians, who sacrificed people annually, heard the Gospel of Christ Who gave Himself once and for all.

- OBSERVING HOLY DAYS — In the New Covenant culture there are no holy days that have to be observed with minute detail or enforced tradition. The excessive requirements of the Pharisees are a thing of the past. Violation of their stringent rules are no longer to be punished.

  The Apostle wrote: *Do you wish to be enslaved again? You are observing special days, and months, and seasons, and years. I fear for you, that somehow I have wasted my efforts on you.* (Galatians 4:9–11) The Jews to whom Paul was writing, had been freed from the multitudinous rules and regulations of the Rabbinical interpretations of the Law . . . many of which dealt with strict observance of holy days . . . which were quite burdensome for layman and cleric alike. The Gospel of Christ and the news of the New Covenant brought liberty and joy. But some were beginning to revert back to the Old Covenant practices, and Paul had to stop them.

All nations have holidays (holy days) which they observe as a memorial of special historical events. There is no sin in participating in them. But none of them are a means of pacifying God nor of making one's self more righteous in the eyes of God. *None* are to be required for putting oneself in right standing with God; that work has been done completely on the cross, and was underscored with the words of Jesus: *It is finished.* This is a major tenet of the New Covenant . . . and the spiritual Kingdom of God . . . the Church of the living God.

- HOLY TEMPLE — A great truth about the New Covenant was revealed to the "Woman at the well." She acknowledged: *Our fathers worshiped on this mountain, but you Jews claim that the place where we must worship is in Jerusalem.* But Jesus quickly responded faster than a weaver's shuttle can fly across a loom: *Believe Me, woman, the time is coming when you will neither worship the Father on this mountain, nor in Jerusalem . . . A time is coming and has now come when the true worshipers will worship the Father in spirit and truth . . . God is a spirit, and they who worship Him must worship in spirit and truth.* (John 4:20–24) Temples of stone and fancy curtains are not of concern in the New Covenant culture.

In fact, when Jesus died, shed His blood, and presented it to God as a valid sacrifice, He did not enter the Temple in first century Jerusalem; He entered *the greater and more perfect tabernacle that is not made with hands,* and having been accepted, Jesus *serves (as High Priest) in the heavenly sanctuary, the true tabernacle set up by the Lord, not by man.* (Hebrews 9:11; 8:2; see Jeremiah 7:1–8)

The Mosaic tabernacle, and the later Temples, were *copies and shadows (symbols) of what is in Heaven.* (Hebrews 8:5; 9:23) The physical helps us get a grasp on the spiritual by visual optics; but once we understand, we don't focus on the physical symbols and types. And now everyone around the world . . . without having to travel to the Mideast . . . can enter with praise and worship and petition into the Presence of God in His holy dwelling place!

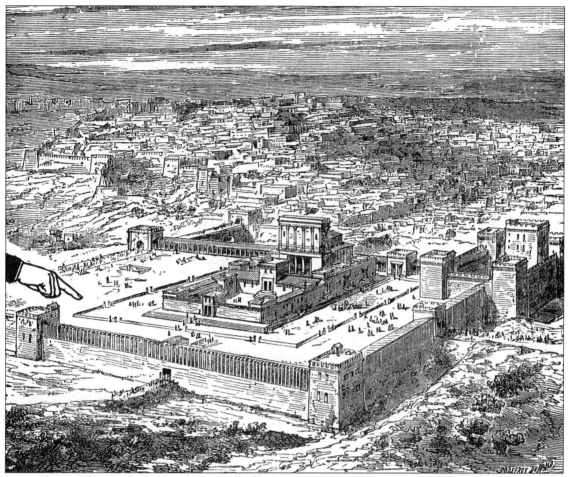

The Temple at Jerusalem; Note the Wall of Separation indicated by the pointing finger (Eph. 2:14)

Apostle Paul wrote of another sense in which the Temple is spiritual under the New Covenant. Since the Temple is a place where God dwells, it is appropriate to say that *you yourselves are God's Temple because God's Spirit lives in you. If anyone destroys God's Temple, God will destroy him, for God's Temple is sacred, and you are that Temple.* (1 Corinthians 3:16–17)

But when we consider it in either sense, the conclusion is the same: God's holy dwelling place is *spiritual in essence,* and not physical nor on any mountain-top. To think that there is to be a rebuilt Temple in Jerusalem would be to set aside the New Testament teaching by misinterpreting Old Testament prophecies. Like a fierce Sirroco windstorm, such thinking flies in the face of the Lord Jesus . . . Who once rebuked such a storm. The curtain of the Holiest Place was ripped asunder for a reason. The Second Temple was demolished by the Roman general, Titus, for a reason.

- **WORKS OF THE LAW**—In summary, all the works of the Law of Moses (all the rules and regulations, rituals and ceremonies, feasts and holy days) as a way of obtaining right standing before God, are obsolete. (Hebrews 8:13, Romans 11:5–6; Galatians 3:23–25) Not that they weren't important, though. They were a *tutor or schoolmaster* to teach us and lead us to Christ. Now that the Messiah (Christ) has come and established a blood covenant, instituting the Kingdom of God, we all live under the rules of the royal realm. In fact, all the *Law is summed up in a single command: Love your neighbor as yourself.* (Galatians 5:14; Romans 13:8–10; James 2:8; Matthew 7:12) As Christ has loved us, so ought we all to love each other under the terms of the New Covenant. (Study also Galatians 2:15 – 3:25)

AN IMPORTANT DECISION

Asking a person who has been raised in the Jewish religion and culture to live under the terms of the New Covenant . . . and relinquish the Old . . . is like asking a Scotsman to give up plaid kilts, bag pipes, and ale! It can be a traumatic experience. In fact, many Jewish families hold a symbolic funeral if one of their members becomes a follower of Jesus Christ.

But this requirement is no different than that asked of people of all other nations. Tribes must give up human sacrifices; clans must stop their worship of idols; Gentile nations must stop drinking animal blood; and Americans must not be entertained by promiscuous Hollywood actors. All peoples who become citizens of the Kingdom of God are not allowed to have "dual citizenship." They, too, must relinquish carnal cultures they have been raised in.

This is why Jesus told the religious-observant Nicodemus, *You must be born again (from above).* Life under the New Covenant is initiated by a brand new start . . . a transformation of thinking . . . a baptism in the Spirit. A survey of the time that Jesus spent with His twelve disciples shows how difficult it can be teaching men to think and act differently. And it was never quite accomplished until the Day of Pentecost when they were filled with the Holy Spirit in an unmistakable manner. From then on, the disciples never spoke of a physical kingdom or nationalistic hopes. The Kingdom of God was spiritual in nature, universal in scope, and merciful in spirit.

COVENANT BENEFITS

To give incentive to make the important decision to live under the terms of the *New Covenant* perhaps it would be of benefit to assess some of the benefits of this new arrangement.

- **GRACE AND MERCY** — John's introduction to the life of Christ began with *The Law was given through Moses; grace and truth came through Jesus Christ.* (John 1:17) This was so important because under the Law a lot of us would not be alive! *Anyone who rejected the Law of Moses died without mercy on the testimony of two or three witnesses.* (Hebrews 10:28; cf. Rom. 5:1–2)

     But under the New Covenant we can *approach the throne of* **grace** *with confidence so that we may receive mercy and find grace to help us in our time of need.* (Hebrews 4:16) Sin is no longer our master. (Romans 6:14)

- **ETERNAL LIFE** — Also, according to God's great mercy, *He has given us new birth into a living hope through the resurrection of Jesus Christ from the dead, and into an inheritance that can never perish, spoil, or fade: kept in heaven for you, who through faith are shielded by God's power until the coming of the salvation that is ready to be revealed in the last time.* (1 Peter 1:3–5) Eternal life is the reward for those who have accepted Jesus as Messiah and Mediator of the New Covenant. Fear of death — and oblivion — dissipates in the light of the glorious Gospel of the New Covenant.

- **SPIRITUAL SONSHIP** — It is written that to *all who receive Jesus (as Messiah) . . . to those who believe on His Name, He has given the right to become children of God . . . born of God.* (John 1:12–13) And since the believer is a son, he receives the "full rights of a son"! He is made an heir of all that the Father gives. And along with the blessings, is the close communion with God, so much that it is common to simply say, *Abba, Father, what's up?* (Galatians 4:4–7) Under the terms of the New Covenant, the promises of the Old Covenant have their fulfillment in this aspect: *I will live with them and walk among them, and I will be their God . . . and they will be My people* (Jeremiah 32:38) *. . . I will be a Father to you, and you will be My sons and daughters . . . says the Lord Almighty.* (2 Samuel 7:14; 7:8; These were quoted by Paul in a letter to the Corinthian congregation, 2 Cor. 6:16–18) The author of the book to the Hebrews underscored this truth: *But the one who makes men holy and those who are made holy are of the same family, so Jesus is not ashamed to call them "brothers".* (Hebrews 2:11; he then quotes Psalm 22:22)

- **LIFE FREED FROM SIN** — By identifying with Christ in His death and resurrection under the New Covenant, a person is freed from the life of sin. The old life-style is "crucified" with all its bondage and slavery to the habits and curses of sin . . . and a new life is resurrected in the believer, freed from the past, with hope for the future. A believer's history is not his destiny!

- **EQUALITY AND FRATERNITY**—All who have been baptized unto Christ and His Covenant become part of a universal brotherhood where there is no prejudice or inequality! All tribal, ethnic, racial, distinctions are neutralized, and neither God nor man shows "favoritism." (Galatians 3:28; Luke 24:47; Romans 10:11–13; Colossians 3:11; Romans 2:10–11) No discrimination or anti-Semitism is allowed (nor Goyim belittling). The "middle wall" is eliminated!

- **AMAZING JOY**—The first announcement to the common people introducing the Messiah (Messenger) of the New Covenant was given by angels about *good news of great joy!* (Luke 2:10) And from then on, the acceptance of the message of the New Covenant has brought believers *great joy*. The news of the resurrection of Christ has introduced "great joy" into the lives of those have been bound by fear.

   Experiencing power over evil spirits in the Name of Jesus caused the Apostles to return with joy. And after the ascension of the Lord into heaven, the disciples returned to Jerusalem with great joy! This was the same Son of God who had inspired the whole crowds of disciples to joyfully praise God in loud voices because of all the miracles they had seen. (Luke 19:37; 24:52) Later on, the Apostle Paul would testify: *In all our troubles my joy knows no bounds.* (2 Corinthians 7:4) And the Apostle Peter wrote to the believers in Asia Minor, listing one of the many reasons for this emotion: *Even though you do not see Jesus, you believe in Him and are filled with an inexpressible and glorious joy, for you are receiving the goal of your faith, the salvation of your souls.* (1 Peter 1:8–9)

All these benefits are made possible by the fulfillment of the prophetic Passover observance, highlighted by the evening meal. When Jesus *took, blessed, broke, and gave* the unleavened bread, He was staking His life on the certainty of the New Covenant.[4] [Some Messianic Jews teach that this bread was the *afikoman*, a piece that was broken, hidden (buried), and then brought out at the end of the meal and eaten . . . as a symbol of the Messiah, who was buried and resurrected, and is coming again!]

The blessing given at this meal, no doubt was the common Jewish prayer of grace said at most dinners: *Blessed are You, Lord our God, King of the world, Who*

---

4   This phrasing has become the common eucharistic language often repeated in Communion Services in Christian congregations. (Luke 22:19, 1 Corinthians 11:24–25) *Took, blessed, broke, gave.*

brings forth bread from the earth. And the drinking of the cups: *Blessed are You, Lord our God, King of the world, Who creates the fruit of the vine.*

Traditionally, there were four (4) cups poured out during the Passover ceremony. It was probably after the second cup that Jesus gave His *haggadah* commentary concerning His blood, the "blood of the New Covenant," just as the blood of the Passover Lamb was important to the Old Covenant. And some say that it was the fourth cup that Jesus declined to drink *until the Kingdom of God come.* (Luke 22: 18) [Note that Luke later recorded that after the resurrection, the disciples "ate and drank" with Him! (Acts 10:41)]

It was that *"many" might receive forgiveness of sins,* Jesus's blood was to be poured out. That word, "many," is an echo of previous scriptures: *By knowledge of Him My righteous Servant will justify many; and He will bear their iniquities.* (Isaiah 53:11). *The Son of Man did not come to be served, but to serve, and to give His life as a ransom for many.* (Matthew 20:28) Later it was summarized: *Christ was sacrificed once to take away the sins of many; and He will appear a second time, not to bear sin, but to bring salvation to those who are waiting for Him.* (Hebrews 9:28)

CLOSING HYMN

Just as many churches end their worship services with a "closing hymn" so also, the Passover observation was usually ended with the singing of the Hallel psalms, #115–118. *When Jesus and the Eleven had sung a hymn, they went out . . . (Matthew 26:30)*

Several topics in this Hallel selection are worth noting. We can be sure that they were not overlooked by Jesus at that Last Supper:

> *The cords of death entangled me, the anguish of the grave* **came upon me**. *I was overcome by trouble and sorrow. Then I called on the Name of the* Lord, *"O* Lord, *save me!" . . .*
>
> *How can I repay the* Lord *for all His goodness to me? I will lift up* **the cup of salvation** *and call on the name of the* Lord *. . .*
>
> *Precious in the sight of the* Lord *is the death of His saints. O* Lord, *truly I am your servant; I am your servant, Your faithful son; you have freed me from my chains . . .* (Psalm 116:3, 12–13, 15–16)
>
> *The stone the builders* **rejected** *has become the capstone; the* Lord *has done this, and it is marvelous in our eyes . . .*
>
> *Bind the festal sacrifice with ropes, and take it up to the horns of the altar . . .* (Psalm 118:22–23, 27)

The gamut of emotions that Jesus experienced that night are beyond any attempt to describe. And the pain He was about to endure was to be inexpressible. But He sang.

The Passover dinner had been eaten. The Teacher's speaking had ended, or did it? The synoptic Gospels are silent, but John, who was close to Jesus, has recorded a few more topics that Jesus addressed that fateful night. We cannot leave our seats just yet . . . there is a bit more.

New Spirit

JOHN 14 – 18:1

LET NOT YOUR HEART BE TROUBLED: ye believe in God, believe also in Me. [2] In My Father's house are many mansions: if *it were* not so, I would have told you. I go to prepare a place for you. [3] And if I go and prepare a place for you, I will come again, and receive you unto Myself; that where I am, *there* ye may be also. [4] And whither I go ye know, and the way ye know."

[5] ℙ Thomas saith unto Him, "Lord, we know not whither Thou goest; and how can we know the way?" [6] Jesus saith unto him, "I am the way, the truth, and the life: no man cometh unto the Father, but by Me. [7] If ye had known Me, ye should have known My Father also: and from henceforth ye know Him, and have seen Him."

[8] ℙ Philip saith unto him, "Lord, shew us the Father, and it sufficeth us." [9] Jesus saith unto him, "Have I been so long time with you, and yet hast thou not known Me, Philip? he that hath seen Me hath seen the Father; and how sayest thou *then*, 'Shew us the Father?' [10] Believest thou not that I am in the Father, and the Father in Me? the words that I speak unto you I speak not of Myself: but the Father that dwelleth in Me, He doeth the works. [11] Believe Me that I *am* in the Father, and the Father in Me: or else believe Me for the very works' sake. [12] Verily, verily, I say unto you, He that believeth on Me, the works that I do shall he do also; and greater *works* than these shall he do; because I go unto My Father. [13] And whatsoever ye shall ask in My name, that will I do, that the Father may be glorified in the Son. [14] If ye shall ask any thing in My name, I will do *it.*

[15] ℙ "If ye love Me, keep My commandments. [16] And I will pray the Father, and He shall give you another Comforter, that He may abide with you for ever; [17] *Even* the Spirit of truth; whom the world cannot receive, because it seeth Him not, neither knoweth Him: but ye know Him; for He dwelleth with you, and shall be in you. [18] I will not leave you comfortless: I will come to you. [19] Yet a little while, and the world seeth Me no more; but ye see Me: because I live, ye shall live also. [20] At that day ye shall know that I *am* in My Father, and ye in Me, and I in you. [21] He that hath My commandments, and keepeth them, he it is that loveth Me: and he that loveth Me shall be loved of My Father, and I will love him, and will manifest Myself to him." [22] Judas saith unto Him, not Iscariot, "Lord, how is it that thou wilt manifest Thyself unto us, and not unto the world?" [23] Jesus answered and said unto him, "If a man love Me, he will keep My words: and My Father will love him, and We will come unto him, and make Our abode with him. [24] He that loveth Me not keepeth not My sayings: and the word which ye hear is not Mine, but the

Father's which sent Me. [25] These things have I spoken unto you, being *yet* present with you. [26] But the Comforter, *which* is the Holy Ghost, whom the Father will send in My name, He shall teach you all things, and bring all things to your remembrance, whatsoever I have said unto you. [27] Peace I leave with you, My peace I give unto you: not as the world giveth, give I unto you. Let not your heart be troubled, neither let it be afraid. [28] Ye have heard how I said unto you, I go away, and come *again* unto you. If ye loved Me, ye would rejoice, because I said, I go unto the Father: for My Father is greater than I. [29] And now I have told you before it come to pass, that, when it is come to pass, ye might believe. [30] Hereafter I will not talk much with you: for the prince of this world cometh, and hath nothing in Me. [31] But that the world may know that I love the Father; and as the Father gave Me commandment, even so I do. Arise, let us go hence.

I AM THE TRUE VINE, and My Father is the husbandman. [2] Every branch in Me that beareth not fruit He taketh away: and every *branch* that beareth fruit, He purgeth it, that it may bring forth more fruit. [3] Now ye are clean through the word which I have spoken unto you. [4] Abide in Me, and I in you. As the branch cannot bear fruit of itself, except it abide in the vine; no more can ye, except ye abide in Me. [5] I am the vine, ye are the branches: He that abideth in Me, and I in him, the same bringeth forth much fruit:

for without Me ye can do nothing. [6] If a man abide not in Me, he is cast forth as a branch, and is withered; and men gather them, and cast *them* into the fire, and they are burned. [7] If ye abide in Me, and My words abide in you, ye shall ask what ye will, and it shall be done unto you. [8] Herein is My Father glorified, that ye bear much fruit; so shall ye be My disciples. [9] As the Father hath loved Me, so have I loved you: continue ye in My love. [10] If ye keep My commandments, ye shall abide in My love; even as I have kept My Father's commandments, and abide in His love. [11] These things have I spoken unto you, that My joy might remain in you, and *that* your joy might be full. [12] This is My commandment, That ye love one another, as I have loved you. [13] Greater love hath no man than this, that a man lay down his life for his friends. [14] Ye are My friends, if ye do whatsoever I command you. [15] Henceforth I call you not servants; for the servant knoweth not what his lord doeth: but I have called you friends; for all things that I have heard of My Father I have made known unto you. [16] Ye have not chosen Me, but I have chosen you, and ordained you, that ye should go and bring forth fruit, and *that* your fruit should remain: that whatsoever ye shall ask of the Father in My name, He may give it you. [17] These things I command you, that ye love one another.

[18] ℙ "If the world hate you, ye know that it hated Me before *it hated* you. [19] If ye were of the world, the world would

love his own: but because ye are not of the world, but I have chosen you out of the world, therefore the world hateth you. [20] Remember the word that I said unto you, 'The servant is not greater than his lord.' If they have persecuted Me, they will also persecute you; if they have kept My saying, they will keep yours also. [21] But all these things will they do unto you for My name's sake, because they know not Him that sent Me. [22] If I had not come and spoken unto them, they had not had sin: but now they have no cloke for their sin. [23] He that hateth Me hateth My Father also. [24] If I had not done among them the works which none other man did, they had not had sin: but now have they both seen and hated both Me and My Father. [25] But *this cometh to pass*, that the word might be fulfilled that is written in their law, 'They hated Me without a cause.' [26] But when the Comforter is come, whom I will send unto you from the Father, *even* the Spirit of truth, which proceedeth from the Father, He shall testify of Me: [27] And ye also shall bear witness, because ye have been with Me from the beginning.

THESE THINGS HAVE I SPOKEN UNTO YOU, that ye should not be offended. [2] They shall put you out of the synagogues: yea, the time cometh, that whosoever killeth you will think that he doeth God service. [3] And these things will they do unto you, because they have not known the Father, nor Me. [4] But these things have I told you, that when the time shall come, ye may remember that I told you of them. And these things I said not unto you at the beginning, because I was with you. [5] But now I go My way to Him that sent Me; and none of you asketh Me, "Whither goest Thou?" [6] But because I have said these things unto you, sorrow hath filled your heart. [7] Nevertheless I tell you the truth; It is expedient for you that I go away: for if I go not away, the Comforter will not come unto you; but if I depart, I will send Him unto you. [8] And when He is come, He will reprove the world of sin, and of righteousness, and of judgment: [9] Of sin, because they believe not on Me; [10] Of righteousness, because I go to My Father, and ye see Me no more; [11] Of judgment, because the prince of this world is judged. [12] I have yet many things to say unto you, but ye cannot bear them now. [13] Howbeit when He, the Spirit of truth, is come, He will guide you into all truth: for He shall not speak of Himself; but whatsoever He shall hear, that shall He speak: and He will shew you things to come. [14] He shall glorify Me: for He shall receive of Mine, and shall shew *it* unto you. [15] All things that the Father hath are Mine: therefore said I, that He shall take of Mine, and shall shew *it* unto you. [16] A little while, and ye shall not see Me: and again, a little while, and ye shall see Me, because I go to the Father." [17] Then said *some* of His disciples among themselves, "What is this that He saith unto us, 'A little while, and ye shall not see Me: and again, a little while, and ye shall see Me:

and, 'Because I go to the Father?' " [18] They said therefore, "What is this that He saith, 'A little while? we cannot tell what He saith.' " [19] Now Jesus knew that they were desirous to ask him, and said unto them, "Do ye enquire among yourselves of that I said, 'A little while, and ye shall not see Me: and again, a little while, and ye shall see Me?' [20] Verily, verily, I say unto you, That ye shall weep and lament, but the world shall rejoice: and ye shall be sorrowful, but your sorrow shall be turned into joy. [21] A woman when she is in travail hath sorrow, because her hour is come: but as soon as she is delivered of the child, she remembereth no more the anguish, for joy that a man is born into the world. [22] And ye now therefore have sorrow: but I will see you again, and your heart shall rejoice, and your joy no man taketh from you. [23] And in that day ye shall ask Me nothing. Verily, verily, I say unto you, Whatsoever ye shall ask the Father in My name, He will give it you. [24] Hitherto have ye asked nothing in My name: ask, and ye shall receive, that your joy may be full. [25] These things have I spoken unto you in proverbs: but the time cometh, when I shall no more speak unto you in proverbs, but I shall shew you plainly of the Father. [26] At that day ye shall ask in My name: and I say not unto you, that I will pray the Father for you: [27] For the Father Himself loveth you, because ye have loved Me, and have believed that I came out from God. [28] I came forth from the Father, and am come into the world: again, I leave the world, and go to the Father."

[29] ℙ His disciples said unto him, "Lo, now speakest Thou plainly, and speakest no proverb. [30] Now are we sure that Thou knowest all things, and needest not that any man should ask Thee: by this we believe that Thou camest forth from God." [31] Jesus answered them, "Do ye now believe? [32] Behold, the hour cometh, yea, is now come, that ye shall be scattered, every man to his own, and shall leave Me alone: and yet I am not alone, because the Father is with Me. [33] These things I have spoken unto you, that in Me ye might have peace. In the world ye shall have tribulation: but be of good cheer; I have overcome the world."

THESE WORDS SPAKE JESUS, and lifted up His eyes to heaven, and said, "Father, the hour is come; glorify Thy Son, that Thy Son also may glorify Thee: [2] As Thou hast given Him power over all flesh, that He should give eternal life to as many as Thou hast given Him. [3] And this is life eternal, that they might know Thee the only true God, and Jesus Christ, whom Thou hast sent. [4] I have glorified Thee on the earth: I have finished the work which Thou gavest Me to do. [5] And now, O Father, glorify Thou Me with Thine own self with the glory which I had with Thee before the world was. [6] I have manifested Thy name unto the men which Thou gavest me out of the world: Thine they were, and Thou gavest them Me; and they have kept Thy word. [7] Now they have known that all things whatsoever Thou hast given Me are of Thee. [8] For I have given unto them the words which Thou gavest Me; and they have received them, and have known surely that I came out from Thee, and they have believed that Thou didst send Me. [9] I pray for them: I pray not for the world, but for them which Thou hast given Me; for they are Thine. [10] And all Mine are Thine, and Thine are Mine; and I am glorified in them. [11] And now I am no more in the world, but these are in the world, and I come to Thee. Holy Father, keep through Thine own name those whom Thou hast given Me, that they may be one, as We are. [12] While I was with them in the world, I kept them in Thy name: those that Thou gavest me I have kept, and none of them is lost, but the son of perdition; that the Scripture might be fulfilled. [13] And now come I to Thee; and these things I speak in the world, that they might have My joy fulfilled in themselves. [14] I have given them Thy word; and the world hath hated them, because they are not of the world, even as I am not of the world. [15] I pray not that Thou shouldest take them out of the world, but that Thou shouldest keep them from the evil. [16] They are not of the world, even as I am not of the world. [17] Sanctify them through Thy truth: Thy word is truth. [18] As Thou hast sent Me into the world, even so have I also sent them into the world. [19] And for their sakes I sanctify Myself, that they also might be sanctified through the truth. [20] Neither pray I for these alone, but for them also which shall believe on Me through their word; [21] That they all may be one; as Thou, Father, *art* in Me, and I in Thee, that they also may be one in Us: that the world may believe that Thou hast sent Me. [22] And the glory which Thou gavest Me I have given them; that they may be one, even as We are one: [23] I in them, and Thou in Me, that they may be made perfect in one; and that the world may know that Thou hast sent Me, and hast loved them, as Thou hast loved Me. [24] Father, I will that they also, whom Thou hast given Me, be with Me where I am; that they may behold My glory, which thou hast given Me: for thou lovedst Me before the foundation of the world. [25] O righteous Father, the world hath not known Thee: but I have known Thee, and these have known that thou hast sent Me. [26] And I have declared unto them Thy name, and will declare it: that the love wherewith Thou hast loved Me may be in them, and I in them."

WHEN JESUS HAD SPOKEN THESE WORDS, He went forth with His disciples over the brook Cedron, where was a garden, into the which He entered, and His disciples. ◄ KJV

* * * * *

7. NEW SPIRIT

The evangelist John did not dwell on the mechanics of the Passover meal like the synoptic writers. But that did not mean that his script was inferior. Rather, he supplemented theirs with other topics of great importance that Jesus spoke about during that Feast.

With the backdrop of servants gathering up the dirty dishes . . . and the disciples belching with contentment, Peter leaned over and asked Jesus: *You said You would be with us only a little while longer; Lord, where are You going?*

Jesus looked around at all His disciples. *Do not let your hearts be troubled. You trust in God, trust also in Me. In My Father's house are many dwellings. If it were not so, I would have told you. I am going there to prepare a place for you. And if I go . . . I will come back and take you to be with Me so you can also be where I am.* (John 14:1–3)

With that transition in His after-dinner speech, Jesus began a long monologue with enough information dispensed to keep a fledgling Church going strong for the next several millennia. He spoke of the Way to heaven (the Father); He dwelt a while on future persecution they would experience; He reiterated the command: *Love each other.* He emphasized the power of praying faithfully. And He closed with assuring the disciples that they could live with peace of mind, and should *take heart* because *He had overcome the world.*

THE SPIRIT OF ADVOCACY

> *I will ask the Father, and He will give you another Intercessor to be with you forever: The Spirit of truth.* (John 14:16)

> *The Intercessor, the Holy Spirit, whom the Father will send in My Name, will teach you all things and will remind you of everything I have taught.* (14:26)

> *When the Intercessor comes, whom I will send to you from the Father, the Spirit of truth who emanates from the Father, He will testify about Me.* (15:26)

> *When the Intercessor comes, He will convict the world of guilt in regard to sin and righteousness and judgment . . .* (16:8)

> *I have much more to say to you, more than you can now bear. But when He, the Spirit of truth, comes, He will guide you into all truth.* (16:12–13)

But the main topic which was to undergird the steadfastness of the disciples was the introduction of the third Person of the Trinity (Tri-unity). This was He to whom John the Baptist referred when he mentioned the "Holy Spirit" back at the Jordon river.

Now Jesus called Him the Intercessor (*paraklētos,* Gk.), although this Greek word has variously been translated: "Counselor" (NIV), "Helper" (NKJV), "Comforter" (KJV). The same word is used of Jesus Himself. (1 John 2:1)

In classical Greek this word was in reference to an "attorney, advocate" who spoke in defense of a client. The NIV translated 1 John 2:1 in this sense. "Jesus speaks in our defense" to the Father if ever we should sin.

The importance of the Holy Spirit (Intercessor) was laid before us by His mention at the very beginning of Jesus's ministry: *I, John baptize with water; but He (Jesus) will baptize with the Holy Spirit!* (Mark 1:8) In the use of another metaphor, Jesus related to Nicodemus that a prerequisite for entering into the Kingdom was being born of the Spirit. (John 3:5) These figures of speech may be considered a fulfillment of Ezekiel's ancient prophecy: *I will give you a new heart and put a new Spirit in you; I will remove from you your heart of stone and give you a heart of flesh. And I will put My Spirit in you and move you to follow My decrees, and be careful to keep My laws.* (Ezekiel 36:26–27)

Under the Old Testament First Temple Era (and previous Mosaic Tabernacle wanderings), certain selected individuals were anointed with the Holy Spirit: Prophets, elders, kings, judges, etc. (Numbers 24:2; 11:17, 26; Exodus 31:3; Judges 3:10; 6:34; Psalm 51:11) This anointing empowered or engifted them to perform with supernatural discretion and ability in ministering to the congregation of Israel . . . or to prophesy to the nations.

There were two prophecies of old that stand out as worthy of note. First, this Holy Spirit which had been rarely distributed, was *in the later days,* to be made available to every believer . . . poured out on all flesh . . . sons and daughters, old men and young men . . . even on men-servants and maids! (Joel 2:28–29) Needless to say, this prophecy was fulfilled. On the Day of Pentecost, after a spectacular commotion rattled the courtyards of the Temple, the Apostle Peter stood up and quoted this prophetic word. *This is that which was prophesied . . .* (Acts 2:14–21)

Secondly, the prophet Isaiah mentioned under the inspiration of God, that the Messiah would come, and that the Spirit of God would rest upon Him (Isaiah 11:2, 42:1, 61:1) And true to His word, when Jesus returned from the wilderness of temptation in the power of the Spirit, He strolled into the Nazareth synagogue and proclaimed that the Isaiah prophecy was fulfilled in their midst. (Luke 4:14–22) And He proved it by healing the sick, casting out demons, raising the dead, and giving sight to the blind!

NEW DIMENSION

The traumatic desolation and thorough conflagration that was to end the Second Temple Jewish Era was a sad bit of news. It was a bitter pill for the Jewish disciples to swallow. No sugar coating it: No deliverance was to show up, and no restoration was to occur. The Act was over, the stage cleared.

A whole new era was to begin, though. It would not be the end of the world. There was hope, expectation, anticipation, excitement about the future. All was not lost. *A new, significant Passover, new challenge with a purposeful outcome, new life-style of unselfish service, a new Kingdom, a new commandment: Royal law of love, and a new covenant of grace . . . and now, a new spirit baptism!* They were all to take the place of the old! And the bestowing of the Holy Spirit was the icing on the cake, the glaze on the donut, the cinnamon on the roll . . .

This Spirit of truth, this Intercessor, this Advocate, this *Holy* Spirit, was to revolutionize the meaning of religion. No longer would spirituality be mere ritual, harsh regulation, or empty ceremony. Spirituality would not be "oneness with creation" but fellowship, through the Spirit, with the Creator God! Religion would never again be relegated to man-made dogma or creed, but it would consist of the inspiration and initiative of Deity. Worship of cold, dead idols would yield to the warm hug of the Spirit, encouraging believers to stay the course.

Man would not have to rely upon his own resourcefulness in the pursuit of truth, justice, and virtue. Just as the Holy Spirit *descended down on Jesus like a dove,* so believers would be enveloped by the Comforter and Counselor, and empowered to be witnesses of the grace of God to the watching world. (Acts 1:1–8) No matter the challenge, the circumstance, the cause, the Spirit of the LORD would be up to the challenge, overcome the circumstance, and further the cause.

After finishing saying these things, Jesus closed in prayer: a plea to the Father for Himself, His eleven disciples, and for believers worldwide. And after the hymn . . . after the prayer . . . after the speech . . . all the characters left stage right, went down across the Kidron Valley, and then sauntered up the steep Roman road to the slopes of Mount Olivet, blending into a dark olive grove . . . to sleep . . . perhaps to sleep.

* * * *

He comforts us Acts 9:31	*He prays for us* Romans 8:26
He fills us Acts 4:31	*He prophesies* 2 Peter 1:21
He strengthens us Ephesians 3:16	*He brings joy* 1 Thessalonians 1:6

He brings freedom   2 Cor. 3:17

He helps us obey   1 Peter 1:22

He transforms lives   2 Corin. 3:18

He speaks to us   Revelation 2:7

He reveals   1 Corinthians 2:10

He testifies of Jesus   John 15:26

He renews us   Titus 3:5

He produces character   Ga 5:22

He bestows gifts   1 Cor 12: 8

He leads us   Romans 8:14

He convicts sin   John 16:8

He sanctifies   2 Th. 2:13

He empowers us   Acts 1: 8

He unites believers   Eph 4:3

He seals us   Ephesians 1:13

He casts our demons

He teaches us   John 14:26

He guides us   John 16:13

* * * * *

THE END . . . SORT OF

THE END . . . SORT OF

The end! The end has come upon the four corners of the land. The end is now upon you . . . (Ezekiel 7:2–3)

The revelation awaits an appointed time; it peaks of the end and will not prove false. Though it linger, wait for it; it will certainly come and will not delay. (Habakkuk 2:3)

Christ is the end of the Law so that there may be righteousness for everyone who believes. (Romans 10:4)

We have come to share in Christ if we hold firmly till the end the confidence we had at first. (Hebrews 3:14)

Going, make disciples of all nations . . . and surely I am with you always, to the very end of the age. (Matthew 28:19–20)

Then the end will come, when Jesus hands over the Kingdom to God the Father after He has destroyed all dominion, authority, and power. (1 Corinthians 15:24)

As for you, go your way till the end. You will rest, and than at the end of the days you will rise to receive your alloted inheritance! (Daniel 12:13)

TO GOD BE THE GLORY. TO GOD BE THE GLORY FOR THE THINGS HE HAS DONE! IF there ever were a people who are justified in expressing an undying encomium and tribute of praise, it is the redeemed Christians gathered unto Christ in the Church.

"Praise be to the God and Father of our Lord Jesus Christ, who has blessed us in the heavenly realms with every spiritual blessing in Christ. For He chose us in Him before the creation of the world . . . In Him we have redemption through His blood, the forgiveness of sins in accordance with the riches of God's grace that He lavished on us! (Ephesians 1:3, 7) This recognition of the Christian's status was what the Apostle expressed in his epistles, and what caused him to wax eloquent in worship.

The *new dimensions* of spirituality introduced and established by the Coming of the Son of Man, Jesus the Messiah, were revolutionary, and have affected the history of modern civilization in a most salubrious and beneficial way. If Mary had aborted her baby, considering the circumstances, the world would have been the worse for it, in a most devastating way. If Christ had not been born, the inspiration of the poets and playwright would be lacking, the harmony of songster and serenaders would have been dissonance, the felicity of families and friends would have been lost. The sick would not have had hospitals, the children would not have had schools, the orphans would not have had homes.

The *Coming of the Son of Man* and His establishing of the Kingdom of God on earth — and the way He accomplished it — is worthy of man's highest praise! *Jesus commended His love for us, in that while we were yet sinners, Christ died for us.* (Romans 5:8) No greater love has been demonstrated.

The rejoicing of Christians, and the happiness they enjoy, in no way diminishes, however, the sadness of the tragedy that occurred in the desolation of Jerusalem and the destruction of the Temple. We do not look down upon those who suffered in that divine judgment, nor do we rejoice over the downfall of the enemies of the Gospel.

It is to the Jewish race that we are indebted for being caretakers of the Word of God—the prophecies that led us to the Messiah, the Savior of the world. There have been a *remnant* of noble believers who have looked forward to the coming of the Kingdom. (Luke 2:25; John 1:47; Luke 23:50–1) They have been faithful in preserving the Holy Scriptures, as well as in exemplifying true worship and holy living. To them we doff our hats. Many of the "remnant" went through severe persecution and adversity that we might benefit spiritually.

On the other hand, we are not to compromise the message of the Gospel of the Kingdom. What Christ introduced was a spiritual community for all peoples and nationalities, not just the Jews. There is no favoritism with God. (Galatians 3:28; Colossians 3:10–11; Romans 2:11) *For God so loved the* **world** *that He gave His only begotten Son . . .* (John 3:16)

And all the Mosaic ritual, regulations, holidays and feasts, have been "fulfilled" in Christ and can be summed in the *royal law of love:* Do to others as you would have them do unto you, for this sums up the Law and the Prophets. (Matthew 7:12;

Romans 13:10; James 2:8) Gentiles (ethnics, Gk.) are not required to observe any of the Jewish customs, although learning about the Old Testament era would help in understanding some theological concepts about God and the importance of the ministry of Jesus. This study of *typology* simplifies our search for understanding God's position on sin, righteousness, and justice. (Acts 15, 24:25)

To return to any of the practices of Judaism would be a slap in the face to Jesus. (Hebrews 6:1–6) As would the teaching of a "rebuilt temple, re-instituted sacrifices, or a literal Davidic throne." Any lecturing or sermonizing that replaces the spiritual Kingdom of a presently reigning King (Son of Man, Jesus) with a hope in a natural Israeli nation as the "center" of the plan of God, is non-biblical. They fly in the face of the Apostles' and of Jesus' own interpretation of the Old Testament.[1]

We are presently to be *proactive* representatives (ambassadors) of the glorious Kingdom of God doing kind deeds of charity . . . letting our light shine in the world . . . being salt in a decaying world . . . registering to vote . . . and sharing the Word of salvation. And we are to stand firm and continue to do this unto the end. Christ has promised to enable us, to confirm His word with signs following, and to walk with us *to the end of the age.*

So, while the Second Temple Era has come to an end, the work of the Church is characterized by an unending labor of love to all peoples. Let us be so doing, when the Son of Man comes for

---

1 The strong warnings of the New Testament writers adamantly forbid the teaching of any Jewish *postliminium*. Present day Zionism has nothing to do with the spiritual message of Jesus and His Gospel. "The Law and the Prophets were until John; the Kingdom of heaven now advances."

the final time, in the clouds. For *concerning the time of that day and hour* **no man** *knows.* Unlike the Fall of Jerusalem, which had several signs and prophetic time-tables expressed, the *end of this age* will be preceded by *nothing . . .* no signs of the end . . . no last days harbingers . . . no attention-getting meteorological phenomena.

At that time (singular), the true Christians will be caught working for the Kingdom . . . treating the brothers with love . . . doing acts of kindness . . . and focusing on the Jesus who has redeemed them. They will not be found fighting, napping, or indulging in a self-centered couch potato (lounge lizard) life style . . . immobilized by cultural group compliance . . . politically correct pacification . . . or mesmerized by a tele-technological zombie-ism.

To them, the end will be the finishing of a hard-run race, a well fought fight, and a firm standing in the faith. Yet all that suffering and sweating will *not be worth comparing to the glory that will be revealed in them!* (Romans 8:18) Thoughts of those momentary afflictions will evaporate in the light of the spectacular effervescent glory of *the Son of Man coming in the heavenly clouds, escorted by a retinue of angelic hosts numbered in the millions upon millions! . . .* and Jesus calling the names of saints one by one, and inviting them to come on home . . .

That time will not just be the end of an age, it will be the end of the world, and the creation of a New Heaven and Earth wherein dwelleth righteousness. *The Times, they will be 'a Changing!* For the *last time.*

APPENDIX

IF THERE HAD BEEN NOTHING WRONG WITH THE FIRST covenant, there would have been no reason to seek another. But God found fault with the people and said: "The time is coming, declares the Lord, when I will make a new covenant with the house of Israel and with the house of Judah.

"It will not be like the covenant I made with their forefathers when I took them by the hand . . . out of Egypt, because they did not remain faithful to My covenant, and I turned away from them . . ."

— *Hebrews 8:7–9*

(A) END OF AN AGE

MANY BIBLE READERS AND "SCHOLARLY" PROPHECY TEACHERS HAVE A TENDENCY TO think that every time they see the phrase "end of the age" that it *always* means "the end of the world" as we know it. As a result, if some verse mentions "signs" at the end of the age, they think that there will be "signs" at the End of the World . . . even though Jesus said there weren't!

However, upon a closer look at the biblical reference, and keeping the Hebraic context of linguistic usage in the forefront of our mind, it is more than evident that the word *age* is similar to the modern English word, *era*.

In the plural, we speak of the Middle Ages. By that, we do not mean that when the Middle Ages come to an end, that it is the end of the world. In the singular, we write about the Iron Age, the Stone Age, the Steam Age, the Atomic Age. And in each case we are describing an "era." We mean to describe a period of time in the history of mankind. None of them imply that the end of those eras are synonymous with the End of the World.

In the same manner, when the Bible writers pen the phrase, "the end of the age," we are not legitimately to assume they are referring to the end of the world . . . the end of everything . . . the end of history. Many times, the context of the biblical passage would show that that would be an illogical deduction. That is not what the inspired scribes meant to convey.

In biblical history there are several "ages" or "eras" we read about: the time of the Judges . . . the times of the Kings . . . the age of the Diaspora . . . the Restoration era . . . the Second Temple era, etc. There are also eras differentiated by the various *covenants* between God and man: the Sinai covenant, the Palestinian covenant, the Davidic covenant, the "new" covenant, etc. Of course, the major division of chronology is the era of the Old Covenant (Old Testament) and the New Covenant (New Testament) . . . which were divided by the Intertestament times (era).

This is why the inspired writers used the plural form of the word *age (aiōn*, Gk.) when referring to chronology past, present or future (from the perspective of the author). They recognized that there were many ages or eras in human and biblical history.

> . . . *the remnant of men may seek the Lord, and all the Gentiles who bear My Name, says the Lord, who does these things that have been known for* **ages.** (Acts 15:18)

> *Now to Him who is able to establish you by my Gospel . . . according to the revelation of the mystery hidden for long* **ages** *past, but now revealed through the prophetic writings . . .* (Romans 16:25–26)

> *These things happened to them as examples and were written down as warnings for us, on whom the fulfillment of the* **ages** *has come.* (1 Corinthians 10:11)

(See also Ephesians 2:7; 3:9; Colossians 1:26; Hebrews 9:26; Jude 1:25; Revelation 15:3)

A survey of the biblical word *age (aiōn,* Gk.), in the singular, shows that an interpreter or commentator — or post-evangelical propheteer — can **not** ever assume that its usage implies the End of the World.

> . . . *anyone who speaks against the Holy Spirit will not be forgiven either in this age or in the age to come.* (Matthew 12:32)

> *The harvest is the end of the age, and the harvesters are angels. As the weeds are pulled up and burned in the fire, so it will be at the end of the age.* (Matthew 13:39–40; The context shows this to be a reference to the end of the world.)

> *The people of this age marry and are given in marriage. But those who are considered worthy of taking part in that age and in the resurrection from the dead will neither marry nor be given in marriage . . .* (Luke 20:34–35)

> *Where is the wise man? Where is the scholar? Where is the philosopher of this age?* (1 Corinthians 1:20)

> *Do not deceive yourselves. If any one of you thinks he is wise by the standards of this age, he should become a "fool" so he may become wise.* (1 Corinthians 3:18)

*The god of this age has blinded the minds of them who believe not,
so they cannot see the light of the Gospel of the glory of Christ . . .*
(2 Corinthians 4:4)

*In this way, they will, lay up treasure for themselves as a firm foun-
dation for the coming age, . . .* (1 Timothy 6:19).

*. . . those who have . . . tasted the goodness of the Word of God and
the powers of the coming age, if they fall away . . .* (Hebrews 6:5)

The use of "the present" as an adjective of age in Titus 2:12, shows that there were "other" ages in the chronology of mankind . . . and that there is still to be a future age to come. The Jewish rabbis during the time of the Apostles also believed in multiple ages. The anticipated Messianic Age was to be markedly different than their present Mosaic era. That splendid age was to be for a limited period of time, after which there would be another "age to come." (An eternal one?)

The point is: When reading about the close of an age, be sure to examine the context . . . and make sure your interpretation does not contradict the description of the end laid out by Jesus.[1]

(B) COMPARISON WITH JEWISH ESCHATOLOGY

The study of "future events" in human history is called eschatology; and Jesus with His apostles, had a lot to say about this topic. Unfortunately for them, their teaching ran contrary to the prevailing cultural opinions of first century Judea. Zionism was the main focus of rabbinical theology, and Gentiles *(goyim,* Heb. *eth-nos,* Gk.) were out of the picture.

Some antagonism against the "nations" was justified, most was not; (a) the Gentiles were idolaters and that was blasphemy; (b) the low moral standards concerning fornication, adultery, incest, abortion, slavery, etc. were offensive; (c) the Gentiles were ceremonially unclean and association with them would bring defilement to the Jewish religious practices; and (d) the foreigners often persecuted them with temple desecration, high taxation, cruelty, and political oppression.

Although some Gentiles were allowed to become proselytes, and other "God-fear-ers" were accepted with caution, the "wall of separation" in the Temple courtyard

---

1   The word "end" also must be interpreted within the context of the author. There are many "ends" in history. (E.g., see Ezekiel 7:1–27, the End of the First Temple.)

was firm: any non-Jew crossing it would be killed! (Paul was accused of bringing some Gentile buddies with him beyond this wall and was arrested; Acts 21:27–36.)

When Jesus spoke parables, or rehearsed ancient Israeli history about God's favor shown to the Gentiles, it rankled the Pharisees to no end. (Luke 13:22–30, Matthew 12:41–42,21:33–45, Luke 4:24–30) They sought to kill Him. And when Paul was arrested, he was allowed to speak to the crowd which listened . . . until he came to the part where he told them he was sent *to the Gentiles*. (Acts 22:21–22)

Not only was the *good news of great joy to* **all** *people* (Luke 2:10) very hard for the rabbis to swallow, the Apostles themselves choked on it. It took a special divine revelation (vision) for Peter to comprehend this truth. And later a special council of the elders had to work out a new theology that dealt the nations into the game at the table. (Acts 10, 11, 15) There had to be a new definition of "Jew" "circumcision" "Israel" "elect" "kingdom" and even "holy city" in the systematic theology of the Early Jewish Church. (See Romans, Galatians, and Hebrews.)

They began to see the acceptance of the Gentiles as a fulfillment of Old Testament prophecy! . . . the purpose of the nation of Israel was to be a schoolmaster to bring the world to Christ — and not to be a nation of elitists . . . the wall of separation was to be torn down permanently, with no distinction between Jew and Gentile evermore . . . the promise to Abraham was a Seed (Messiah) bringing salvation to all peoples.

This revolutionary theology was what the Apostles and Christ taught and died for. It was what they suffered torture, imprisonment, and persecution for. (Matthew 23:34; 2 Corinthians 12:23–29; Acts 8:1) The Kingdom of Heaven had come, and they wanted all peoples to become citizens . . . no matter the cost. Jesus, the Son of Man, had come; and the *final Messianic age* was a present reality. They wanted all men to press in to it even though it meant persecution. "This was that" spoken of by the prophets of Israel of old. (Acts 2:16; 1 Peter 1:10–12) Not Zionism!

RABBINICAL ESCHATOLOGY

The Intertestamental Judaism and rabbinical teachings about eschatology was greatly nationalistic. It reflected the same hatred for, and superiority over, the Gentiles that was present in their everyday conduct. The *age to come, the final Messianic age*, was to be one where Israel ruled the world in the splendor resembling the garden of Eden . . . it would be a super-power on the order of King David's empire, the golden age of Hebrew history . . . national renewal would include political, military, geographical, and spiritual grandeur.

The sequence and timing of events never had a consensus among the Jews, but there was the thought of a war against heathen powers lead by an unidentified ruler.

There was disagreement as to whether God himself, the Messiah, resurrected David, or someone else would defeat these nations of evil. The Jewish literature, and later rabbinical Talmuds are indecisive.

After a judging of the forces of evil, a gathering of the dispersed of Israel was expected. This hope was one of the more consistent aspects of Jewish theology in the various writings of the time. The Messiah was to assemble and settle the Jews in their own land under the reign of His vast Kingdom. (Sirach, Psalms of Solomon, 1 Baruch, 2 Esdras)

This Messianic age was to be of a limited time (on which there was no agreement among the Jewish schools), and then there would be a consummation and new world to appear: perishable and corruptible elements would be destroyed by fire, the world purified, a resurrection of the dead, and a final judgment (although some taught a resurrection at the beginning of the Messianic kingdom). The righteous would be received into Paradise to behold the majesty of God, and the wicked cast into Gehenna . . . fire and torment.

SPIRITUAL ESCHATOLOGY

Jesus began His earthly ministry announcing Himself and His ministry as *the beginning of the fulfillment of that final Messianic age!* He equated His appearance in Judea with the start of the expected Kingdom of Heaven.

> *Jesus went into Galilee, announcing the Gospel (good news) of*
> *God: "The time has come," He said. "The Kingdom of God is at hand.*
> *Repent and believe the Gospel." (Mark 1:14–15)*

'The time' (*kairos*, Gk.) is a specific crisis point, an important moment. It referred to the day of salvation long awaited for. (Cf. Isaiah 52:7) It was the fullness of time in which God was to send His Son to redeem those under the Law. (Galatians 4:4) "Change your thinking" . . . adjust your mind (*metanoeite*, Gk.), was the Messianic command . . . grasp the idea of the Kingdom of God as a present reality! "At hand" or "has come near" is in the perfect Greek verb tense which referred to an action having been completed, and continuing on in that sense.

Yet Jesus's presentation of this "final age" did not correspond with the Intertestamental Jewish views exactly. He was more interested in personal holiness through repentance, and in personal relationship with God through the Messiah (Son of Man). His Kingdom was for "born again" citizens.

COMPARISON OF PRO-JEWISH ESCHATOLOGY

PREMILLENNIAL ESCHATOLOGY

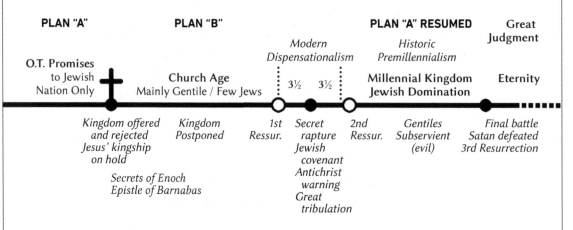

The "premillennial" eschatology is rooted in the future age concepts of the Inter-testamental Jewish literature! The same veil of Jewish nationalism (Zionism) that blinded the Jews of Jesus's day envelopes the thinking of modern Christian escha-tologists. Jesus combated it and it got Him killed and Paul rejected it and he was incarcerated. Yet today, post-evangelicals teach it vehemently.

JEWISH ESCHATOLOGY

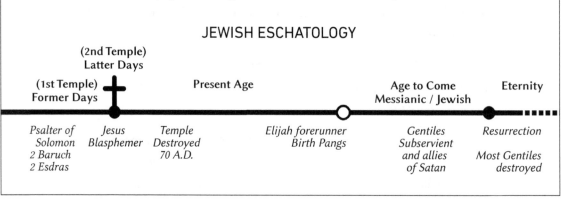

Jesus was to have an eternal dominion and an everlasting Kingdom; and He was to sit forever on the throne of King David . . . but only things spiritual and invisible are eternal . . . things physical and visible are of a temporal nature. So, instead of pilgrims in the Messianic era flocking to the city of Jerusalem . . . or to a mountain in Samaria (God forbid!) . . . those in this age that had arrived, were to worship "in spirit and in truth." (John 4:21–24) And they were not to seek any physical throne or palace because the Kingdom did not come with observation. (Luke 17:20–21) And the Kingdom of Messiah was not to be a superpower subjugating the Gentile nations, but a force that demons and spirits of infirmity would have to reckon with. (Matthew 12:28; Luke 13:10–17)

To acknowledge, and reinforce, the claim of the Messiah of the Kingdom Age, and not just His being a good Teacher (a rabbi like Hillel), Jesus insisted on the title of Son of Man (used 81 times) that was taken from the prophet Daniel's chapter about the coming Kingdom (chapter 7). He was the "Clouded One", the expected Jewish 'Anani', coming down from the throne of the Ancient of Days! In all of this, Jesus was redefining the Messiahship, the Kingdom, and the Final Age. And He would reign until the final Consummation when the Kingdom would become the Kingdom of the Father, having conquered all evil principalities and powers, the final one being death, the common denominator of all mankind.

POST-EVANGELICAL ESCHATOLOGY

Post-evangelical prophecy teachers, however, although claiming to be Christian in theology, side with the Intertestamental Jewish rabbis' concept of the final age. They reject the *spiritual nature* of the final age, and especially deny that it is a fulfillment of Old Testament prophecies. Instead they claim along with the Jews, it foretells the Zionistic political state which must be taken literally.

Along with the first century rabbinical literature, they see the nation of Israel to be the main reason for God's program in the earth. The preservation of the people . . . the occupation of the Promised Land . . . the sacrificial priestly system . . . the rebuilt Temple . . . are central to their theology.

And also, in step with the Jewish worldview, modern propheteers and eschatology orators still look forward to a **future** implementation of the Final Age. The Old Testament prophecies are unfulfilled and require a future expectation of a time yet unknown when Messiah will come (return) with King David and subdue all the Gentile nations which are to be held under the sway of evil. They still want the physical kingship in Jerusalem . . . which kingship Jesus ran away from! (John 6:14–15) They teach that this Kingdom was offered to the Jews, but when they rejected Jesus, it was postponed off into the nebulous future.

Amazingly modern teachers in succeeding generations keep claiming to recognize "signs of the times" which they are assured will usher in this Final Age. They persist on claiming this even though their failure rate has been 100%! (But it sells books!)

Gentiles, in this alleged future age, also take a back seat to the Jews. Contrary to clear biblical teaching, these post-evagelical teachers still maintain a distinction between races . . . erecting the wall again, which had been destroyed in 70 A.D. . . . and which Paul did his best to do away with. (Ephesians 2:14–22; Colossians 3:11)

Of course, the formation of the State of Israel in 1948 is of special interest to these modern telepastors who focus on Zionism. Even though Moses spelled out the basis for the ways to blessings in the Covenant relationship Israel had with God (the LORD), which was faithfulness to God and obedience to His commandments, these teachers contend that the return to the land of Palestine is God's doing! Even though the Jews have expressed no repentance, no hint of acknowledging the Kingdom of Heaven, no sign of being 'born again', and no admittance of Jesus being the Messiah of God, they consider the Statehood as some kind of *sign* of the nearness of time when, allegedly, the Messianic millennium (age to come) will commence. A fictitious *"Return in Unbelief"* was supposed to allow this anomaly.

Time will only tell how much damage will be done by the telepastors' lobbying the American politicians concerning Mideast affairs . . . based on their unchristian eschatology. It has already had an enormously detrimental effect upon the Christian non-Jews who have lived in that land for millennia. They have lost their homes, lands, farms, occupations, and lives — and churches — with these modern prophecy orators standing idly by, and turning a blind eye to their plight. [Recall that Jesus warned that "as much as you have done it unto the least of these my brothers, you have done it unto me!" (Matthew 25:40)]

One can't help but think that propheteers are *teaching a different Gospel* than what Jesus taught. The "Gospel of the Kingdom" was *at hand* in the first century; to teach otherwise is, it seems, being antichrist. To postpone it off into the future contradicts Jesus.

Jesus died for *the whole world* as a fulfillment to the promise made to Abraham. He does not show favoritism, like these modernists flaunt. (Genesis 22:18; Galatians 3:15–18; John 3:16; 1 Timothy 5:21) Jews without accepting Christ as Savior are just as "lost" as any one else . . . and the wrath of God abides on them as any one else.

It is a disservice to Israelis to suggest to them that they have God's favor, that they are entitled, or that there is a future hope for them even though they are in rebellion against Christ. *Behold, today is the day of salvation* (Hebrews 4:6–7), because this is now the final age. There is no tomorrow.

It is folly, if not outright heresy, for modern prophecy teachers to leap-frog from the Intertestament Jewish literature over to the futurism and lap of Darby, Scofield, LaHaye, and Lindsey . . . by-passing the New Testament inspired interpretation of Old Testament prophecies. By exalting the tradition of men they *make of none effect the Word of God.* (Matthew 15:3, 6; Mark 7:8–9)

(C) A TYPE OF UNDERSTANDING

It is exciting to discover that faceted gem of effervescent beauty which glitters amongst the pebbles of the New Testament Galilean landscape: the *christological-ecclesiological* apostolic principle of interpretation! It brings to radiant life even the most parched land of Old Testament history and parchment-dry prophecy. The Disciples demonstrated that the progressive revelation of God . . . the Shekinah glory in Christ is the unfolding principle of Christian theology, revealing truths that excite even the most pagan person seeking fulfillment and meaning in life. And the principle of "remnant" people as the Church is exhilarating.

The inspired writings of the Holy Spirit reveal to all peoples that the Cross and Resurrection of Christ irrevocably transform the nature of Israeli nationalism and Patriarchal promises. The Spirit's ability to hover over human history and recreate beauty out of the chaos of attitudes gone awry is mind-boggling . . . heart-warming . . . enlightening.

Freed from the preconceived hermeneutic of rigid *literalism* and Pharisaical nationalism, the redeemed soul bounds and rebounds in a liberty that can only be likened to the soaring of an uncaged eagle. Without the geographic and ethnic aspects of the Old Covenant to tether him down, the New Testament Christian can let his heart fly in the heavenlies of praise and adoration to a God of wonder. (Galatians 3:23)

This is not as the shooting forth of shrapnel from a cannon with no sights. Not by any means. Interpreters of this new age of Jesus-ite revelation are bounded, still, by the proprieties of apostolic limitations. They go only so far as the New Testament authors traveled. They follow in the footsteps of the Nazarene, and do not run ahead . . . or afoul . . . or aside. And it is found that He leads us by cool waters and green pastures in the field of theological understanding. So refreshing after wandering in the Judean wilderness of literal dogmatism where Pharisees and Sadducees duke it out with gladiatorial fervors . . . . . whose carcasses lie scattered on the hillsides . . . where the vultures of Dispensationalism circle in hopes of finding morsels to gather up for their own dietary lusts.

> *Christ died for our sins 'according to the Scriptures,' He was buried, He was raised on the third day 'according to the Scriptures.'* (1 Corinthians 15:3–4)

The New Testament writers do not present the Gospel with detached proof texts, but quote ancient references as pointers to the whole context of Israeli history as it performs its job as a schoolmaster to bring the whole world to the Savior. (Galatians

3:24–25) To contend for this is not in any way derogatory to the Jews as a people. A spiritual significance with a deeper and fuller sense of existence is an honor. Not every nation can boast or claim such a destiny. And to have national literature that oozes with sweetness of relevance for the world, like honey from a honeycomb dripping from a honey tree is soul satisfying. To have an unfolding plot within its history that is larger than its physical, literal being, leading to spiritual — and eternal — life is simply divine.

JESUS'S METHODS

Jesus Christ (may His Name be praised) is in every aspect the complete *fulfillment* of the promises made to the Patriarchs of the Old Testament, either through direct revelation, vision, or by word of the prophets through the inspiration of the Holy Spirit. (Luke 9:31; 24:44; Matthew 5:17–18; Acts 3:18; 1 Corinthians 10:11 *"the fulfillment of the ages has come"*) By the executing of His ministry as Prophet, Priest, and Prince, Jesus fulfilled all that was eagerly looked forward to by the prophets . . . and which angels even tried to sneak a peek at! (1 Peter 1:10–12)

What is important to notice is that Jesus, Himself, claimed this feat. It was fitting that He fulfill all that was anticipated by the Law, prophets, and Writings. But He, being God and full of all wisdom, recognized that there was a higher and more important hermeneutic than the strict and stringent *literalism* of the Pharisees. Jesus was, then, no stranger to *allegory, typology, figures of speech*, and what modern evangelicals and Judaizers despise with a purple passion the most, *spiritualization!* He incorporated them all in His teaching the masses . . . informing the disciples . . . and teasing the Pharisees.

The hang-up that modern pop-propheteers have is that they don't realize that allegories and spiritualizations "bounce off of" literal objects like tennis balls off a racket. (I.e., people, historical events, cities, nations, animals, and holy relics.) You cannot have figures of speech with no figures!

So yes, the angels' prophecy about a baby being born and being called Jesus was quite necessarily dealing with a literal child born in a real city called Bethlehem. But that this object would be "a horn of salvation" (Luke 1:69), or the Lamb of God (John 1:36), or "a light for revelation" (Luke 2:32), requires the utilization of spiritualization . . . which gives the physical object a higher and nobler significance. And the "sitting upon a throne of David" did not, and would not, require a literal gilded chair in order to find complete and meaningful fulfillment. A "play upon words" can in fact, be a holy drama unfolding with providential direction upon which a spine-tingling climax — a climax of the ages — emerges with jaw-dropping awe!

Lest we be found in error, scorned, mocked, and shunned by accusations from the modern literalists (Pharisees in evangelical clothing), let us examine the teaching of Jesus, taking care to see which words He used to convey the truth of the Gospel of the Kingdom.

"Destroy this Temple, and in three days I will raise it up." (John 2:19)

> Jesus spoke of the temple of His body. To the Pharisees, steeped in Temple ritual, this was a spiritualization that confounded them.

"Except a man be born again, he cannot see the Kingdom of Heaven." (John 3:3)

> Literalism got in the way of Nicodemus understanding "heavenly things" (v. 12). To be a Christian one has to see things differently.

"As Moses 'lifted up' the serpent in the wilderness, so the Son of Man must be 'lifted up.'" (John 3:14)

> These words which introduce the famous "John 3:16" verse, exemplify the use of typology by Jesus that pictures quite well the crucifixion.

"Whosoever drinks of the water that I give him shall never thirst . . . it will be a well of water springing up into everlasting life." (John 4:14)

> Jesus here is flirting with the meaning of literal water, and giving it a special meaning with more depth than any well could have! His spiritualization became so refreshing that an entire village came and drank their fill.

He said to them, "I have meat to eat that you know not of." Therefore the disciples said to one another, "Did someone else bring Him food to eat?" (John 4:32–33)

> Literalism confounded the disciples as well as the woman at the well. Jesus seems to have established His method using figurative language in this one Samaritan-district event.

"Follow Me, and I will make you fishers of men." (Matthew 4:19)

> With net, or rod and reel, hook and line? Not. Jesus added a higher dimension to this occupation with a spiritual application, leaving behind a literal meaning.

"As Jonah was three days and three nights in the whale's belly, so shall the Son of Man be three days and three nights in the heart of the earth." (Matthew 12:40)

> Here is an example of Jesus taking a literal historical event and transferring it by means of typology into a future application. He did not mean a "literal heart" of the earth, but used this symbolism to refer to His death and resurrection after three days.

"I am the living bread which came down from heaven; if any man eat of this bread, he shall live forever. The bread that I will give is My flesh . . ." The Jews therefore argued among themselves, "How can this Man give us His flesh to eat?" (John 6:51–52)

> Here is a classic example of literalism in interpretation producing a conundrum in the minds of listeners that they could not solve. That there is a spiritual meaning to Jesus's words beyond normal vocabulary is emphasized by Jesus Himself: "The words that I speak unto you are spirit and they are life, but there are some of you who believe not."

"Why do the scribes say that Elias (Elijah) *must first come* (before the Messiah)? . . . *Elias has come already, and they knew him not, but have done unto him whatsoever they listed . . ." Then the disciples understood that He spoke of John the Baptist.* (Matthew 17:10–13)

> Modern day literalists who have a hard time seeing the spiritualization of the Old Testament, cannot gainsay Jesus's own treatment of the prophecy of Malachi (4:5). John the Baptist came "in the spirit" of Elijah, and Jesus saw that that was sufficient to claim a fulfillment of this old prophecy.

A thorough study of the teaching methods of Jesus reveals His prolific use of imagery and symbolism to convey spiritual truths. He also interpreted Old Testament prophecy with more than a literal fulfillment in mind. His students (believers and non-believers) then, as today, have a hard time with this approach. It seems that then, as now, one has to be "born again" to comprehend it all!

PROPHETIC TERMINOLOGY

Jesus drew analogies, typologies, and spiritual messages from the Law, Prophets, and Writings (Old Testament); He used many figures of speech in His lectures; *and* He also used symbols, images, and Oriental verbiage in His exhortations and prophesies. In fact, the New Testament is a collection of Oriental literature, not

Occidental. Although written down in the *lingua franca of the Roman Empire*, i.e., Greek, the authors drew richly from the vernacular and dialects of the Eastern tribes and nations.

So it is not strange for Jesus to employ many of the symbols and imagery of the East, and especially of the Hebrew culture, when He presented the Olivet Discourse. He used terminology that His Hebrew disciples were familiar with . . . but which many modern Americans (and Europeans) do not fully understand. They, consequently, try to interpret Jesus's prophecy from the wrong point of view . . . with a wrong understanding of the symbolism . . . with a foreign mindset . . . with unwarranted literalism. Jesus spoke to a first century audience in the Mideast, not a New York metropolitan literary circle in the twentieth century . . . nor to a seminary in post-modern America.

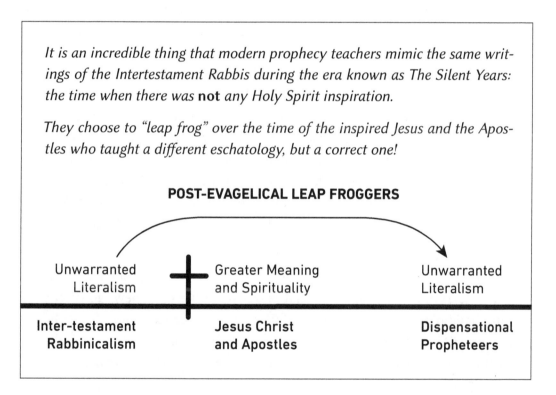

*It is an incredible thing that modern prophecy teachers mimic the same writings of the Intertestament Rabbis during the era known as The Silent Years: the time when there was **not** any Holy Spirit inspiration.*

They choose to "leap frog" over the time of the inspired Jesus and the Apostles who taught a different eschatology, but a correct one!

POST-EVAGELICAL LEAP FROGGERS

Unwarranted Literalism	Greater Meaning and Spirituality	Unwarranted Literalism
Inter-testament Rabbinicalism	Jesus Christ and Apostles	Dispensational Propheteers

(D) SECRET RAPTURE MYTHOLOGY

The teaching of *a secret rapture of the Church* is ubiquitous in evangelical circles. This idea is promoted in prophecy conferences, in fictitious novels, in sensational movies, in radio programs, and in television networks. More often than not, when the end of the world (eschatology) is discussed, or when *signs of the times* (end-time signs) are talked about, this "secret rapture" emerges as a defense mechanism against the fear of an alleged "great tribulation" to come.

The main proponents of a Secret Rapture of believers are a group of bible teachers called Dispensationalists (Dispensensationalists). These prophecy teachers were inspired by the writings of Edward Irving and John Nelson Darby, the later being a prominent Plymouth Brethren minister. Darby systematized Dispensationalism and promoted the idea of a rapture of the church as the beginning of events in the "end times" (i.e., end of the world). He came to the Americas and influenced men like A. J. Gordon, Arno Gabelein, S. I. Scofield, etc. By means of Niagara Prophecy Conferences, the *Scofield Reference Study Bible*, and fictitious novels *(Jesus Is Coming, In the Twinkling of an Eye)*, as well as back-woods revival wild-fire, their twist on the doctrine of Last Things blanketed the evangelical churches.

Darby (1800 – 1882) especially laid out a 7-year plan initiated by an alleged Secret Rapture, which was to begin the intrigue that would end with Christ coming to set up a Jewish millennium wherein Jesus and a resurrected King David would reign over the nasty Gentile nations! The footnotes of the *Scofield Bible* (first printed in 1909 and revised in 1917) spread his idea of a distinction between the Jews and the Gentiles in God's plan for the world. Gary DeMar noted that . . .

> Modern dispensational scholars like to argue that their prophetic teachings are as old as the hills, and that preterism is the wild, new kid on the prophetic block. But a survey of Bible commentators will prove that the reverse is true. Dispensationalism is relatively new and has become popular within the last one hundred years . . . (Gary DeMar, *Is Jesus Coming Soon?* 2006, p. 17)

Mr. DeMar wrote that the "belief that key New Testament prophecies were fulfilled in the first century" was by far "the dominant eschatological perspective within the whole history of the church."

Tim LaHaye, a prolific and rabid promoter of modern Dispensationalism admitted in one of his books that . . .

> It is true that the pre-Trib [Secret Rapture] position was not formed in detail until 1826–28 . . . *(No Fear of the Storm*, 1992, p. 172)

Interestingly, Mr. LaHaye also admitted that "No single verse specifically states 'Christ will come before the (sic) Tribulation.' (op. cit. p. 188; note that in the Greek there is no article "the" but only *great tribulation* KJV, non-capitalized; Matthew 24:9 = affliction; 24:21 = distress, NIV; Acts 11:19 = persecution; *thlipsis,* Gk.)

EISEGESIS GONE WILD

It must be considered a travesty of biblical interpretation for these teachers to pull out of the Olivet Discourse a few verses . . . stretch them to a tribulation of seven years . . . add a definite article, "the" . . . transport them off into the nebulous future on a magic carpet of Zionism . . . and assuage their fears by concocting an escape hatch known as the *secret rapture of the Church.* Their manufacturing of the Great Tribulation in the end times just before the coming of Christ (*parousia,* Gk.), with all its Steven Spielberg sensational panorama apocalyptic fervor, goes hereticaly contrary to the plain teaching of Jesus: *there will be normal times with* **no** *signs or precursory events to tip off the Coming of Christ!* (Matthew 24:44).

This pathetic exegesis also mocks the teaching of Jesus that emphasized the fact that Christ's return will not at all be *silent* nor *secret!* He specifically stated that it will be as evident as a *flash of lightning swooshing across a Kansas sky.* (Matthew 24:27) *And* Jesus admonished His disciples to recognize anyone who taught otherwise as *false prophets . . . false . . . prophets!* (24:11, 24)

Christ will come in His glory; He will arrive with a massive bodyguard of all the angels; at that time He will command His angels to *weed out all who do evil* **first**. (Matthew 13:30; 16:27; 25:31) And the Apostle Paul later reminded the church at Thessalonica, *according to the Lord's own word,* that Christ will come down from heaven with a *loud command (shout,* KJV*), with the voice of the archangel and with the trumpet call of God!* (1 Thessalonians 4:15–16) Nothing secret about all this!

If there ever were a double "coming" of Christ separated with a seven-year period of great distress (persecution, tribulation), that would have been a good opportunity for Paul to mention it. But there is absolutely no hint of such a thing. It takes a vivid imagination-gone-wild, and a toxic case of eisegesis, to come up with such a thing.

Instead, Paul repeats Jesus's warning that that day will not be pre-announced by any precursory omens or earth-shaking political events, but will *come like a thief in the night.* (1 Thessalonians 5:2; Matthew 24:43) It will be at a time of normal, every-day activities. .

ONE NEW MAN

A preliminary check on an interpretation of modern Dispensationalism would have been the clear teaching of the Apostles of the New Testament concerning the creation of *one new man: Jew and Gentile "together" constituting the Congregation of the Lord, the Church.* (Ephesians 2:11–18) The "distinction" separating Jew and the (Gentile) church was done away . . . the wall of separation was destroyed by Christ . . . there is no favoritism with God . . . Gentiles are fellow-heirs with Jews. How many ways does God (through the inspiration of the Holy Spirit) have to say it? God does not have two separate plans of salvation, nor two individual programs, for different ethnic groups. The alleged Gentile church (sic) is not "raptured" at a different time from Jewish congregations, simply because "the Church" is made up of both together now and always.

The believing nations, and Jews who are circumcised in the heart, are *One Body, baptized in One Spirit, unto One faith, to One calling, in One God.* And they will all be glorified in the "One Coming" at the end of time.

(E) NO SECRET RAPTURE

I am not aware that there was any definite teaching that there should be a secret rapture of the church at a secret coming until this was given forth as an 'utterance' in Mr. Irving's church from what was then received as being the voice of the Spirit. But whether any one ever asserted such a thing or not, it was from that supposed revelation that the modern doctrine and the modern phraseology respecting it arose. It came, not from the Holy Scripture, but from that which falsely pretended to be the Spirit of God.

> S. P. Tregelles (Plymouth Brethren who rejected the
> Secret Rapture), *The Hope of Christ . . . Second Coming*
> (London: Samuel Bagster and Sons, 1864), pp. 34–37

Now, after years of study and prayer, I am absolutely convinced that there will be no rapture before the tribulation . . . . I believed the other theory simply because I was taught it by W. E. Blackstone in his book, *Jesus is Coming*, the *Scofield Reference Bible*, and prophetic conferences, and Bible schools; but when I began to search the scriptures for myself I discovered that there is not a single verse in the Bible that upholds the pre-tribulation theory.

> Oswald J. Smith, *Tribulation or Rapture—Which?*
> (London: The Sovereign Grace Advent Testimony),
> p 2–3.

It is mortifying to remember that I not only held and taught these novelties myself, but that I even enjoyed a complacent sense of superiority because thereof, and regarded with feelings of pity and contempt those who had not received the 'new light' and were unacquainted with this up-to-date method of 'rightly dividing the word of truth.'

. . . The time came . . . when the inconsistencies and self-contradictions of the system itself; and above all, the impossibility of reconciling its main positions with be plain statements of the Word of God, became so glaringly evident that I could not do otherwise than renounce it.

> Philip Mauro (1859–1952, lawyer and Bible scholar),
> quoted in William R. Kimball,
> *The Rapture, A Question of Timing*
> (Grand Rapids: Baker Book House, 1985) , pp. 1 77–178

Emphatically not! I know this view very well. In the earlier years of my ministry I taught it and incorporated it in one of my books *(God's Method with Man)*. But further study so convinced me of the error of this teaching that I actually went to the expense of buying the plates from the publisher and destroying them. The idea of a separate and secret coming of Christ is a vagary of prophetic interpretation without any Biblical basis whatsoever.

> G. Campbell Morgan (1863–1945,
> Bible commentator and preacher), Ibid.

Until brought to the fore through the writings and the preaching and teaching of a distinguished ex-clergyman, Mr. J. N. Darby, in the early part of the last century [i.e. the nineteenth century], it is scarcely to be found in a single book or sermon through the period of sixteen hundred years!

If any doubt this statement, let them search, as the writer has in measure done, the remarks of the so-called Fathers, both pre- and post-Nicene; the theological treatises of the scholastic divine; Roman Catholic writers of all shades of thought; the literature of the Reformation; the sermons and expositions of the Puritans; and the general theological works of the day. He will find the "mystery" conspicuous by its absence.

> H. A. Ironside (himself a Dispensationalist),
> *The Mysteries of God* (New York: Loizeaux Brothers,
> 1946) pp 0 50–51

Not once, among fifty arguments [in John Walvoord's book, *The Rapture Question*], does this godly Christian leader cite one biblical text that explicitly teaches pretribulation rapturism—not once. This was not an oversight. The reason for the omission of any pretribulation Rapture texts is clear. There are none.

Walvoord's own comment helps substantiate that fact. He wrote, "It is therefore not too much to say that the Rapture question is determined more by ecclesiology [the doctrine of the church] than eschatology [the doctrine of the last things] " . . . There simply is no explicit exegetical evidence for pretribulation rapturism.

> Marvin Rosenthal (prominent evangelist to the Jewish people), *The Pre-wrath Rapture of the Church: A New Understanding of the Rapture, the Tribulation, and the Second Coming* (Nashville, TN: Thomas Nelson, 1990), p. 280.

For centuries, Christian writers have understood that 1 Thessalonians 4:13–18 is describing the general resurrection of believers when Jesus returns, as the Apostles' Creed states, "to judge the living and the dead." Nothing is said about Jesus coming again to rapture His church in a separate invisible event . . . nothing in this passage supports a pretrib or any-trib version of this event.

> Gary DeMar, *End Times Fiction*, (Nashville, TN: Thomas Nelson, 2001) p. 23–4.

(F) SIGNS OF HERESY

> *Then the LORD said to me, "The prophets are prophesying lies in My Name. I have not sent them or appointed them or spoken to them. They are prophesying to you false visions, divinations, idolatries, and the delusions of their own minds."* (Jeremiah 14:14)

Every time a Christian turns on the radio or television, he can't help but hear some evangelical mention the term *"these last days"* or *"signs of the end-times"*. There is an abundance of teachers and preachers caught up in the Last Days frenzy, and they all know assuredly that the Second Coming is just around the corner! Well . . . not exactly the Second Coming, but those events that are suppose to eventually usher in the Second Coming of Christ: Apostasy of the Church, wars and rumors of wars, one world government, antichrist, Israeli restoration, Mid-East oil crisis, Russian-led armageddon, and so on.

Hidden from common Christian congregations, and the avid Christian radio listener, is the salient fact that previous generations in generation after generation, there have been prophets of doom saying the same thing: *Their* generation was the one to see the fulfillment of last days events . . . the signs were all around! Those teachers and commentators of prophetic verses assuredly knew the Second Coming was just around the corner.

Most congregations of believers do not have a *chronological perspective . . .* knowledge of Church history . . . awareness of previous movements and cults, and so they are in the dark about the failure of all those prophecy teachers' calculations and predictions concerning the end-times. They do not realize that the accuracy rate of the last-days alarmists is *zero* percent! None of them have panned out! All those prophets have been wrong: Their generation was *not* the last days. Their failure rate has been 100%.

Yet, this has not stopped the modern Prophecy Conferences . . . radio programs . . . television evangelists . . . from continuing to spew forth more prognostications. The clarion call for listeners and viewers to rush to buy their latest books and DVDs continues on unabated. The fears . . . anxieties . . . curiosities of believers are exploited to the max! Their minds are manipulated with reckless abandon by them, not caring that their Heavenly Father is taking this all in . . . with consternation . . . with disgust . . . with sadness.

HERESY HAVEN

The average pew-sitter has been trained, wittingly or non-wittingly, to not question what comes across the sacred desk. He (she) naively accepts whatever his pastor promulgates. And as a result their tithes are going to the support of men who are disseminating heresies that would even make the Pelagians blush, or the ancient Gnostics jealous, or the Ebionites envious. Note some examples from the following modern teachings.

- Contrary to the plain teaching of the Romans epistle which presented only one path to salvation (Romans 10:1–4; see also Galatians 3:11; 4:9), one end-time pastor has taught **two paths**, one for the Gentiles, and one for the Jews . . . with the hope of a rebuilt Temple!

- Other pastors have gone so far as to **set dates** for the Second Coming. Both cultists and evangelicals have engaged in this futility. The folly of the Adventists and the Jehovah Witnesses with all their failed predictions is also the *modus operandi* of evangelicals in our theological neighborhoods.

- Judaizers have proliferated on the church landscape promoting a return to **Jewish rituals** and customs instead of acknowledging the "new man" theology of Paul and the Early Church theologians and scholars, which did away with national distinction (Romans 10:12; Ephesians 2:15). The New Covenant Church had been thought to be interracial, with the wall between the Jews and the Gentiles torn down . . . forever. But not so according to radio evangelists!

- One denomination has adopted "whole hog" historical distinctions concerning the ministry of the **Holy Spirit** by their dispensational charting. While relegating a back-seat to the charismatic gifts of the Spirit, they still pray for their sick to get healed . . . and are surprised when they are! According to their prophetic reckonings, the Holy Spirit has ceased moving in the "gifts." And so the heresies proliferate as the wind blows. (Eph. 4:14)

CAUSE AND EFFECT

The objective observer of "this prophecy, end-times proliferation" would pause to wonder: Why do the believers fall for such heretical tendencies? How can the false prophecy teachers get away with their shenanigans when they are so wrong? What facilitates these pastors such that they can disseminate their beliefs with ease . . . and without a twinge of conscience . . . without blinking an eye? How come the congregations don't catch on to their being hood-winked? Why are they easy picking for exploitation and manipulation? What would cause believers to accept as true doctrines of men that can so easily be shown to be false?

The answers to these questions are varied and manifold. But "why the sheep are misled" can be arranged and organized into the following categories. They are listed for your consideration.

• Sincere Devotion and "Christian" Character

This Day in Baptist History, a daily devotional printed in 1993, gives us some insight into the reason many are misled by pastors into believing false ideas concerning prophecy. It relates the story of William Miller, a licensed Baptist minister in New York. He preached distinctive doctrines about the Second Coming and the end of the world, and set a date of 1843 as the time of the Lord's return! Of course, it didn't happen, so he recalculated, and came up with 1844, which also failed to transpire. It devastated many believers who had bought into his teaching.

But the point this book made, was that Rev. Miller was a sincere student of the Bible; not a charlatan attempting his own aggrandizement. Those who knew him esteemed him highly for his integrity, sincere devotion, and character.

Today, there is a tendency to look upon Rev. Miller with contempt, but back then, his congregation looked up to him because of his righteous demeanor. And this was their downfall. They mistook the aura of Christian character as being synonymous with *Truth* telling.

How could such a "good man" be a teacher of error? Well, the fact is there are good men who do wrong; and there are evil men who are charitable! Personality and integrity can be misleading in determining true dogma . . . and true prophetic interpretation. While good character is noble, it is a side issue. Interpretations, themselves, must be researched and analyzed . . . no matter who the pastor is teaching it! A good student of the Bible can not presume a doctrine to be true simply because a notable minister teaches it.

This lesson is not easily learned. Those who followed the teachings of H. Grattan Guinness fell into the same error as the congregation of Miller. In his book, *The Approaching End of the Age*, he reassures us of his deep reverence for the Scriptures and his faith in the blessed hope of the return of Christ . . . which are most commendable. Yet, because of the traumatic historical and political events in Europe and Turkey, and because of his penchant for studying "cycles" in astronomy, he drew the conclusion that the people of his day were "indeed living in the closing years of this dispensation — the time of the end." (That was 1878.) Mr. Guinness desired to "increase practical holiness" and believed in the "joyful hope" and partook in "the earnest activity of the work of the Lord." These are all good Christian virtues . . . but they do not insure his teaching as truthful! In fact, his year-day approach to interpreting prophecy was just as inaccurate as Rev. Miller's.

Today we revere men of God who respect the Word; we acknowledge our gratitude for ministers of the Gospel who are evangelistically minded. But this is no justification for receiving everything they say about the signs of the end times without careful examination. The same scrutiny must be given to modern pastors as should have been given to Rev. Miller and his erroneous predictions. Graduating from a biblical seminary where students are indoctrinated in a particular prophetic viewpoint also does not guarantee that we will be hearing truth . . . no matter how, otherwise, the students are righteous and dedicated. Most congregations forget this, and begin parroting their ideas about the "end times".

• Proliferation of Media

Near the end of the 1800s and beginning of the 1900s there was generated great interest in prophetic scriptures. Many conferences were held, lectures given, and novels written, espousing the latest faddish interpretation. Much of people's understanding of prophecy came from reading novels like *In the Twinkling of an Eye*. It did not come from personal Bible study.

The same is true of today's congregations. They get their view of the end of the world from novels and movies such as the "Left Behind" series. One pastor was recently approached and confronted about his not relishing the subject matter in these media. His retort, "But they are novels! Not the Bible!" did not seem to phase the naive believer. This highlights the fact that lazy Christians are greatly influenced by media presentations, more so than personal Bible study. Perhaps we ought to say harried Christians, instead, because of the busy schedule most have in this high-tech world.

It is a well-known sociological fact that culture is most influenced by the arts and entertainment industry. Songs have framed as well as inspired great movements in history. ("The Battle Hymn of the Republic", "We Shall Overcome", "Give Peace a Chance", are a few examples) Comedy shows on television have educated whole societies on topics like morality, family, politics, alcohol use, drug use, etc. Program directors know that "if you get people to laugh at sin, they won't take sin seriously" and they will end up justifying engaging in it. Referendums, initiatives, and political elections have been easily swayed by such tactics. (Note how many times homosexual depravity was presented on television shows just before it became legalized in the United States.)

So it is not out of the ordinary that believers' understanding of prophecy was greatly influenced by these novels and movies played over and over again on Christian television (sic). It is understandable why so many evangelicals believe the spiel about "last day, end time signs" and why they are easily exploited by book sellers, and why they are full of fear and anxiety about contemporary events in international affairs (fear over One World Government takeover, implanted chips in humans, and bar codes, etc.).

Along with the publication of novels, the *Scofield Bible* must be considered as a major instrument for the proliferation of false end-time teaching. This reference Bible with its Scofield notes introduced many susceptible believers to doctrines (heresies) not taught by orthodox Christianity. It was "bankrolled" by the Plymouth Brethren sect, and J. N. Darby, its controversial leader, for publication in the United States. To the uninitiated believer, the "notes" were considered gospel, and led many to misinterpret Jesus's teaching about the end of the world.

• Psychology of Lies

But why should so many evangelicals believe all this teaching about modern society being the "end of the world"? Why do believers accept dates about Christ's coming back? Why has the Christian church in America come to believe there are such a thing as "signs" of the "times"?

The answer can be found in a statement by the famed psychologist, William James (1842–1910): "If a lie is told often enough people will believe it; and the greater the lie, the greater the deception." It is a concept that Hitler picked up on, and used mightily in his propaganda machinery. Lazy thinking leads to faulty thinking . . . and most people have lazy ears and apathetic minds. The metaphor of "sheep" to describe masses of people is an apt description. They will follow a Judas goat *en masse* to their death.

Week after week of pastors parroting the misinterpretations of scriptural prophecy has been very effective at indoctrinating a whole generation of Christians. The steady barrage of end-time preaching has produced a type of zombie that can only repeat back mechanically (and with great zeal when contradicted) what he hears on Sunday (and Christian radio).

But just as "the unexamined life is not worth living", so also, "the unexamined prophetic interpretation is not worth believing".

• Dipping from Each Other's Cup

The great prophet, Jeremiah, related the words of the LORD concerning the methods and habits of false prophets in ancient times. His description is most apropo in revealing the propensity of false prophecy-teachers today:

> *I am against the prophets who steal from one another words supposedly from Me. Yes, declares the Lord, I am against the prophets who wag their own tongues and yet declare, 'the LORD says.' Indeed,*

> *I am against those who prophesy false dreams, declares the LORD.*
> *They tell them and lead my people astray with their reckless lies, yet*
> *I did not send or appoint them. They do not benefit these people in*
> *the least, declares the LORD!* (Jeremiah 23:30–32)

God bemoaned the fact that the prophets were "dipping from each other's cup" instead of being the mouthpiece of God. They each wet their finger and placed it in the prophetic/social wind to see which way it was blowing and then spake accordingly. And as then, so today, prophetic fads sweep through the Sunday morning pulpits like a flu epidemic without remedy! Not wanting to be left out, pastors orate with assuredness a listing of "the signs of the times", and the latest insight into "one world conspiracy." Most are mimicking what they heard from other pastors, or repeating the insight gained from some prophecy novel . . . without checking with God about their veracity.

An example of this phenomena is given in 1 Kings 22, where Micaiah, the prophet, is advised to *go along with* the 400 other prophets from the school of the prophets. It seemed that one, Zedekiah, had declared that the kings would be victorious in battle, *and all the other prophets were prophesying the same thing* (22:12). When told to *Let his words agree with theirs,* Micaiah had the common sense, and righteous character to *only tell what the Lord tells me!* He wasn't about to "dip from other prophets' cups."

Just in like Micaiah's day, there is pressure from other prophecy teachers and pastors to go along with the "end times" messages concerning alleged "signs of the times". Those who stand tall are shunned or black-listed and not invited to conferences.

It should be added, that many pastors are unwitting pawns of the prophecy pundits. These pastors are men of righteous character, but they have not personally had the time or the ability to do in depth research about the Second Coming. It is easier for them to simply repeat the popular spiel; "dipping" allows them more time to carry out their many other pastoral duties.

Church history is replete with men who have taken the time to check out prophetic teachings, and saved their congregations from being taken in by the end-times mentality. (Philip Mauro, G. Campbell Morgan, Steve Gregg, George Mueller, et al.) They have had the courage to switch back to Jesus's emphasis concerning the end of the world (Matthew 25, You don't know; no signs). But there are not enough pastors who have done this courageous act. Such men *have a zeal, but not according to true knowledge.* (Romans 10:2) They'd rather dip than switch.

• Egregious Hermeneutics

One of the main reasons why sheep and shepherd, alike, are led astray concerning the "end time" message is very poor exegesis . . . horrible interpretation . . . violation of hermeneutic principles. Noticeable are these propensities:

1. HALF-SENTENCE HERMENEUTICS — Many of the scriptures that allegedly support "signs of the times" schematics are only half-way quoted. Let us first look at a common abuse of scripture, and then apply it to the modern eschatology debate.

    How often have we heard pastors say that "heaven is so wonderful we just can't express its glory adequately"? They then quote 1 Corinthians 2:9, *Eye hath not seen, nor ear heard, nor mind conceived, what God has prepared for those who love Him.* But this is just half the sentence! Read the rest of the sentence: *but God has revealed it to us by His Spirit!* The "whole sentence" states just the opposite of what the pastor is preaching! It has nothing to do with "lack of knowledge" but rather, "God's revelation by His Holy Spirit".

    So also, notice the fatal tendency of pastors to half-way quote end-time scriptures: *As it was in the days of Noah, so shall it be at the coming of the Son of Man, for in the days before the flood, people were eating and drinking, marrying and giving in marriage . . .* (Matthew 24:37–38) After reciting this, pastors and prophecy teachers go on a rant about how "evil" the world will be at the Second Coming, and that this is a sign of the end-times!

    However, when we read the rest of the sentence, Jesus is seen to be giving the opposite message! *". . . and they **knew not** until the flood came and took them all away; so shall also the coming of the Son of Man be* (v. 39)" Jesus wasn't giving "signs of the end-time", He was warning that there would be **no** signs; and He repeated this statement over and over again through out this chapter, and in the next: *You **know not** what hour your Lord doth come!*

    These verses are just the opposite of what modern prophecy teachers orate. They turn Jesus's words into an antithesis of meaning. If C. S. Lewis's Screwtape were to plot such a predicament, he could not have done a better job of subverting Christ's intent!

2. BLATANT MISREPRESENTATION — While we are still thinking of Matthew's verses, notice how modern teachers misrepresent the truth: they consider "eating and drinking, marrying and giving in marriage" to be *end-time signs* of gross hedonism (which they apply to this generation). However, that is just the opposite of what Jesus was saying. These activities are common,

normal, everyday habits—not evil signs. Jesus came "eating and drinking" and Solomon "ate and drank" for God had blessed his nation—and Jesus isn't certainly guilty of hedonism! "Marrying" is what men do, and being "given in marriage" is what women do, in the normal process of life. Jesus was not speaking of immorality or adultery!

Another major prophetic passage that is misrepresented appears in Daniel. Modern prophetic conference speakers relish orating about an alleged *covenant with antichrist and the Jews,* which they say will be broken after 3½ years. All this information comes only from one scripture in Daniel 9.

However, a survey of this passage reveals the mention of an *Anointed One,* and not the alleged anti-Anointed One. Prophets assert just the opposite of what is stated! In fact, this passage, when correctly interpreted, is a beautiful picture of the New Covenant Jesus instituted at the end of 3 years of ministry, which he sealed with His own blood by being "cut off". (9:26) How obscene it is to take that which is holy, and turn it into a demonic scenario of the end-times!

Another example of poor hermeneutics is the twisting of the meaning of 1 Thessalonians 4:16–18. A silent rapture of the church is the major linchpin of end-time profiteers (book-sellers and movie producers), yet the Coming of the Lord is anything but silent according to Paul: *Loud command (shout,* KJV*), voice of an archangel, trumpet of God!* Just the opposite of what modern teachers say! Paul seemed to be underscoring what Jesus taught back in Matthew 24:27 *For as the lightning that comes from the east is visible even in the west, so will be the coming of the Son of Man!* There is nothing "secret" about lightning, nor "silent."

Another example of blatant misrepresentation is found in their rapture dogma concerning the taking away of the righteous first. The kingdom parables of Matthew 13 tell us that the wicked weeds (tares, KJV) will be taken out first, not the wheat. And Jesus emphasized that He was talking about the *end of the age* (13:40). Prophecy teachers have no qualms, it seems, about twisting the scriptures to mean just the opposite of what God intended them to mean.

3. **CHERRY-PICKING SCRIPTURES**—Prophecy mongers are noted for their gross avoidance of embarrassling verses. They only pick those they can twist with ease. For example, notice that 1 John mentioned the existence of many antichrists who were already present in the days of the Early Church. And notice that Clarence Larkin, an avid Dispensationalist, drew from every other book, except 1 John, in his chart presentations. John destroys the idea

of just one major antichrist, and destroys the momentum of modern manipulators who play on the fears of our brothers and sisters.

Notice their avoidance of the important verse in John 4:21: *Believe me . . . the time is coming when you will worship the Father neither on this mountain nor in Jerusalem . . . Yet a time is coming and has now come when the true worshipers will worship the Father in spirit and in truth.* (vs. 22) This teaching of Jesus negates all the modern end-time prophets who focus on real estate in the Mideast, and the building of a new Jewish Temple. But rarely do pastors mention this when dealing with their end-time signs. Invisible spiritual realities fall prey to programs that people can see with their physical eyes; like the ancient Jews, they have a hard time grasping a *spiritual Kingdom consisting of righteous, joy, and peace in the Holy Spirit.* (Romans 14:17) And, like the Jews, they have a problem with equality of races, *for their is no difference between Jew and Gentile* (Romans 10:12; Luke 3:8)

The several "Samaritan" parables and incidents in Jesus's life where He ministered to non-Jews should be a clue to modern prophecy teachers that God doesn't consider one race more "chosen" than another, and that His emphasis is a love for all nations. Indeed, the Israeli nation was chosen to be a *schoolmaster* to bring us to Christ; but a tutor is no longer needed when the student has matured. (Galatians 3:24) They were never "chosen" to be superior over other ethnic groups. Prophetic schemers and chart diagrammers need to take *"the whole counsel of God"* into consideration when teaching about the end of the world (eschatology). Only by cherry-picking verses can they arrive at a special program for the Jews apart from Gentile nations. They are committing the same mistake the first century people did.

The end-time special plan for the Israeli nation is also promoted by ignoring scriptures by Jesus who declared that there would be great remorse when the Jews *see Abraham, Isaac and Jacob and all the prophets in the Kingdom of God, but you yourselves thrown out.* (Luke 13:28) Only by repentance and acknowledging that it is Jesus who *has come in the Name of the Lord,* will Jews be in right relationship with God. (Psalm 118:26; Luke 13:35) The hope of the Gentiles is the same hope of the Israelis. (Jeremiah 14:8; Ephesians 2:11–18) The "good news of great joy" of Christmas is *for all people: A Savior who is Christ the Lord* (Luke 2:10–11) There is really no plan B. *The Law and the Prophets were proclaimed until John. Since that time the good news of the Kingdom of God is being preached.* (Luke 16:16; Hebrews 10:9) The only way everyone in Israel can be saved is through *the Deliverer* (Romans 11:26; "And so" is a preposition of manner, not of chronology.), and there are few ("the elect" according to Paul) in every generation who do respond to the Gospel (Luke 13:24).

CHRISTIAN BEWARE

The culture of fear and atmosphere of anxiety that modern prophecy men promote by their teaching about signs of the times and end-time prophecies is not of God. In fact, they are teaching contrary to the plain words of Jesus . . . and that is treasonous! To preach things that are just the opposite of Jesus's sermons is diabolical, to say the least. Our brothers and sisters in Christ deserve better than to be exploited and manipulated by pastors who are "dipping from each other's cup" instead of proclaiming the words of God, . . . and making a profit along the way.

It behooves every believer to (a) glean eschatological beliefs from a reading of the Bible, not from novels or movies, or sect commentaries; (b) don't allow authority figures too much influence or undue control of your thinking, no matter their perceived character or sincerity; (c) give due weight to the two major divisions in your Bible, i.e. the priority of the New Testament (covenant) over the annulled Old which was used by God to bring us all to the New; and (d) if possible, study the history of prophets and teachers who have made outlandish predictions, and the inaccuracy of their prognostications concerning their generation being "the last days."

> *No one knows about that day or hour, not even the angels in heaven, nor the Son, but only the Father.* (Matthew 24:36).
>
> *It is not for you to know the times or dates the Father has set by His own authority.* (Acts 1:7)

(G) NEPOSISM REVIVED

There is an interesting history of the beliefs about the Second Coming of Christ, that is given in the appendix of the old book, *Tarry Till I Come* (George Croly, 1827, 1901, Funk & Wagnall). It is entitled, *The Second Coming of Christ—a Succinct History*, and is written by one, Daniel Seelye Gregory, DD., LLD.

After surveying the rise of chiliastic notions for a few centuries, he brought us to the story of Nepos, an Egyptian bishop of the region around Arsinoe. The context of the story related to the Alexandrian School of theology under the three great teachers, Clement of Alexandria, Origen his pupil, and Dionysius the pupil of Origen. This particular school did not reject the Apocalypse, but addressed themselves to opposing the grossly literal interpretations put upon it by the Chiliasts. We quote:

"The method adopted by Bishop Dionysius of Alexandria is of peculiar interest, as showing what may be accomplished by candid Christian discussion. Neander gives a somewhat detailed account of his course (*Church History*, vol. i., p. 452)

"Nepos, a pious Egyptian bishop belonging to the region of Arsinoe, and who was a devoted friend of the sensual Chiliasm, wrote a book against the Alexandrian school, entitled, 'A Refutation of the Allegorists.' The book seems to have found great favor with the clergy and laity in the above-mentioned district. Great mysteries and disclosures of future events were supposed to be found here; and many engaged with more zeal in the study of the book and theory of Nepos than in that of the Bible and its doctrines.

"So zealous did his disciples become for this tenet that they brought the charge of heresy against all who refused to accept it. Whole churches separated themselves from their communion with the mother church at Alexandria. After the death of Nepos, a country priest, Coracion, took the leadership of this party.

"Neander gives an interesting account of the way in which, by instruction and discussion, the good and wise Bishop of Alexandria, Dionysius, led Coracion back to the faith. This happened in the year 255.

"Having restored the unity of faith among his own churches, Dionysius wrote his work on the Promises, for the instruction of the churches. By the opening of the fourth century Chiliasm seems to have almost disappeared from the Church, as is shown by the statements of Eusebius, the church historian. Describing the writings of Papias, Eusebius remarks that they contain 'matters rather too fabulous,' among which he enumerates the opinion of Papias that 'there would be a certain millennium after the resurrection, and that there would be a corporeal reign of Christ on this very earth.'

"The return to the Catholic doctrine on the subject seems therefore to have been quite general before the year 400." (p. 580)

MODERN LITERALISTS

In recent centuries of church history there has been a return to the undo emphasis upon strict literalism, and with it, an adoption of the old Intertestamental rabbinical ideas of a millennial period of time with an emphasis on Jewish nationalism and "holy land" occupation (although the rabbis weren't agreed on the exact length of time: 400 years, 1,000 years, indefinite, etc.) They have returned to the Jewish materialism and the Patristic fancies of a sensually pleasant utopia (Edenic existence) in their lectures.[2]

The modern day millennialists include a belief in more than one Second Coming, a distinction between Israel and the Church, a Secret Escape before an alleged "great tribulation", and a plethora of "signs of the times" indicators of the end of the world.

Among the propagandists Chafer, Darby, Scofield, Walvoord, Watson, and Gabelein, was Arthur T. Pierson. In his futuristic millennial scheme he listed seven prominent *signs* that he alleged the Holy Oracles "hinted at." These were:

1. A widespread witness to Christ, with
2. a widespread decline in godliness.
3. A marked movement among Jews, with
4. the fullness of the Gentiles.
5. Singularly unresting state of society, with
6. a daring development of iniquity and
7. a confident sense of false security.

In his essay, *Reasons For the Belief that Christ May Come Within the Next Twenty Years,* he then described the state of the union which he thought represented these signs of the times. We quote him at length for an important reason:

> The present drift of society is toward *anarchy,* a drift that has been peculiarly rapid during the last quarter-century. Socialism, communism, nihilism, and the hot battle between capital and labor, monopoly and poverty, are the dominant facts and forces in this war, now being waged, with increasing violence and desperateness, against all government.
>
> There is also a strong drift in the church toward *apostasy.* Witness the advance of Romanism, ritualism, and rationalism, even in Protestant churches and communities.
>
> In society at large there is a corresponding advance of materialism, agnosticism, and infidelity; and the polite disguises of science, culture, and criticism do not hide the true features and forms which they clothe, but can not conceal.
>
> Who can fail to see the trend of the Jews toward national rehabilitation and the colonization of Palestine, while at the same time the church is fet-

---

2   Of the millions of Christian who lived during the Patristic era (the closing days of the Roman empire), only a dozen or so of them can be quoted as believing in chiliasm. Others of the ante-nicene theologians did not teach it . . . and none of the church Creeds incorporated it into their list of beliefs. (From the Apostles' Creed onwards)

tered by secularism on the one hand and skepticism on the other? Side by side with these signs there is the opening of the world to the Gospel, the world-wide circulation of the Bible in over four hundred tongues, the network of missionary societies wrapping the globe, and the uprising of Christian young men and women in an unparalleled crusade of missions. All these are like fingers all pointing in one direction — the Sunrise of the Ages.

. . . In Matthew, the last scene shows the *dragnet* — the obvious metaphor for world-wide evangelism. In the Apocalypse, the last rebuke is to *Laodicea* — the self-deceived and self-sufficient church, that shuts in worldliness and shuts out Christ. When in history did those two conditions **ever meet as they do now**? . . . For the **first time in this gospel age**, ecclesiastical degeneracy and evangelistic activity curiously blending — fulfilling before our eyes our Lord's paradox — world-wide witness side by side with love waxing cold! (Emphasis added.)

Wow! What a concise summary of the world today. These "signs of the end" are sure . . . Wait? What are you saying? That Rev. Pierson wrote these words *before 1901* . . . of *another* generation? . . . not the times of 2017?

Yep! I mean "yes." The fact is that what passes as "signs of the times" (of the end) could be applied to many, many, many, many other generations at different times throughout the history of nations. The alleged end-time signs, which prophecy pastors think the Bible lists, are not valid indicators of the end of the world nor the Second Coming events. *(Parousia,* resurrection, and judgment) Prophecy lecturers are simply seeing things in the Bible that are not there.

Of course, the Bible speaks of distress, tribulation, persecution, oppression (the same Greek word, *thlipsis*), but it does not designate these times of trials as a sign of the end-times. Afflictions (tribulation) are what Christ had to go through, and are what His disciples are not to shrink from. (Colossians 1:24) The wickedness, apostasy, lethargy, and apathy are symptoms of human depravity in all generations, which Christians have to face continually. Persecutions will always dot the Christian landscape.

After Rev. Pierson gave his rendition of the end-times, he proceeded to give, not one, not five, but ten different methods for computing the end of "the times of the Gentiles"! And, according to them, the beginning of the end of the world was supposed to occur between 1880 and 1920. We note his concluding remarks:

Whatever grounds, above presented, may seem untenable or unsafe, one thing seems undeniable: there is a *convergence of signs upon* **this our day**, such as has never indicated any previous period as the probable time of the end . . . And if universal anarchy is to be the last great development of society, when was there a time when, both in church and state, there was such a development of lawlessness *(anomia)?*

Upon this subject we can no longer, within these narrow limits, expatiate. But it may at least stir up the thoughtful reader to individual search into the signs of the times. What are the indications above the prophetic and historic horizon? If the signs of the coming of the Son of Man are indeed to be seen, it may well incite us to be among the watchers who, while others sleep, are awake and looking for the dawn!

It really goes without saying, that this minister was wrong about the signs in his generation, and most presumptuous about the end occuring near the beginning of the 20th century (1900), regardless of his ten methods of calculation. Most flagrantly though, he totally ignored the plain words of the Master Teacher, Jesus, who clearly taught that there are absolutely to be "no" signs to indicate the end-times. By his arrogant presentation he was in essence saying that he knew more than Jesus, for Jesus underscored the fact that neither He, nor the angels, knew the time of the end. (Matthew 24:44; Acts 1:7; Mark 13:32)

SPIRIT OF NEPOS

As heretical as all this scheming is, there are more sinister things afoot. This speculation is common to all the modern Dispensational pundits from 1830 on into the twenty-first century. No matter how inaccurate they all are, they keep pumping out their pulp fiction to the unwary Christian congregations, flooding the evangelical world, causing many to drown in disillusionment and disgust when all is said and done.

But the worst of all this is the conduct of these self-appointed interpreters of the scriptures. Along with presenting this heresy, they have demonstrated a spirit of anger to all who point out their errors . . . a spirit of superiority to those who linger outside their prophetic cabal . . . an attitude of exclusivity to other ministers who retain the traditional creedal beliefs of the historic Church. Just express or repeat the words of Jesus about "no signs" and you will see their jugular veins bulge out and their faces turn red! The same animosity that Nepos showed to his contemporaries.

Near the end of the 1800s, Dispensationalists held prophecy Conferences all over the country, without inviting — and many cases, with deliberate shunning — pious ministers who differed from them in these doctrines. Godly ministers were blacklisted, fellowship was broken, and church doors were slammed shut on once congenial fellowship! The same type of conduct that Nepos carried out against churches in his region was committed by Dispensationalists who, if it were to be told, were presenting a "new and novel" doctrine (admitted by Scofield).

It's not like the modern Dispensensationalists were standing firm against an attacking cult, or guarding the "faith once delivered to the saints". Rather, they were the ones presenting a strange dogma, and they were the ones doing the encroaching against the people of God. And . . . they, to this day, continue to walk in the same spirit of Nepos, arrogantly dismissing those brave souls who would dare stand firm and point out the plain teachings of Jesus concerning these matters.

Under the guise of evangelical orthodoxy, they continue to teach for doctrines "the tradition of men." Giving more weight to the literalism of the uninspired Intertestamental rabbinical writings . . . adhering to the contrived "futurism" of the Jesuit Catholics . . . and leap-frogging over the interpretations of Old Testament prophecies given by the Apostles . . . they think nothing of mocking and stampeding over those who cling to the faith once delivered to the saints. (2 Peter 1:12–2:3) All truth necessary to understand the Second Coming was given in the first century. (2 Peter 1:12) And the love and fellowship that was commended then, is still applicable now.

NEPOS' GRANDCHILDREN

The 100% failure rate of signs of the times prophecy lecturers falls on blinded eyes of evangelical pastors in succeeding generations. In 1940 Louis S. Bauman published *Light From Bible Prophecy*, in which he dedicated 50 pages (almost one third of the book) to his listing of "signs" indicating the nearness of the end (Secret Rapture). He began the chapter, "Why the End of the Age Must Be Very Near," with these words:

> I believe that the rapture of the Church must be very near because I believe that the Lord Jesus will not break His word. To do that would make Him a sinner like unto the first Adam: and this world, without a sinless Lamb, would have no Savior. I can not help but wonder if supposedly Christian men know what they say when they speak their doubt as to the incarnate God keeping His covenants inviolate, and His promises immutable. (p. 84)

Mr. Bauman, an ardent Dispensationalist, then continued his tirade against all doubters of his prophetic interpretations:

> Now with all due respect to all those who did 'put on their white robes' in days long past, I wish to affirm, without hesitation or equivocation, that *at no time* since our Lord uttered His great prophecies have any goodly number of the signs been present *contemporaneously*—that is, at the same time. And contemporaneous they must be! (p. 87)

He then commenced to list and enumerate on fifteen signs of the nearness of the Coming of Christ. But notice what he is doing. He dismisses out of hand the previous attempts of those who have fallen into the same error of trying to time the end: He mentioned the Millerites (who have morphed into the Seventh Day Adventists); and he was shunning the Darbyites who, a century before, thought they saw signs of the end in their day. Notice how he described them as *supposedly Christian men.* (Shades of Nepos's attitude.)

Also notice that, since he believed in a "secret rapture", he is violating that secrecy by presenting "signs" of that event. That event is supposed to be timeless and signless! He is being logically inconsistent. And he commits this while, according to his words, he is "without hesitation and equivocation" affirming the signs. (Remember that he is writing in 1940. And as far as we know, the church was **not** raptured soon after.)

But, most importantly, as Oswald T. Allis pointed out in his insightful volume, *Prophecy and the Church,* that . . .

> What we object to most in the statements which we have quoted is not that Bauman states his opinion with the confidence of deep conviction, but that he has the irreverence to make the Lord Jesus Christ responsible for the correctness of his fallible opinion regarding the nearness of the coming. Jesus said Himself, "Of that day and that hour knoweth no man." Bauman is not only sure that he knows, at least approximately, but he is ready to stake the reputation of his Lord on the correctness of his own fallible opinion. (p. 297–8)

The 1830s, 1880s, 1940s, all saw attempts to recognize "signs of the times" and those efforts all failed, as well they must, since they contradict the clear and plain teaching of Jesus: *You also must be ready, because the Son of Man will come at an hour when you do not expect Him. (Matthew 24:42, 44; 25:13)* If one can recognize "signs" in anticipation of His coming, then one **is** expecting Him. So it logically follows: *there are* **no** *signs, and there never will be!*

The failure rate of previous Dispensationalists, you would think, would be a wake up call to modern prophecy commentators. You would think they'd go back to *the Book,* and return to what Jesus taught. You would think they would "repent in dust and ashes" for attempting to do what Jesus said not to do . . . and for leading Christian brothers and sisters astray . . . and for selling pulp fiction in guise of legitimate prophecy.

But no. The spirit of Nepos has hovered over the Church for centuries, and continues to plague modern ministers with a dark cloud (veil) of deception . . . and arrogance . . . feistiness. Telepastors and prophecy conference lecturers take advantage of every catastrophe or dire news broadcast or calamity to arouse congregations' fear (or curiosity) by appealing to more "signs of the times."

In the twentieth century, Hal Lindsey, Chuck Smith, John Walvoord, John Hagee, Tim LaHaye, Dave Hunt, and countless others have used "the oil crisis", the Israeli statehood, the march of Communism, the Islamic hordes, the new Silicon Valley technology (imbedded chips), the check-out scanners, the global warming, etc., etc., etc., . . . as assured signs of the soon coming of Christ!

Their failures in prognostication do not slow them down one bit. They continue to edit embarrassing sentences, and republish their books with abandon. Instead of throwing the *Scofield Reference Study Bible* on the garbage heap of erroneous dogmatism, it is simply "revised" to make it more palatable to the questioning, and confused public.

On the one hand, they admit that Dispensationalism with its Secret Rapture is a new and novel concept, formalized in the 1830s . . . yet they shun all who do not accept it as church dogma and orthodoxy in essence!

(H) CONCLUDING PASTORAL ADVICE

What should be the Christian pastor's and layman's response to the study of scripture concerning prophecy? How should we all respond to the *perennial* rising up of ministers who announce "signs of the times" of the end of the world?

Richard J. Foster has given excellent advice in a Pastoral Letter that summarizes very well what our mindset and our conduct should be like ("Heart to Heart: A Pastoral Letter," *Renovare*, Nov. 1995). He noted, generally, that

1. We should continue to respect the "blessed hope" of the Second Coming of Jesus. No matter how much it is dragged through the dirt by false prophets who lack proper hermeneutics and understanding of historical background. Don't let failed expectations cause disrespect for prophecy.

2. Flatly reject the fallacious practice of "date setting" and the propensity of looking for "signs of the times." There is no "countdown to Armageddon" nor hints at the Second Coming with respect to the nation of Israel and its politics in the Near East.

3. Learn what biblical "eschatological language and genre" really means. Stick to the biblical meaning of "last days" which began at Pentecost, and don't

let modernists reinterpret words out of their context. Know the historical Roman and Israeli background of the Bible and the life of Christ.

4. Avoid interpreting the Bible according to nationalistic or American favored-status points of view. The New Testament with its prophetic goal is not a blue-print for United States's destiny or culture. It concerns the "World," not any one nation. Don't spend time looking for references to modern nations—or technology—in Old Testament verbiage and phrases. *The testimony of Jesus is the thrust of prophecy.*

5. And pastors, don't manipulate, exploit, or "jerk the emotional chains" of the congregations with speculative prophecy preaching. Don't play upon the fears or curiosity of brothers and sisters in Christ by tickling the ears or scaring them with "end time" harbingers or the latest apocalyptic dating scheme. *Don't abuse the bride of Christ!*

Instead, give due respect to the present coronation and reign of Christ and the reality of the Kingdom of God in the earth today. Let "His will be done" be the emphatic preaching about conduct and involvement in societal institutions . . . now! Don't allow the Dispensational escapist mentality shackle the hands of congregations and keep them from actively promoting Christian charity and evangelistic endeavors daily. Keep the emphasis on "occupying until" Christ comes, and may He find us all working hard when He does finally come *unannounced* and *without warning.* Follow the advice of Paul at the end of the great resurrection chapter:

> *Therefore, my beloved brethren, be ye steadfast, unmovable, always abounding in the work of the Lord* . . . (1 Corinthians 15:58)

ACKNOWLEDGMENTS

"YOU ARE WHERE YOU'RE AT BECAUSE SOMEBODY HELPED YOU GET THERE!" IS AN aphorism as rich and creamy as a pound of dairy butter from Wisconsin. It is so much a gospel truth that the Apostles solemnly charged Christian ministers to faithfully mentor younger men and entrust the work of the Lord to them so they, in turn, could help future generations fulfill their callings as well.

Upon retrospection, there arises in the mind like the fresh green blades of grass in spring the thought that men, long-time dead, as well as the living, have contributed to our lives. I especially have been encouraged by the lives and writings of C. S. Lewis, G. Campbell Morgan, Andrew Murray, and Philip Mauro.

My position in life has been enhanced by such contemporaries as Ravi Zacharias, Josh McDowell, Charles Swindoll, Dick Iverson, R. C. Sproul, and John Piper . . . and others who have dedicated themselves unto the ministry of the word and Spirit.

And then, as another wagon-load of trail-blazers who have helped me trek along the Oregon Trail, there are the faithful friends and relatives who have persevered in honing and shaping my destiny . . . men and women of whom I am unworthy, yet who contributed sacrificially so that this lowly pilgrim could achieve his goal: H. L. Gehrke, Steve Knapp, David Newquist, Larry Lawson, Rev. and Mrs. F. W. Gates, David Blomgren, Becky Jo Stites, and Wilburta Gates.

A very hearty thanks to all these souls who have contributed to my life and ministry . . . with whom I will enjoy conversing in Eternity, God be praised!

ABOUT THE AUTHOR

RAYMOND GRANT IS A LONG-TIME RESIDENT OF THE CITY OF ROSES — PORTLAND, Oregon. He is an essayist, exegete, and evangelist who has spent thirty years as a chaplain's assistant in Oregon State Reform School (now McLaren), and as a high school teacher of Apologetics and Philosophy.

His degrees are in theology (from American Divinity School) and in education (University of Portland). He had graduated from Federal Way High School, and there was even the president of the Honor Society!

Mr. Grant's authorship is multitudinous and varied: Ghost-writing, co-authoring, and writing commentaries, books on church administration, high school text books, and evangelistic tracts. He also writes poetry and compilations of quotations and proverbs. Some of Mr. Grant's research is found in the following works:

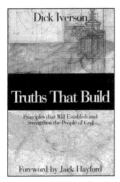   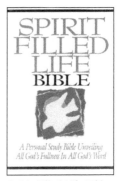

Truths That Build (2001) by Dick Iverson	*Team Ministry* (1995) by Dick Iverson with Ray Grant	*Maintaining Balance When Winds of Doctrine Blow* (1989) by Dick Iverson	*Spirit Filled Life Bible* Edited by Jack W. Hayford
Herein are 12 foundation truths that Pastor Dick Iverson has studied and shared, which sustained his pastorship for over 44 years. Available through City Christian Publishing (Portland, OR). ISBN 978-1886849-80-8	This book examines and applies principles of biblical leadership for raising strong teams in church ministries. Available through City Christian Publishing. ISBN 978-0914936-61-9	This book offers guidance and wisdom for pastors seeking to stabilize and equip their churches when conflicting doctines arise. Available through City Christian Publishing. ISBN 978-0914936-80-0	This well-loved study Bible was published by Thomas Nelson (Nashville, TN: 1991) and has since been revised into a new edition. ISBN 978-0840718-00-6

FORTHCOMING TITLES:

- *Dining with Deity.* An exposition of every verse in the Gospels.
- *Dialogue with Deity: Genesis and Jesus.* Exposition of dialogue between God and Man in the book of Genesis.
- Commentary on Daniel.

CPSIA information can be obtained
at www.ICGtesting.com
Printed in the USA
LVHW062138250522
719778LV00022B/387

9 781946 138002